TRANSFORMING MODERN MACROECONOMICS

This book tells the story of the search for non-Walrasian microfoundations for macroeconomic theory, from the disequilibrium theories of Patinkin, Clower, and Leijonhufvud to recent dynamic stochastic general equilibrium models with imperfect competition. Placing this search against the background of wider developments in macroeconomics, the authors contend that this was never a single research program, but involved economists with very different aims who developed the basic ideas about quantity constraints, spillover effects, and coordination failures in different ways. The authors contrast this with the equilibrium approach of Phelps and Lucas, arguing that equilibrium theories simply assumed away the problems that had motivated the disequilibrium literature. Although equilibrium Walrasian models came to dominate macroeconomics, non-Walrasian theories never went away and continue to exert an important influence on the subject. Although this book focuses on one strand in modern macroeconomics, it is crucial to understanding the origins of modern macroeconomic theory.

Roger E. Backhouse is Professor of the History and Philosophy of Economics at the University of Birmingham, where he has taught since 1980, and at the Erasmus University Rotterdam. He is co-editor (with Philippe Fontaine) of *The History of the Social Sciences since 1945* (2010) and (with Bradley W. Bateman) *The Cambridge Companion to Keynes* (2006). He is co-author (with Bradley W. Bateman) of *Capitalist Revolutionary: John Maynard Keynes* (2011) and author of *The Puzzle of Modern Economics* (2010), and *The Ordinary Business of Life* (2001), published in the United Kingdom as *The Penguin History of Economics* (2002).

Mauro Boianovsky is Professor of Economics at Universidade de Brasilia, where he has taught since 1996. He is the editor of *Business Cycle Theories: Selected Texts, 1860–1939* (2008) and co-editor (with Kevin Hoover) of *Robert Solow and the Development of Growth Economics* (2009). He has written for a number of journals including the *History of Political Economy*, the *Cambridge Journal of Economics*, the *European Journal of the History of Economic Thought*, *Structural Change and Economic Dynamics*, and the *Journal of the History of Economic Thought*.

HISTORICAL PERSPECTIVES ON MODERN ECONOMICS

General Editor:
Craufurd D. Goodwin, *Duke University*

This series contains original works that challenge and enlighten historians of economics. For the profession as a whole, it promotes better understanding of the origin and content of modern economics

Other Books in the Series:

Arie Arnon, *Monetary Theory and Policy from Hume and Smith to Wicksell: Money, Credit, and the Economy*

William J. Barber, *Designs within Disorder: Franklin D. Roosevelt, the Economists, and the Shaping of American Economic Policy, 1933–1945*

William J. Barber, *From New Era to New Deal: Herbert Hoover, the Economists, and American Economic Policy, 1921–1933*

Fillipo Cesarano, *Monetary Theory and Bretton Woods: The Construction of an International Monetary Order*

Timothy Davis, *Ricardo's Macroeconomics: Money, Trade Cycles, and Growth*

Anthony M. Endres and Grant A. Fleming, *International Organizations and the Analysis of Economic Policy, 1919–1950*

Jerry Evensky, *Adam Smith's Moral Philosophy: A Historical and Contemporary Perspective on Markets, Law, Ethics, and Culture*

M. June Flanders, *International Monetary Economics, 1870–1960: Between the Classical and the New Classical*

J. Daniel Hammond, *Theory and Measurement: Causality Issues in Milton Friedman's Monetary Economics*

Samuel Hollander, *The Economics of Karl Marx: Analysis and Application*

Samuel Hollander, *Friedrich Engels and Marxian Political Economy*

Susan Howson, *Lionel Robbins*

Lars Jonung (ed.), *The Stockholm School of Economics Revisited*

Kyun Kim, *Equilibrium Business Cycle Theory in Historical Perspective*

Gerald M. Koot, *English Historical Economics, 1870–1926: The Rise of Economic History and Mercantilism*

David Laidler, *Fabricating the Keynesian Revolution: Studies of the Inter-War Literature on Money, the Cycle, and Unemployment*

Odd Langholm, *The Legacy of Scholasticism in Economic Thought: Antecedents of Choice and Power*

(*continued after index*)

Transforming Modern Macroeconomics

Exploring Disequilibrium Microfoundations, 1956–2003

ROGER E. BACKHOUSE
University of Birmingham

MAURO BOIANOVSKY
Universidade de Brasilia

CAMBRIDGE
UNIVERSITY PRESS

CAMBRIDGE
UNIVERSITY PRESS

32 Avenue of the Americas, New York NY 10013-2473, USA

Cambridge University Press is part of the University of Cambridge.

It furthers the University's mission by disseminating knowledge in the pursuit of education, learning and research at the highest international levels of excellence.

www.cambridge.org
Information on this title: www.cambridge.org/9781107023192

© Roger E. Backhouse and Mauro Boianovsky 2013

First published 2013

A catalogue record for this publication is available from the British Library

Library of Congress Cataloguing in Publication data
Backhouse, Roger, 1951–
Transforming modern macroeconomics : exploring disequilibrium microfoundations, 1956–2003 / Roger E. Backhouse, Mauro Boianovsky.
pages   cm. – (Historical perspectives on modern economics)
Includes bibliographical references and index.
ISBN 978-1-107-02319-2
1. Macroeconomics – History.   2. Equilibrium (Economics) – History.
I. Boianovsky, Mauro.   II. Title.
HB172.5.B3335   2012
339.5–dc23   2012017765

ISBN 978-1-107-02319-2 Hardback
ISBN 978-1-107-43538-4 Paperback

Dedicated to the memory of Edward Backhouse (1919–1988)
and David Luiz Boianovsky (1932–1996)

Contents

Figures

Preface

We began working on the topic of disequilibrium macroeconomics when we were both visiting Duke University, in the first semester of 2003. By 2005, we had three papers written, but we were having problems dividing the material into self-contained papers of a length with which journal editors would be happy. Our first paper, from which material for several chapters of the current book was drawn, grew to around 20,000 words, while the other papers, though of more reasonable length, took material out of the broader context. Although reactions to the papers were favorable, the almost universal response was "But you also need to say something about x, y, and z." We also came to see that disequilibrium macroeconomics was far more central to the transformation of macroeconomics that has taken place since the 1950s than we had realized. For several years, we both put this work aside and turned to other projects. Prompted by the growing interest in the history of recent economics, and macroeconomics in particular, we eventually decided that it was time to write our material into a book on the search for disequilibrium microfoundations for macroeconomics, adding the material that was needed to fill out the story. This book is the result. Although based on our earlier discussion papers, and although Turnitin would no doubt detect matching text, the material has been completely rewritten.

For one of us (Backhouse), this project presents a new challenge in that we are writing about a literature to which he once tried to contribute. However, sufficient time has passed (the work dates from 1974, was used in a thesis in 1976, and then was published between 1980 and 1982) for it to be possible to look back on this as a historical episode. More important, having subsequently chosen to specialize in the history and methodology of economics, not in macroeconomics, no credibility issues are at stake. In any case, these papers, published when the profession was moving away from this subject, were incidental and are mentioned only in footnotes.

We are grateful to participants in the story we tell who were willing to
write, sometimes at great length, responding to questions and commenting
on draft material: Robert Barro, Jacques Drèze, John Fender, Jean-Michel
Grandmont, Frank Hahn, Geoff Harcourt, Peter Howitt, Axel Leijonhufvud,
Edmond Malinvaud, Richard Portes, Robert Solow, and David Winter. We
owe a particular debt to Jean-Pascal Bénassy for his careful reading of a
large part of the manuscript and his advice on how the structure of the book
could be improved. We also benefited from the comments of two anonymous referees who made many valuable suggestions. The usual caveat
applies: none of them should be blamed for the use we have, or have not,
made of their ideas.

None of the material here has been previously published, though much
of it was circulated, in 2004–2007, as discussion papers and was discussed
at conferences and seminars, including the History of Economics Society,
the European Society for the History of Economic Thought, the Brazilian
Economic Society (ANPEC), the University of Birmingham, Université
Catholique de Louvain, London Metropolitan University, University of
Paris I, and Hitotsubashi University. A version of the material in Chapter 7
was presented at a conference on "General Equilibrium as Knowledge" at
the University of Paris I (Sorbonne-Pantheon), in September 2007. We are
grateful to participants in these events for helping us clarify many ideas and
drawing out attention to points that we had overlooked.

Some chapters in this book draw on material from the Patinkin, Clower,
Leijonhufvud, Modigliani, and Solow Papers, held as part of the Economists'
Papers Project in the David M. Rubenstein Rare Book and Manuscript
Library at Duke University. We are grateful to the archivists, including Will
Hansen and Elizabeth Dunn, who have been unfailingly helpful. We are
grateful to Robert Barro, Earlene Clower, Jan Kregel, Axel Leijonhufvud,
Robert Solow, and Roy Weintraub for permission to quote from unpub-
lished papers and correspondence.

Dramatis Personae

This provides selected biographical information on the leading figures in the search for disequilibrium microfoundations, focusing on facts that are relevant to this. Further biographical information on many of these figures is provided in the main text. If no country of birth is given, it is the United States. Qualifications other than the Ph.D. are given only if the person did not obtain a Ph.D. or an equivalent. Honorary and higher doctorates are ignored. Affiliations listed are, with some exceptions, confined to the economists' main positions and exclude visiting and emeritus positions.[1] There is ambiguity in listing emeritus positions, which reflects the ambiguity over the point at which many academics cease to be actively involved in research.

Abbreviations: CEPREMAP – Centre pour la recherche economique et ses applications; CNRS – Centre national de la recherche scientifique; INSEE – Institut national de la statistique et des études économiques; LSE – London School of Economics; MIT – Massachusetts Institute of Technology; UCLA – University of California Los Angeles.

Alchian, Armen A. (1914–; Ph.D. Stanford 1944; UCLA and RAND 1946–) An industrial economist known mainly for his work on industrial economics and property rights, he was an early contributor to the literature on decision making when information is costly. Although he did not contribute directly to the disequilibrium macroeconomics literature, he was an important contributor to the Phelps volume (Phelps et al. 1970) and an influence on the early work of Axel Leijonhufvud.

---

[1] Economists are highly mobile and full listings of affiliations would exhaust the reader's patience. More detailed information can be found in volumes such as Blaug (1999) from which many of the dates have been taken (corrected and updated from a variety of sources, notably the subjects and their universities' Web pages). For some, the affiliations listed here represent a great simplification of their institutional connections.

Arrow, Kenneth J. (1921–; Ph.D. Columbia 1953; Stanford 1953–68, Harvard 1968–79, Stanford 1979–) An influential figure in many fields of economics and creator, with Gérard Debreu, of what became the canonical model of general competitive equilibrium; he listed, in 1959, a series of "scandals" in general equilibrium theory that stimulated others to construct models of general equilibrium with imperfect competition. He co-authored with Frank Hahn a graduate textbook *General Competitive Analysis* (1971) that covered Keynesian problems.

Barro, Robert J. (1944–; Ph.D. Harvard 1970 Brown 1968–73, Chicago 1973–84, Rochester 1975–87, Harvard 1987–) When at Brown, he co-authored, with Herschel Grossman, one of the most-cited articles on disequilibrium microfoundations (1971). After his move to Chicago, he became one of the most prominent new classical macroeconomists, his work on Ricardian equivalence and output-inflation trade-offs being particularly influential.

Bénassy, Jean-Pascal (France 1948–; Ph.D. Berkeley 1973; CEPREMAP 1973–, CNRS 1975–, Laboratoire d'économie politique, Ecole Normale Supérieure 1984–88) His Ph.D, supervised by Gérard Debreu and Bent Hansen, on disequilibrium theory extended the theory of general equilibrium to non-clearing markets. He continued to work on disequilibrium microfoundations and sought to integrate the economics of non-market clearing with imperfect competition.

Blanchard, Olivier (France 1948–; Ph.D. MIT 1977; Harvard 1977–83, MIT 1983–) A leading new Keynesian, he wrote widely used textbooks including a graduate macroeconomics textbook co-authored with Stanley Fischer.

Clower, Robert Wayne (1926–2011; MLitt Oxford 1952, DLitt Oxford 1978; Washington State 1948–49, 1952–56, Northwestern 1957–71, UCLA 1972–86, South Carolina, 1986–2001) As author of the "dual-decision hypothesis," he is, along with Axel Leijonhufvud, with whom he worked at UCLA, one of the two economists usually credited with being the origin of disequilibrium macroeconomics.

Debreu, Gérard (France, 1921–2004; DSc (mathematics) Paris, 1956 CNRS 1946–48, Cowles Commission at Chicago 1950–55, Cowles Commission at Yale 1955–61, Berkeley 1962–86) Creator with Kenneth Arrow of the canonical model of general competitive equilibrium, he did not work on disequilibrium theory himself, but supervised the Ph.D.s of Jean-Pascal Bénassy and Jean-Michel Grandmont.

Dixit, Avinash (India, 1944–; Ph.D. MIT 1968, Berkeley 1968–69, Oxford 1970–74, Warwick 1974–80, Princeton 1981–) An economic theorist working primarily on industrial economics, international trade, and investment, he was co-author with fellow MIT student Joseph Stiglitz of a significant paper on disequilibrium macroeconomics.

Drazen, Allan (1950–; Ph.D. MIT 1976; Chicago 1976–82, Tel Aviv 1982–90, Maryland 1990–) One-time assistant to Don Patinkin, author of an important survey of the disequilibrium macroeconomics in 1980. His subsequent work focused on macroeconomics and political economy.

Drèze, Jacques (Belgium, 1929–; Ph.D. Columbia 1958; Carnegie Tech 1957–58, Louvain 1958–89, Chicago 1964–68) Economic theorist and industrial economist focusing on decision making under uncertainty, he was author of a widely discussed concept of equilibrium with rationing in 1975. He was closely associated with the group centered on CEPREMAP.

Fischer, Stanley (Zambia, 1943–; Ph.D. MIT 1969; Chicago 1969–70, MIT 1973–, World Bank 1988–90, IMF 1994–2001, Citigroup 2001–05, Bank of Israel 2005–) Macroeconomist and author, with Chicago graduate and MIT colleague Rudiger Dornbusch (1942–2002), of a widely used intermediate macroeconomics textbook and, with Olivier Blanchard, of an influential graduate macroeconomics textbook. Author of important survey articles on inflation and monetary economics in the mid-1970s.

Flemming, John S. (United Kingdom, 1941–2003; MA Oxford 1966; Oxford 1963–80; Bank of England 1980–91, European Bank for Reconstruction and Development 1991–93, Oxford 1993–2003) Author of article applying ideas of disequilibrium and rationing to the consumption function in 1973.

Grandmont, Jean-Michel (France, 1939–; Ph.D. Berkeley 1971; CNRS and CEPREMAP 1970–96, École polytechnique 1992–) His Ph.D. supervised by Gérard Debreu, he was the author of a series of papers, many co-authored with colleagues associated with CEPREMAP, on equilibrium in a monetary economy.

Grossman, Herschel I. (1939–2004; Ph.D. Johns Hopkins 1965; Brown 1964–2004) Co-author with Robert Barro of the influential 1971 article. He worked on both disequilibrium and equilibrium models of the effects of monetary policy, and from there, he moved into positive analysis of economic policy more generally.

Hahn, Frank H. (Germany, 1925–; Ph.D. London 1951; Birmingham 1948–60, Cambridge 1960–66 and 1972–92, LSE 1967–72, Siena 1989–) An economic theorist who focused on general equilibrium and the theory of money, he contributed to the early development of models of general equilibrium with imperfect competition and the study of non-tâtonnement processes. He co-authored, with Kenneth Arrow, *General Competitive*

Analysis (1971) and, with Robert Solow, a book on macroeconomic theory (1995). In the late 1970s, he worked with a group of young theorists on information and missing markets and explored what he called "conjectural equilibria."

Hansen, Bent (Denmark, 1920–2002; Fil Dr. Uppsala 1951; Uppsala 1947–55, National Institute of Economic Research [Stockholm] 1955–64, Institute of Planning [Cairo] 1962–65, Berkeley 1966–87) Hansen's doctoral thesis, which turned into *A Study in the Theory of Inflation* (1951), took what could be called a general disequilibrium approach to inflation. Author of a book-length survey of general equilibrium systems, he was, with Gérard Debreu, one of the supervisors of Jean-Pascal Bénassy's important Ph.D. thesis.

Harcourt, Geoffrey C. (Australia, 1931–; Ph.D. Cambridge 1960; Adelaide 1958–85, Cambridge 1982–98) The author of a macroeconomics textbook and a very widely cited survey of capital theory, he became involved with assisting John Hicks in organizing an International Economic Association conference on the microfoundations of macroeconomics in 1975, published in 1977.

Hart, Oliver (United Kingdom, 1948–; Ph.D. Princeton 1974; Essex 1974–75, Cambridge 1975–81, LSE 1982–85, MIT 1985–93, Harvard 1993–) An economic theorist who focused on the theory of firms and market structure. At Cambridge in the late 1970s, he was part of a group of young economists working with Frank Hahn on problems of information and missing markets, using monopolistic competition to show how Keynesian problems could arise.

Hicks, John R. (United Kingdom, 1904–1989; BA 1925; LSE 1929–35, Cambridge 1935–38, Manchester 1938–46, Oxford 1946–65) Widely regarded as Britain's leading economic theorist in the 1930s, he was responsible for the IS-LM model (1937) and *Value and Capital* (1939), which inspired much post-war work on general equilibrium theory. In the 1970s, he questioned the Keynesianism he had helped to create and he was the inspiration behind the 1975 International Economic Association conference on the microeconomic foundations of macroeconomics (Harcourt 1977).

Howitt, Peter (Canada, 1946–; Ph.D. Northwestern 1973; Western Ontario 1972–96, Ohio State University 1996–2000, Brown 2000–) He worked on problems of coordination and monetary economics in the 1970s, co-authoring papers with both Robert Clower and Don Patinkin, contributing to the *American Economic Review* symposium on disequilibrium macroeconomics in 1979. He eventually came to be close to Leijonhufvud in promoting computable, agent-based modeling.

Johnson, Harry G. (Canada, 1923–79; Ph.D. Harvard 1958; St Francis Xavier 1943–44, Toronto 1946–47, Cambridge 1949–56, Manchester 1956–59, Chicago 1959–74 and 1979, LSE 1966–74, Geneva 1976–79) A specialist in international economics and one of the most prolific economists in the 1960s and 1970s, he was an influential interpreter of the Keynesian revolution and publicist for the work of Axel Leijonhufvud.

Keynes, John Maynard (United Kingdom, 1883–1946; MA 1905; Cambridge 1908–42) The economist whose work lies behind the search for disequilibrium microfoundations.

Kornai, Janos (Hungary, 1928; Hungarian Academy of Sciences 1955–58 and 1963–93) A specialist on planning in centrally planned economies, his book *Anti-Equilibrium* (1971) contributed to the growing interest in disequilibrium theory in the early 1970s.

Lange, Oskar (Poland, 1904–65; LLD Krakow 1928; Krakow 1931–35, Michigan 1943, Cowles Commission at Chicago 1943–45, Warsaw 1955–65) While in Chicago he attempted to reinterpret Keynesian theory in terms of Walrasian general equilibrium theory and helped establish the neoclassical synthesis view of Keynesian economics. His work provided the starting point for Don Patinkin, who had attended his lectures in Chicago.

Laroque, Guy (France 1946–; DEA 1971; INSEE 1982–) Working with Jean-Michel Grandmont and others, he was responsible for a series of papers on temporary equilibrium with rationing in the mid-1970s.

Leijonhufvud, Axel (Sweden 1933–; Ph.D. Northwestern 1967; UCLA 1964–94, Trento 1994–) His Ph.D. dissertation, which became *On Keynesian Economics and the Economics of Keynes* (1968), inspired many economists to work on problems of disequilibrium. Along with his UCLA colleague Robert Clower, he remained distant from the literature drawing on Barro and Grossman (1971) that emerged in the 1970s, and focused on more general problems of coordination, eventually taking up computable economics.

Lucas, Robert E. (1937–; Ph.D. Chicago 1964; Carnegie Mellon 1963–74, Chicago 1974–) Arguably the key figure, along with Robert Barro, Thomas Sargent, and others, in the rise of the new classical macroeconomics on account of two papers, published in 1972 and 1976.

Malinvaud, Edmond (France 1923–; Diplôme 1948; INSEE 1948–56, 1967–71, 1974–87, ENSAE 1957–66, College de France 1987–) Author of many works on the theory of intertemporal allocation of resources and econometric theory in the 1950s and 1960s and of a graduate microeconomics textbook, he wrote a very widely cited account of disequilibrium theory (1977).

Mankiw, N. Gregory (1958–; Ph.D. Princeton 1984; Harvard 1985–) A leading New Keynesian macroeconomist and author of widely used textbooks on introductory economics and intermediate macroeconomics.

Modigliani, Franco (Italy 1918–2003; Ph.D. New School 1944; Barnard College 1942–44, New School, 1943–44 and 1946–48, Illinois 1949–52, Carnegie Tech 1952–60, Northwestern 1960–62, MIT 1962–2003) The author of an article (1944) that interpreted Keynesian economics in terms of wage stickiness, he was one of the leading Keynesians in the age of the neoclassical synthesis, as well as being active in macroeconometric model building and writing, with Merton Miller, influential papers in the theory of finance.

Muellbauer, John (Germany 1944–; Ph.D. Berkeley 1975; Warwick 1969–72, Birkbeck College London 1972–81, Oxford 1981–) A specialist in the economics of consumption he was co-author, with Richard Portes, of a dynamic extension of disequilibrium theory in 1978.

Neary, Peter (Ireland, 1950–; DPhil Oxford 1978; Economic and Social Research Institute Dublin, 1970–72, Trinity College Dublin 1972–74 and 1978–, Oxford 1976–78) A specialist in the theory of international trade, he co-authored, with Joseph Stiglitz, a model that modeled expectations of quantity constraints on behavior (1983).

Negishi, Takashi (Japan 1933–; Ph.D. Tokyo 1965; Stanford 1958–60, Tokyo 1965–94, Aoyama Gakuin 1994–) A general equilibrium theorist, he developed some of the earliest models of equilibrium with monopolistic competition and in subsequent years produced a range of theories that he summed up as *Economic Theories in a Non-Walrasian Tradition* (1985).

Patinkin, Don (1922–1995; Ph.D. Chicago 1947; Illinois 1948–49, Hebrew University Jerusalem 1949–97) His *Money, Interest, and Prices* (1956, 1965), both laid a theoretical foundation for the neoclassical synthesis and derived the quantity-constraint spillover effects that were central to the disequilibrium macroeconomic literature. After this book, most of his time was spent on other areas of economics, from the Israeli economy to the theory of money and the history of the Keynesian revolution.

Phelps, Edmund S. (1933–; Ph.D. Yale 1959; Yale 1959–66, Pennsylvania 1966–71, Columbia 1971–) He was responsible for the "Phelps volume" (Phelps et al. 1970) that opened up the information-theoretic explanations of unemployment that were developed by Robert Lucas into what became the new classical macroeconomics, though his own work took him in different directions.

Portes, Richard (1941; Ph.D. Oxford 1969; Princeton 1969–72, Birkbeck College London 1972–94, London Business School 1995–) A specialist in the control of enterprises in centrally planned economies, who overlapped briefly with Richard Quandt at Princeton, he co-authored a dynamic extension of the fixed-price model in 1978 and undertook a series of papers, many co-authored with David Winter, on estimating disequilibria in East European countries.

Quandt, Richard (Hungary 1930–; Ph.D. Harvard 1957; Princeton 1956–) A microeconomic theorist (and author of a widely used textbook) and econometrician, who focused on the estimation of non-linear models and of markets with rationing.

Samuelson, Paul A. (1915–2009; Ph.D. Harvard 1941; MIT 1940–2009) One of the leading U.S. Keynesians who created the 45-degree line model that, together with the IS-LM model, dominated the teaching of Keynesian economics. He invented the term "neoclassical synthesis."

Solow, Robert M. (1924–; Ph.D. Harvard 1951; MIT 1950–) One of the most prominent Keynesian economists of the Keynesian era, he co-authored, with Joseph Stiglitz, a model of macroeconomic disequilibrium that was published in 1968, three years before the Barro-Grossman model. A later paper, co-authored with Ian M. McDonald, added to the new Keynesian literature a model of a monopoly union, and he co-authored a book with Frank Hahn challenging the new classical conception of how markets work.

Stiglitz, Joseph E. (1943–; Ph.D. MIT 1966; MIT 1966–67, Yale 1967–74, Stanford 1974–76 and 1988–2001, Oxford 1976–79, Princeton 1979–88, World Bank 1997–2000, Columbia 2001–) He was the co-author, with Robert Solow, of an early model of equilibrium with rationing, but his main work has been on markets with asymmetric information. He became a prominent New Keynesian on account of his use of asymmetric information to explain why labor markets might not clear and why there might be rationing in capital markets.

Weintraub, E. Roy (1943–; Ph.D. Pennsylvania 1969; Rutgers 1968–70, Duke 1970–) A general equilibrium theorist he wrote a prominent survey that focused attention on the term "microfoundations" in 1977.

Weintraub, Sidney (1914–83, Ph.D. New York University 1941; New School 1951–57, Pennsylvania 1950–83) A Keynesian economist who was responsible for developing Keynes's theory as a theory of aggregate demand and supply, which he applied to problems of inflation and income distribution. He is often credited with being the first to use the term "microfoundations."

Winter, David F. (United Kingdom, 1945–; MA Pennsylvania 1970; Sussex 1974–75, Birkbeck 1975–77, Bristol 1977–) Co-author, with Richard

Portes, of a series of articles on the estimation of disequilibrium systems in Eastern European countries.

Woodford, Michael (1955–; Ph.D. MIT 1983; Columbia 1984–86 and 1995–, Chicago 1986–95) Author of *Interest and Prices* (2003), widely taken to be the definitive statement of the new neoclassical synthesis that integrated real business cycle theory with new Keynesian economics.

Younès, Yves (Tunisia, 1937–1996; Tunis; CEPREMAP) A co-author, with Edmond Malinvaud, Jean-Michel Grandmont, and others at CEPREMAP, of articles on the theory of general equilibrium with quantity rationing in the mid-1970s.

ONE

Introduction

THE SEARCH FOR MICROFOUNDATIONS

This book tells the story of the search that took place, in the second half of the twentieth century, for a more rigorous macroeconomic theory. This was a time when many developments in macroeconomic theory were driven by economic events and by new policy challenges. In the 1960s, economists needed to explain economic growth – why some countries grew rapidly and others remained poor – and why prices were rising even when the shortages associated with the Korean War had ended. After 1973, the problem of stagflation, simultaneously rising inflation and unemployment, suddenly emerged, making the need for new theories even more urgent. However, the shape of the new theories that emerged was driven just as much by the concern, shared by most economists, to develop a macroeconomic theory that could be derived rigorously from theories about how individual households and firms responded to the circumstances they faced. In the language that economists started using in the 1970s, they sought a macroeconomic theory that had rigorous microfoundations.

The approach to the problem of microfoundations that was to become dominant involved modeling households and firms as optimizing agents, operating in perfectly competitive markets. Most economists took this as an approach with which they had to engage, even if they did not agree with it and wanted to work with other types of model. The most rigorous instantiation of this theory was the theory of general competitive equilibrium, in which formal axiomatic methods were used to analyze equilibrium in models with arbitrary numbers of agents and very general assumptions about technology and consumers' preferences. Using miniature general equilibrium models involving one or two "representative" agents, many macroeconomists concluded that, unless people had limited information

1

(a situation that would not last very long, because people would learn from experience) the economy must be in equilibrium: the combination of optimizing agents and competitive markets implied that supply must equal demand in all markets. The concept of involuntary unemployment, the essence of which is that the supply of labor exceeds demand, did not make sense. The most prominent work in this genre was the new classical macroeconomics and, shortly after that, real business cycle theory. Although these models were very different from his, this conception of equilibrium was widely named "Walrasian," after the nineteenth-century pioneer of general equilibrium theory Léon Walras, whose *Elements d'economie politique pure* (1874), was taken to have originated this approach. The approach contrasted with the Keynesian models that, prior to the 1970s, formed the basis on which the macroeconomic consensus rested.

However, the search for microfoundations, which was well under way long before the 1970s, for reasons that clearly had nothing to do with the macroeconomic challenges of that period, also involved economists who argued that Walrasian models were not suitable for analyzing the real world. These economists sought to derive "disequilibrium" or non-Walrasian microfoundations for macroeconomics that could displace the unrealistic and inappropriate assumption of perfectly competitive equilibrium.

MYTHS ABOUT THE SEARCH FOR MICROFOUNDATIONS

The story of the evolution of macroeconomics from the 1950s to the 1990s has been told many times, but usually by practitioners reflecting on their subject in textbooks (e.g., Blanchard 2003) or through public reflections on the progress that the field has made (e.g., Mankiw 1990; Woodford 1999; Blanchard 2000) or in claims that the field has gone wrong (e.g., Solow 1997; Krugman 2009).[1] The problem with most of this literature, we argue,

---

[1]   An important exception is Hoover (2012), who traces the search for microfoundations back to Keynes, arguing that before the 1970s great importance was attached to the heterogeneity of agents. Extended discussions can also be found in *The New Palgrave Dictionary of Economics*, the first edition of which covered the topic in three articles: "Macroeconomics: Relation with Microeconomics" (Howitt 1987) and "Disequilibrium Analysis" (Bénassy 1987a) and "Rationed Equilibria" (Bénassy 1987b). In the second edition, these were replaced with an article on "Microfoundations" (Janssen 2008), "Dynamic Models with Non-Clearing Markets" (Bénassy 2008a), and "Non-Clearing Markets in General Equilibrium" (Bénassy 2008b). Bénassy (1995, 2006) has also edited and discussed two substantial collections of articles on the topic. Other significant surveys discussions include Silvestre (1992), Janssen (1993), and Busetto (1995). Weintraub (2008) provides a skeptical note about the (ir)relevance of modern developments for the microfoundations debate. His earlier work on the search for microfoundations (E. R. Weintraub 1977, 1979)

is that, with very few exceptions, it either misses important developments in macroeconomics that were increasingly spurned in and after the 1970s or does not see their full significance. Like most intellectual historians, we are interested in blind alleys and ideas that proved mistaken as much as in ideas that were ultimately successful. However, the story is intriguing because, as we show, many of these abandoned theories were aimed at addressing problems for which the successful theories had no solution.

An example of failure even to mention the search for disequilibrium microfoundations is the account provided by Michael Woodford (1999), whose textbook became very influential after the millennium. The starting point in his account is the Keynesian revolution, the contribution of which he argues was to shift attention from the business cycle to statics to the simultaneous determination of prices, the rate of interest, output, and employment. Although it involved neglecting important problems, it focused attention on problems that had to be solved if the field was to make progress. Initially, there was a methodological gulf between Keynesian macroeconomics and classical microeconomics, but this was, he claimed, bridged by viewing macroeconomics through the lens of general equilibrium theory. The resulting neoclassical synthesis involved the "redefinition of the scope of Keynesian analysis as relating purely to the period before wages and prices were able to adjust" (Woodford 1999:10). Despite this achievement, "the perceived incompleteness of the theoretical foundations of Keynesian economics continued to motivate important work of criticism and refinement" (Woodford 1999:11), notably analyzing components of the Keynesian model such as the consumption function and the demand for liquid assets in terms of individual optimizing behavior.

The challenge to the first neoclassical synthesis, Woodford argues, came with "the great inflation," which caused a crisis in Keynesian economics. The need for analysis of the relationship between policy and inflation,

is discussed in Chapter 8. Solow (2004) provides an example of the clear recognition by a leading macroeconomic theorist of the notion that macroeconomic models have always had microfoundations, even if less formal microfoundations than those found in the modern literature. There have been some other accounts of the search for microfoundations (e.g., Van Ees and Garretsen 1990; Garretsen 1992; Janssen 1993; Kirman 1993; Rizvi 1994; Hartley 1997; Gallegati and Kirman 1999; De Antoni 2006; De Vroey 2006; and Arena 2010). However, while they have made some valuable points (e.g., Van Ees and Garretsen have pointed out that the concerns of the disequilibrium macro were far more ambitious than merely explaining wage stickiness), their concerns are substantially different from ours. Janssen's concerns are methodological, while Garretsen is concerned with developing an interpretation of Keynes. Rizvi, though providing a discussion that covers many of the works that we discuss, focuses on evaluating general equilibrium theory. De Vroey (2006) and Arena (2010) are focused on material outside the story on which we focus.

which Keynesian economics, being essentially static, could not provide, led
to a reassessment and the rise of new theories.

Most notably a framework was needed that would clarify the links between macroeconomic policy and the eventual changes in the general price level that would
result from it. Attention to this problem soon pointed up other weaknesses of
Keynesian models, such as their neglect of the endogeneity of expectations and
of the determinants of supply costs. Together with the lingering conceptual problem of the relationship between macroeconomic and microeconomic theory, these
issues provided fuel for a series of fundamental critiques of Keynesian economics,
that have often been described as "revolutions" or "counter-revolutions" in their
own right. (Woodford 1999:14)

From here, Woodford discusses "monetarism," "rational expectations
and the new classical macroeconomics," and "real business cycle theory,"
noting that it proved "possible to incorporate rational expectations – and
indeed, intertemporal optimizing behavior – into models of nominal wage
and price rigidity" to obtain "new Keynesian models" (1999:24). By the
1990s, this variety of approaches, distinguished by attitudes to wage and
price flexibility and by methodological differences, set the scene for what
he labels, with a modest question mark, the new neoclassical synthesis. Like
the synthesis represented by Patinkin, this approach uses the tools of general equilibrium theory to bridge the divide between macro and micro, but
it does so using dynamic models.

Today this [using general equilibrium theory] means using intertemporal general
equilibrium analysis to model the complete dynamics of the macroeconomy – just
as is done in modern theories of financial markets, industry structure and so on –
rather than simply using a static general-equilibrium model to describe the long-
run position toward which the economy should tend asymptotically. In practice
this means that the methodology of the new synthesis is largely that of the real business cycle literature, even though wage and price rigidities are allowed for, and the
determinants of (individually) optimal wage and price-setting decisions are modeled in detail. (Woodford 1999:29)

Although based on real business cycle methodology, which in turn drew
on the new classical macroeconomics, Woodford's was a synthesis in the
sense that it finds a role for both Keynesian and classical ideas. The two
views are relevant in different situations. He disparaged the idea of describing the synthesis as Keynesian on the grounds that such nomenclature was
not appropriate in science: one does not, for example, have "Einsteinian
physicists."

A number of features of Woodford's account need to be challenged. The
first is that he is concerned with policy: it is the policy challenges that drew

attention to the problems in Keynesian economics and hence prompted the need for re-evaluation of macroeconomic theory. There is no suggestion that a reappraisal of Keynesian economics was well under way before the new policy challenges arose; neither is there any suggestion that these challenges had to do with the general equilibrium framework itself. Second, Keynesian phenomena are equated with wage and price inflexibility, without suggesting that this explanation might have been one of the major issues under debate.

Woodford is not the only author to have removed disequilibrium theory from the history of macroeconomics. In his macroeconomics textbook, Blanchard (2003:572–81), is silent, jumping straight from "the neoclassical synthesis" to "the rational expectations critique" and "modern developments." Even a distinguished historian of economic thought, Mark Blaug (1992, ch. 12), offers a methodological interpretation of the history of macroeconomics between the 1960s and 1980s as a debate between Keynesians and monetarists in which disequilibrium macroeconomics is barely mentioned. By the late 1980s and early 1990s, most surveys of competing schools of macroeconomic thought either omitted disequilibrium macro altogether (e.g., Phelps 1990), or treated it as a finished episode (e.g. Snowdon, Vane, and Wynarczyk 1994:109–23), which, by forcefully bringing into the picture the issue of the microfoundations of macroeconomics, led both to the revival of interest in the market-clearing approach (New Classical school) and to attempts to rationalize wage and price stickiness (New Keynesian economics). The latter may be correct, but, as we hope to show, it is a limited view.

A clue that something significant is be missing from the argument is that many of the names that dominated the period's macroeconomic literature are either absent from Woodford's account, or play minor roles: Robert Clower, Axel Leijonhufvud, Robert Solow, Robert Barro, Herschel Grossman, Frank Hahn, Jacques Drèze, Jean-Pascal Bénassy and Edmond Malinvaud. Not only is what was, in 1988, almost twenty years after its publication, the most-cited article in the *American Economic Review*, "A General Disequilibrium Model of Income and Employment" (Barro and Grossman 1971; see Anonymous 1988) not mentioned, but the entire literature to which it was a contribution is passed over. Barro and Grossman's article was cited 325 times, and in addition, their subsequent book (1976) was cited 285 times. Citation counts do not prove that an article is important, but they sound a warning.

Figure 1.1 shows that there was a sizeable literature on disequilibrium analysis and that it began before the dramatic events of 1973. In the words of Peter Howitt (1990:10), "for a brief period in the early 1970s," disequilibrium

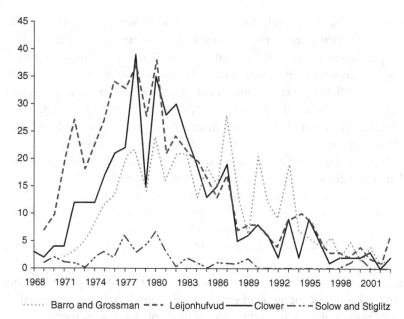

Figure 1.1. Citation counts for Clower (1965), Leijonhufvud (1968), and Barro and Grossman (1971)

macro was "the hottest topic in macroeconomics". It also shows that interest in these works continued well into the 1990s.

Not all histories ignore disequilibrium macroeconomics as completely as does Woodford's. However, where the topic is discussed, it is almost invariably as the prelude to the New Keynesian macroeconomics (see, e.g., Mankiw 1990:1655–56; Blaug 1997:672–73, 685–87; Blanchard 2000:1386–87). Disequilibrium macroeconomics is presented as the economics of price rigidity. Economists realized, so the New Keynesian stories run, that conventional theories, based on perfect price flexibility, could not provide an adequate explanation of Keynesian unemployment, and so economists explored the implications of wages and prices being sticky: the result of price stickiness was that markets do not clear, creating spillover effects in other markets. Disequilibrium could imply a demand multiplier under conditions of Keynesian excess supply in both goods and labor markets, or a supply multiplier with generalized excess demand in those markets, depending on the price vector. Such results were "tantalizing" in the macroeconomics of the 1970s (Blanchard 2000:1386). However, there was the problem of which scenario was more likely, which could only be settled by a theory of price formation.

As suggested by Gregory Mankiw (1990:1655), general disequilibrium models "à la Barro-Grossman do not fit easily into the history of post 1970 macroeconomics. In contrast with most of macroeconomic theories put forward after that, they were not directly aimed at correcting the flaws that provoked the breakdown of the consensus that prevailed until the early 1970s." More recently, Mankiw (2001:C49n1) has claimed that New Keynesian theories started in the mid 1980s should be interpreted as "explaining why the [excess supply] regime in general disequilibrium models is the normal case." In the same vein, Huw Dixon (1997:176–79) has argued that the essential insights of disequilibrium macroeconomics about firm rationing in the output market are based on the notion that price exceeds marginal cost, as later developed in the imperfect competition New Keynesian models. New Keynesian economics then enters as a natural development from this, in that it provides explanations of why prices are sticky and does not simply assume it. As in Woodford's account, the story remains a tale of clear progress.[2] Both versions of what happened to macroeconomics around 1970 – be it Woodford's writing the search for disequilibrium microfoundations out of the story or presenting disequilibrium macroeconomics as no more than a primitive forerunner of New Keynesian Economics (of which both Mankiw and Dixon are supporters) – miss important elements of the history and hence distort it.

REVISING THE HISTORY

Our claim is that if we are to understand the way macroeconomics developed during this period, it is essential to have a much fuller account of the search for disequilibrium microfoundations. The New Keynesian theories capture part of what went on but they nonetheless leave important parts of the story out. The first point is that, as we have already mentioned, disequilibrium theory began before the crisis of the 1970s: the search for a new macroeconomics was not just a response to economic events. It involved many of the leading figures in the discipline, and, crucially, it was an attempt to find an alternative to a theory of general competitive equilibrium believed to be both unrealistic and logically flawed. The second point is that though fixed-price models were important, the literature went well beyond that. Models with price rigidities were used as a first step in the analysis because it was believed that they were a better approximation to

---

[2] Backhouse (1995, part III) presented one account in this vein. This book can be seen either as a criticism or as a development from that.

the way real-world markets behaved than were models of market-clearing competitive equilibrium. Where we part company with the new Keynesian accounts cited earlier is that the literature went further than this in important respects:

(1) Price rigidity was believed to arise because disequilibrium was the inevitable result of adjustments to equilibrium having to take place in real time: it did not arise simply because of institutional market imperfections such as unions or barriers to entry. When market conditions change, prices need to change and, outside organized, centralized markets (such as stock exchanges or commodity markets), this process takes time with the result that some trades take place at disequilibrium prices. Non-Walrasian theories were thus intended as general theories about how markets worked.

(2) For a significant number of contributors to the literature, the theory was needed because the theory of general competitive equilibrium was logically deficient in that the model contained that no one who could change prices. The story was sometimes told of an "auctioneer" who would cry out prices, with no trading taking place till an equilibrium set of prices had been worked out—the so-called *tâtonnement* process—but this was clearly a fictitious person who was not part of the model. However, though some markets operate like this, most markets do not. More important, if there were such an individual (or agency), it would involve costs, which immediately invalidates the assumption that trading can take place costlessly.

(3) The literature, contrary to the claims of those who see only fixed-price models, did extend to theories in which prices were endogenous. Models were developed in which agents had the power to set prices. Obviously, this meant that the models were, in a sense, models of imperfect competition. However, as explained in point (1), imperfect competition did not arise because of institutional barriers to competition: it arose simply because, in the absence of a deus ex machina, agents had to be the ones who set prices, and if so, they had to have the power to do so, if only whenever prices are out of equilibrium.

A NOTE ON TERMINOLOGY

Discussion of this literature is beset with terminological problems, and different labels abound: non-Walrasian theory, disequilibrium theory, equilibrium with rationing, non-tâtonnement theory, fixed-price models. Before proceeding, it is important to clarify the way these terms are generally used.

One of the earliest terms was "disequilibrium macroeconomics," following the title of Barro and Grossman's article (1971) "A General Disequilibrium Model of Income and Employment." Equilibrium meant simply market clearing – equality of supply and demand in each market – and "disequilibrium" that this was not so, arising because agents (both households and firms) faced not only a budget constraint but also constraints on what they could buy or sell.

However, the term *equilibrium* can also mean, following its physical meaning as a state of rest or a balance of forces, the solution to a model. In traditional theory, these two meanings were the same, for the only forces were demand and supply understood as the amounts that agents wanted to buy and sell at the prices they faced. In models with rationing, on the other hand, agents were assumed to face constraints that forced them off conventionally defined supply and demand schedules, so the two meanings of disequilibrium diverged. It was possible to have equilibrium (in the sense of a balance of forces) in which there was disequilibrium (in the sense that supply and demand are unequal in one or more markets). This was the essence of disequilibrium models, for the claim was that markets would not converge to a position where all markets cleared.

This terminological problem becomes particularly obvious in the case of general equilibrium models. When Barro and Grossman wrote of a "general" disequilibrium model they meant one in which there could be disequilibrium in any or all markets, not simply, as in much of the literature, just the labor market. Theirs was, however, a macroeconomic model in that it dealt with aggregates: there were markets for labor and commodities.[3] However, the term "general equilibrium theory" had come to mean a particular type of model – microeconomic in that it modeled an arbitrary number of potentially heterogeneous agents, but general in that it modeled all markets simultaneously and that very general assumptions were made about consumers' preferences and about technology. Moreover, general equilibrium analysis focused on proving that equilibrium existed and investigating whether it was unique and stable. The result was that when price rigidities and imperfect competition were analyzed within this framework, producing models in which markets did not clear – disequilibrium models according to one meaning of the term – they were still called

---

[3] There is a need for a third market in the background, but this does not need to be modeled explicitly.

general equilibrium models, because of the genre of which they clearly formed a part.

Equilibrium can also mean that agents face situations in which, given the constraints they encounter (which of course include market conditions) they have no reason to change their behavior – that consumers are maximizing utility and firms are maximizing profit. In the traditional general equilibrium model, in which supply and demand schedules described behavior, equilibrium in this sense implied market clearing. However, once we depart from that framework, problems arise. If competition is imperfect, or monopolistic, individual agents have some market power in that they can change the prices at which they trade. Equilibrium, in the sense of a situation where maximizing agents will not wish to change their behavior, will not imply market clearing, for it will not be profitable for sellers to lower their prices to the market clearing level. Similarly, if agents have mistaken expectations or asymmetric information, or are bound by long-term or even implicit contracts, they may choose to remain in situations in which markets do not clear.

A widespread feature of this literature is rationing, the term "equilibrium with rationing" being common. It is particularly important in the general equilibrium literature for, if agents are not identical, the rationing scheme may matter. For example, when there is a shortage of goods, is everyone forced to consume less, or do some people get all they want and others nothing (as when some people are fully employed and others have no work)? Or, if there is a shortage of goods, are they allocated by first-come first-served, queuing, a lottery, or some other mechanism? Rationing raises further questions. Does rationing imply that agents are not maximizing utility or profit? One answer is that they are maximizing subject to a constraint on the quantity that they can buy or sell. However, this raises the question as to why they do not offer higher prices to obtain goods that are in short supply, or offer to reduce prices to sell goods or labor for which there is insufficient demand. Surely, some economists argue, rationing caused simply by the fact that prices have not adjusted to equilibrium must imply non-maximizing behavior.

Rationing also raises a question about competition. Perfect competition refers to a market in which agents are price takers – they cannot change price – and they can buy or sell as much as they wish at the prevailing prices. Rationing violates that assumption, which implies that competition cannot be perfect if there is rationing. Equilibrium with rationing thus becomes equilibrium with imperfect competition. Thus, if out-of-equilibrium transactions are seen as an inevitable consequence of economic activity taking place in time, and if this is taken to imply rationing, it follows that markets have to be modeled as imperfectly competitive (the terms "imperfect competition" and "monopolistic competition" are used interchangeably).[4] It is only in imperfectly competitive markets that agents can set prices – important given that there is no one else to set prices. Against that, some economists prefer to reserve the term imperfect competition for markets in which agents have monopoly power in equilibrium and to see the ability to change prices out of equilibrium as something different from imperfect competition.

Earlier, the term "state of rest" was equated with a balance of forces. In a simple, static model, the two are the same. However, during the 1970s, economists moved toward the analysis of models that were dynamic in two senses. One was that agents were modeled as making inter-temporal choices, notably with consumers maximizing lifetime utility. The other was that the environment they faced was assumed to be stochastic: economies were hit by random shocks, coming from either monetary policy or technology. The new classical models developed by Robert Lucas and others were equilibrium models in that, at any moment, agents were taking optimal decisions given the information they had available, but they were not in a state of rest, for economic activity was fluctuating in response to shocks. Agents optimized but random, unpredictable shocks would cause them to make mistakes. Although this term is peripheral to the literature covered by this book, it leads to the concept of a stochastic equilibrium, in which variables are characterized by a stable probability distribution.

Once established, terminology changes slowly. Terms that had once been relatively unproblematic because different meanings coincided, ceased to correspond in a simple way with the models that were being developed. Perhaps the simplest solution would be to use the term "Walrasian" to refer to models of competitive markets in which, aside from random shocks, agents are maximizing utility or profit and markets clear in the sense that any unemployment is "voluntary" (the result of decisions by workers to hold out for a better wage than they can currently obtain). The literature with which we are concerned can then be called "non-Walrasian," for it deals with equilibria in which one or more of the conditions for a Walrasian equilibrium are not satisfied.

---

[4] In other contexts, this interchangeability of imperfect and monopolistic competition would not be legitimate (the theories of the two economists who first used the terms, Edward Chamberlin and Joan Robinson, were very different), but for the literature we are dealing with, it presents no problems.

At this point, the inclinations of the historian and the economist part company. The economist, developing a theory, will opt for consistent use of terminology. In contrast, the historian will generally favor using the terminology that was used by those whose work he or she is discussing, because terminological shifts can be significant. In this book, therefore, because different participants described their work in different ways, the terminology varies. In some cases, to avoid pedantically defining every use of common terms, meaning has to be inferred from the context. Our hope is that, provided that readers are aware of the multiple meanings discussed in this section, this should not cause problems.

THE ARGUMENT TO FOLLOW

The search for disequilibrium foundations took place against the background of much broader changes in macroeconomics, outlined in Chapter 2. These include the Keynesian revolution that, for many reasons, forms the starting point for modern macroeconomics. Salient economic events are discussed along with changes in monetary economics and the theory of economic growth. Monetary theory is an important part of the background for the search for microfoundations because debates about models are sometimes hard to separate from debates about stabilization policy. Growth theory matters because the new models that came into macroeconomics in the 1970s paid much more attention to the supply side: this and their concern with dynamics took them into the domain of growth theory.

After that, the book adopts a broadly chronological structure. It starts in the 1950s with Patinkin, whose work arguably provides the starting point for the literature on non-Walrasian theory (the qualification is inserted because Patinkin's work, as we explain, was in turn inspired by the work of his teacher, Oskar Lange). It then moves on to the 1960s and the two figures most widely credited with having initiated the search for new theoretical foundations for Keynesian economics, Robert Clower and Axel Leijonhufvud. Although they bring in some other early work, Chapters 5 through 8 then focus on the 1970s. Chapter 5 covers models of equilibrium with price rigidity – fixed-price models – taking the story from the models of Robert Solow, Joseph Stiglitz, Robert Barro, and Herschel Grossman up to the new Keynesian rationalizations of wage stickiness that were being developed by the end of the decade. Chapter 6 then tells the parallel story of the search for "equilibrium" microfoundations, associated with Edmund Phelps and Robert Lucas, ending with the story of Barro's and Grossman's abandoning of disequilibrium modeling, and Barro's emergence of one of the most prominent new classical macroeconomists.

Chapter 7 steps back from purely macroeconomic models to consider the less-well-known general equilibrium literature that emerged in parallel with it. The starting point here is the developments in general equilibrium theory in the 1950s and 1960s, from Kenneth Arrow and Gérard Debreu to Frank Hahn and Takashi Negishi, without which the work of Jean-Pascal Bénassy, Jacques Drèze, Jean-Michel Grandmont, and Guy Laroque could not be understood. It focuses on the development of models of imperfect competition that could explain how price adjustment took place. Discussion of the 1970s concludes with Chapter 8, which reviews some of the main attempts to take stock of the literature on microfoundations, the focus being on the surveys by E. Roy Weintraub, Grandmont, and Allan Drazen and a widely cited series of lectures by Edmond Malinvaud. These were important in helping frame the way economists thought about microfoundations, whether Walrasian or non-Walrasian.

As will be made clear, disequilibrium theory did not end with the 1970s. Chapter 9 considers the main ways in which it was taken forward, culminating in a discussion of the relationship of disequilibrium theory to the new neoclassical synthesis, the dominant approach to macroeconomics around the millennium. Conclusions are then drawn in the final chapter.

The literature involved is large and complex, involving many of the profession's leading figures – many distinguished economists not mentioned here participated at some point. Furthermore, the boundaries of the literature are ill defined. For example, we need to consider Hahn and Negishi on non-tâtonnement models, for this is essential to understand non-Walrasian models of imperfect competition, but we do not need to cover the entire literature on the stability of non- tâtonnement processes in general equilibrium models. Simple characterizations are dangerous, but an attempt is made to provide a visual account in Figure 1.2.[5] This is far from comprehensive, as regards both the individuals named and the connections among them, but it provides a picture of some of the main economists involved, leaving aside those working in the Phelps tradition. Economists are grouped roughly into locations, though there is considerable arbitrariness here, not least because of mobility. Leijonhufvud is placed at University of California, Los Angeles (UCLA), on the grounds that, though his Ph.D. was from Northwestern University, he completed the thesis and the subsequent

---

[5] We note that some readers urged us to remove this diagram as oversimplified though others encouraged us to retain it as helping to provide an overview, if only a partial one.

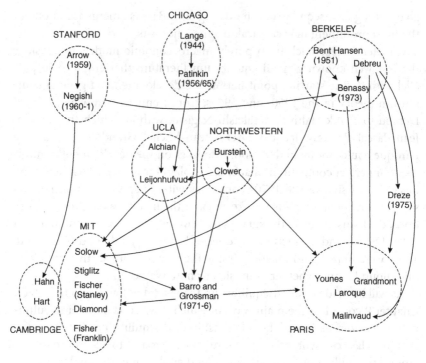

Figure 1.2. An overview of the search for disequilibrium microfoundations

book at UCLA where Alchian was an important influence on his work. In contrast, Bénassy is placed at Berkeley, because this is where he completed his Ph.D. Grandmont, on the other hand, is significant in our story because of his later work with Younès, Laroque, and others, so is placed in Paris. The two Cambridges are shown as overlapping because of the extensive collaboration between them. Connections within the Massachusetts Institute of Technology (MIT) are not shown even though Stiglitz, Fischer, and Diamond had obtained their Ph.D.s from MIT, and hence had been taught by Solow, as were Woodford and several others not shown in the diagram.

A HISTORIOGRAPHIC NOTE

The search for microfoundations of macroeconomics forms part of a much broader transformation of economics that took place from, roughly, the 1960s to the 1980s. An important manifestation of this broader change was the rise of rational choice theory and of the "economic" approach to human behavior in general. Not only did economics become more mathematical during this period,[6] but the rational choice model also became the generally accepted perspective, and explanations that did not involve individual rational choice were increasingly seen as inadequate (Backhouse 2002, 2008, 2010a, 2010b; Rodgers 2011). These developments, which affected all of the social sciences, undoubtedly fit into the context of the Cold War, and many of those involved in this story were linked with institutions such as RAND, the histories of which have been told elsewhere (see, for example, Amadae 2003). This transformation of economics went along with an ideological change in which economics played a central role. There was increasing skepticism about whether government intervention could improve on the performance of free markets, whether at the level of the economy as a whole or that of individual industries. The assumptions of rational individuals and competitive markets, which are central to our story, were intertwined with arguments about how free markets would perform better than the state. It is possible to discern differences between the intellectual cultures in the United States and Europe that no doubt influenced the way macroeconomic theories were developed on each side of the Atlantic. For example, the Keynesian "social democratic" consensus of the early post-war decades that gave way to free-market liberalism propagated by Ronald Reagan and his contemporaries had much deeper roots in Europe than in the United States. It is hard to believe that this had no connection with differences in the way macroeconomics was undertaken.

Our reason for not paying more attention to these broader factors is not that we consider them unimportant (one of us has recently argued very strongly not only that economics should be placed in the context of broader intellectual developments, but also that it should not be considered apart from the other social sciences).[7] The search for microfoundations was clearly driven by a belief that economic theory should become more rigorous, according to a very specific understanding of rigor, and by a belief that explanations of economic phenomena should be grounded on assumptions about individual behavior. Although economists might be reluctant to admit this, such understandings are historically contingent. Explaining behavior in terms of rational individuals may not be ideologically neutral, and for some contexts that may matter. However, we felt that it was appropriate to leave such ideas aside in order to sort out what happened in what we believe to be a fascinating story, even without taking them into account.

---

[6] This can be documented. Backhouse (1998) provides statistics on the use of mathematics in the main academic journals for the period up to 1960, and the trends documented there continued.

[7] See Backhouse and Fontaine (2010a, 2010b).

The main place where our narrower perspective may be thought a problem relates to the connection between economic theory and policy. The story
of macroeconomics in the 1970s has been told in terms of the displacement
of Keynesianism by monetarism, where both terms have clear ideological
resonance. It may well be true that, for many of the economists we discuss,
the appeal of one macroeconomic theory rather than another was ideological. Many of the new classical economists were certainly in favor of less
government intervention while their Keynesian opponents were more lib-
eral (in the U.S. sense of the word). In this sense, there was a left-right split.
It is, moreover, plausible to argue that the empirical results that economists
produced, and the studies they chose to believe, were influenced by their
prior beliefs. We do not dispute this.[8]

However, even though ideological commitments are, no doubt, tangled
up with the story we tell, we are not convinced that it would have made
sense to try to work them into the book. Disentangling the relation between
economic thinking and ideology is difficult and can probably be done
only at the level of intellectual biography.[9] Lucas, Kydland, and Prescott,
for example, would presumably claim that they are critical of government
intervention because their work shows that such policies will be damaging.
Arguing that their motivations were different would require a type of argument that goes beyond anything we can provide here. More important than
that, many of the ideas discussed in this book cut across political views.
There are clearly economists in our story whose political positions are well
known, whether on the right or the left, but they formed part of a community in which ideas passed from economists of one political persuasion to
another and in which the political positions of many are not on the public
record. This position echoes the conclusion of intellectual historian Daniel
Rodgers (2011), who has argued that the rise of thinking in terms of individuals, including the "economic" approach to human behavior, transcends
any left-right distinction. Although it sounds perverse to argue this, the role
of ideology in our story is both obvious and impossible to disentangle. To
frame our history around it would require writing a very different type of
history – one to which the history told here would be complementary.

---

[8]   This is discussed in Backhouse (2010a).
[9]   See, for example, Cherrier (2011) on the relationship between Friedman's economics and
      his ideology.

TWO

Macroeconomics after Keynes

THE KEYNESIAN REVOLUTION AND THE AGE OF KEYNES

For most of those involved, the search for non-Walrasian or disequilibrium microfoundations was a continuation of the task begun by John Maynard Keynes in *The General Theory of Employment, Interest and Money* (1973[1936]). In that book, he had tried to show why the market for labor might never achieve equilibrium – why, in other words, capitalist economies might exhibit long-term, involuntary unemployment. Much of the literature on disequilibrium microfoundations, therefore, was about reappraising the Keynesian economics that had come to dominate economic thinking since the Second World War. The reason why Keynesian economics had come to dominate macroeconomic theory to such an extent that reappraising Keynesian theory could be seen as close to synonymous with reappraising the foundations of macroeconomics was not that his book bore no relation to previous economic thinking; it was that it brought together in a coherent framework key ideas developed during the 1920s and 1930s, an extremely creative period in which economists had grappled with theories of money and the business cycle as they confronted problems from German hyperinflation in the early 1920s to the Great Depression of the 1930s (Laidler 1999). Keynesian concepts proved useful not just for tackling the problem of mass unemployment but also for controlling inflation and allocating resources during the Second World War. They also proved a good fit with the mathematical tools to which economists were increasingly turning, a change driven in part by the involvement of economists in operations research. At the same time, Keynes's view that government had a responsibility to manage the economy chimed with changed expectations of what government needed to do. The experience of Roosevelt's New Deal and the experience of wartime economic

17

planning were taken to show what government could achieve, while the emerging rivalry between the United States and the Soviet Union provided a clear reason why government needed to take responsibility for economic performance. Keynesianism dominated both as an economic theory and as a framework for thinking about economic policy (see Backhouse 2008, 2010a, 2010b; Backhouse and Bateman 2011).

The result was that when people looked back to the period before the Second World War, they saw a different world from the age of Western prosperity that was clearly emerging by the 1950s. The Keynesian revolution – a product of changes in economic ideas combined with new ways of doing economics at a time of dramatic social and political change – became the dominant event in twentieth-century economics. So much so that, by and large, pre-Keynesian economics became almost invisible to economists trained after the war. If they looked back, they saw only what Keynes wanted them to see – an arid "classical theory" that was neither rigorous nor a good fit for modern circumstances. However, although the Keynesian revolution was effectively the label that had come to be attached to one element in a complex and inter-related set of historical changes, spanning society, politics and economics, economists did not see it that way. Instead, they saw it as the result of a decisive theoretical innovation. After all, if the classical economists had been, as Keynes (1973[1936]:16) described them, "Euclidian geometers in a non-Euclidian world," it was only to be expected that their writings should pass into history when a new theory was developed.

So, by the mid-1950s, macroeconomics was effectively Keynesian economics. Keynesian theory was used to explain unemployment and inflation, and was also the basis for thinking about the business cycle and economic growth. If economists wanted to work on macroeconomics, they more or less had to work on Keynesian macroeconomics. However, even though it was the dominant approach, economists did not fully understand the Keynesian system. Moreover, Keynesian theory still needed to be developed, for although Keynes had provided many invaluable conceptual tools, he had not worked them out with the degree of mathematical rigor that was increasingly expected. Many of his ideas, such as his theories of what determined the two main categories of private spending – consumption and investment – needed to be taken further if they were to be the basis for the new empirical models that were being demanded, capable of providing numerical forecasts of the effects of policy changes. This all required that further work be undertaken on the conceptual foundations of macroeconomics.

In addition, as the 1950s wore on, new policy problems came to the fore. In the 1940s, there had been great concern about long-term stagnation, for it was widely feared that once the war, which had massively increased demand for goods and services, was over, the world would return to conditions of stagnation such as had prevailed in the 1930s. All previous major wars had been followed by periods of depression, and it was not clear why this should not happen again. However, by the 1950s, a return to the conditions of the 1930s was looking increasingly unlikely. Instead, inflation and economic growth became more important problems. Inflation had, of course, been a problem during the Second World War (as it has been during all wars), but the cause had been clear. Military spending had created severe excess demand, and civilian consumption had to be restrained either by price increases or by other measures. "Inflation gap" theories, relating inflation to the gap between aggregate demand and the supply of goods and services made good sense under such conditions. However, after the war, the problem of inflation was different. There was a burst of inflation caused by spending on the Korean War, but even if this were discounted, it was clear that inflation posed a continuing problem.

In many countries, inflation was serious because the international financial system had been reconstructed, at Bretton Woods, around a system of fixed exchange rates. Most countries fixed their exchange rates in relation to the U.S. dollar, which in turn was fixed to gold. The result was that countries experiencing higher inflation than their trading partners became uncompetitive, and their balance of payments would fall into deficit, forcing them to borrow from abroad in a world in which financial markets were much more constrained than they became after the 1970s. Governments were thus more or less forced to keep inflation from getting out of line with inflation in other countries, something that, because of the dollar's role as the main international reserve currency, related to policy in the United States. Devaluation was an option, but governments generally considered this a sign of defeat and sought to avoid it, often at great cost. More commonly, growth would be reined back in an attempt to restrain both inflation and demand for imports.

By the 1960s, even though inflation was not significantly different from what it had been for most of the post–Second World War period (with the exception of the Korean War), it was perceived as more important problem than it had been the case a decade earlier, for it was clear that it was taking place even in the absence of war. Thus, when the American Economic Association (AEA) organized sessions on contemporary economic problems for its 1960 meeting, its president could write to one

potential contributor that he would not be surprised to learn that inflation was thought to be one of those problems.[1] There was also great concern with unemployment. During the 1960s, the Kennedy administration's
Keynesian Council of Economic Advisers, headed by Walter Heller, believing that under Eisenhower, unemployment had been allowed to remain too
high, designed a package of measures to reduce it to a more acceptable level.
From 1963 onward, unemployment fell each year. Despite that, inflation
was still less than 2 percent per annum by 1965, and though it rose to 3 percent by 1967, this was still not out of line with what had been experienced
in the 1950s when unemployment had been higher. However, by the end
of the 1960s, escalating expenditure on the Vietnam War combined with
Lyndon Johnson's unwillingness to abandon his Great Society program had
begun to raise the inflation rate, which reached almost 6 percent by 1970,
higher than at any point since the Korean War. Unemployment began to rise
for a couple of years, and inflation slipped back to 4 percent. Meanwhile,
world commodity prices had been rising, and in 1973, the Organization
of Petroleum Exporting Countries (OPEC) managed to create an effective
cartel and oil prices, which had been static for many years, suddenly rose.
An Arab embargo on oil exports to countries that supported Israel in its
war against Egypt and Syria together with an almost fourfold rise in prices
in 1973–74, which dramatically shifted purchasing power to oil-exporting
countries and rendered much energy-intensive technology obsolete, moved
the world economy, which had been booming in 1973, dramatically into
recession. Output and employment fell and inflation accelerated. U.S. inflation peaked at 12.3 percent in 1974, and a year later, unemployment, which
since 1970 had been around 5 percent, rose to 8.5 percent of the labor
force[2]. This was followed, six years later, by a further doubling of oil prices
after the Iran-Iraq War, and U.S. inflation reached a second peak of 13.5
percent in 1980. There were similar rises in inflation, accompanied by high
unemployment, across the world. In some countries, inflation rose even
higher. In Britain, for example, where liberalization of the banking system
had produced a massive increase in the money supply at the same time as
fiscal expansion had dramatically cut unemployment, inflation was running at more than 25 percent in 1975.

[1]   Lee Bach to Paul Samuelson and Robert Solow, April 6, 1959. Paul A. Samuelson
      Papers, Box 14. David M. Rubenstein Rare Book and Manuscript Library, Duke
      University.
[2]   U.S. Bureau of Labor Statistics data. Inflation is December-to-December rise in the
      Consumer Price Index (CPI) for urban areas. Note that using annual averages would give
      different figures, so rapidly was inflation changing.

The second major problem that emerged by the 1960s was economic growth. In the 1940s, as the war ended, the main concern, as has been explained already, was avoiding a recurrence of the Great Depression; there was also the urgent need to keep Europeans alive (literally, given the devastation caused during the last year of the war) and to reconstruct the European economies. However, even as these problems were solved, two factors made growth an increasingly prominent problem. One was increased awareness of the gap between rich and poor countries, with differences in incomes being far higher than had been realized. This became more important as European empires were dismantled and former colonies became independent, the most significant being India and Pakistan in 1947. The newly established United Nations gave these new countries a voice they had not previously had.

The other factor was the Cold War, in which military rivalry between the United States and the Soviet Union was inextricable from economic and technological rivalries. The military strength of the Soviet Union during the Second World War clearly reflected the industrialization and economic growth produced under Stalin's Five Year Plans. There had been military assistance from the West to the Soviet Union, but the vast bulk of the resources needed to defeat Germany had been domestically produced. After the war, Soviet statisticians produced impressive estimates of the rate at which the Soviet economy was growing, which compared favorably with growth rates achieved in the West. The United States appeared to be lagging behind, a fear dramatically reinforced by the undeniable achievements of Soviet technology, including the rapid development of nuclear bombs, the launch in 1958 of the first orbiting satellite, Sputnik, and then the first man in space.

These two reasons for concern with growth were, of course, linked, because the two countries were offering rival economic systems to the Third World. To persuade countries such as India to adopt a capitalist model, it was necessary to show that U.S. capitalism was more successful than Soviet planning. On top of that, growth was needed to achieve domestic objectives: full employment and rising living standards. If workers demanded higher wages, productivity growth was needed to avoid inflation.

Although these concerns with inflation and economic growth can all be traced back, on one way or another, to the Second World War, a useful benchmark is 1956. By the mid-1950s, the stresses of the immediate post–Second World War era were over. There was nuclear balance, with both the United States and the Soviet Union having the bomb. The Korean War had ended with the country divided, and the Soviet suppression of the Hungarian uprising signaled that the Soviet Union was not relaxing its grip on Eastern Europe, while the Suez crisis made it clear that Britain and France were no longer major powers. On the other hand, Western Europe was emerging from reconstruction and beginning the spell of rapid growth known, in France, as *les trente glorieuses*. The rationing of essential commodities left over from the war was ending, and the foundations of the welfare state had been laid. In 1956, the Treaty of Rome, which marked the beginning of what would eventually become the European Union, was signed.

However, although 1956 was a significant year for the world as a whole, it also saw significant developments within macroeconomics. It saw the publication of the volume containing Milton Friedman's restatement of the quantity theory of money, the starting point for what came to be almost universally known as "monetarism," the doctrine that challenged the Keynesian consensus on how best to design macroeconomic policy. There was, Friedman contended, a connection between the quantity of money in circulation and the price level, and therefore, anti-inflation policy should involve controlling the growth rate of the money supply. The same year also saw the publication, in articles written independently by Robert Solow and Australian economist Trevor Swan, of the neoclassical theory of economic growth, as well as the first edition of *Money, Interest and Prices*, Don Patinkin's magisterial treatment of monetary theory. The neoclassical growth model ignored short-run problems of unemployment and paid no attention to inflation: it provided a theory of how, assuming competitive markets for output, capital and labor, the rate of growth of national output would, in the long run, converge on the rate determined by technical progress and the growth rate of the labor force. *Money, Interest and Prices*, in contrast, sought to provide a rigorous account of the short run – of the world in which Keynesian problems occurred.

Of these three theoretical innovations, it is Patinkin's book, discussed in detail in Chapter 3, that is the key to the story told here. As we explain later, its purpose was to provide theoretical foundations for monetary economics and, as part of that, a theory of employment. It represented a theoretical instantiation of the neoclassical synthesis that Paul Samuelson had proclaimed a year earlier in the third edition of his best-selling introductory textbook, *Economics* (1955). Patinkin's work was rooted in the concept of general competitive equilibrium, but it contained elements that pointed toward the disequilibrium microfoundations for which economists were searching during the next twenty years. However, to understand the history of this literature and what happened to this search, we need to look outside it and to consider what happened to, on one hand, the theory of money and inflation and, on the other, to the theory of supply. These take us not just to Patinkin but also to Friedman and Solow.[3]

THEORIES OF MONEY AND INFLATION

Although this was no part of Keynes's message, the prevailing view in the Keynesian era was that monetary policy was of minor importance compared with fiscal policy; indeed, in a country with a developed financial system, what mattered was the structure of credit as a whole, a view represented most clearly in Britain by the Radcliffe Report (Committee on the Working of the Monetary System 1959). Money was not something given from outside, but was determined within the financial system, as made clear by John Gurley and Edward Shaw in *Money in a Theory of Finance* (1958). In the 1960s, this was considered the "new view" of money, represented in the work of the prominent Keynesian economist James Tobin, based at Yale: agents did not demand anything called money but a range of assets – currency and different types of bank deposit – that were imperfect substitutes for each other in agents' portfolios and that exhibited the characteristics of money to different degrees.[4] Not only was there no clear relationship between the money supply and the price level; there was no need even to define any aggregate called "money."

Not all economists subscribed to the view that the money supply was less important than the financial system of which it was a part. The most prominent opponent of this position was Milton Friedman, whose essay "The Quantity Theory of Money: A Restatement" (1956) aimed to reinstate the quantity theory by presenting it as a theory of the demand for money. The ratio of money to income – the velocity of circulation – might not be stable, but the inclusion of a suitable range of variables was consistent with a stable demand function for money. In addition, although the money supply clearly responded to economic events – it was endogenous to the system – it was not completely endogenous. It could, and did, change for reasons quite unrelated to the demand for money. The stock of money could therefore be an important causal factor behind both inflation and the business cycle. Friedman, in conjunction with various colleagues at the University of Chicago and the National Bureau of Economic Research, notably Anna

[3] The model was developed independently by Solow and Swan, but it was Solow's version that was more widely cited.
[4] Tobin (1971) collects his most important papers.

Schwartz, developed these ideas, engaging in debates with Keynesians, such as MIT economist Franco Modigliani and Yale economist James Tobin. This research culminated in *A Monetary History of the United States, 1867–1960* (Friedman and Schwartz 1963) which argued that, far from being impotent, a disastrous collapse in the money supply had been the main factor turning what might have been a normal recession into the Great Depression.

Friedman's aim was to argue not just that monetary policy was important but also that the right monetary policy was to fix the growth rate of the money supply at a constant rate. This would stabilize the economy through preventing monetary shocks from being a source of disturbance, and it would control the rate of inflation. To make this case, he had not only to reinstate the idea that the quantity of money was a key variable in the economy, but he had also to develop a theory of how prices and output changed when changes in the money supply brought about changes in the level of aggregate demand. The prevailing Keynesian approach was to treat prices as determined by factors that were largely independent of the level of aggregate demand. It was recognized that sustained high or low levels of aggregate demand might lead to higher or lower inflation, but this was not the prime determinant of inflation. Hence, inflation could be analyzed in terms of "cost push" (rising import prices, or unions pushing up wages faster than productivity) or "demand pull" (high demand causing prices to rise). However, in 1958, Bill Phillips, at the London School of Economics (LSE), analyzed the relationship between inflation (the rate of change of money wages) and unemployment across almost a century. Although he was not the first to see this relationship, it came to be known as the Phillips curve. When Paul Samuelson and Robert Solow were asked to write on the theory of inflation in one of the sessions on current problems at the 1960 AEA meeting, they took up this curve and explored how it could be used to analyze anti-inflation policy. They conjectured that it might be possible to move up and down the Phillips curve, and to that extent, it provided a menu of policy choices, but that if attempts were made to exploit it, aiming for low unemployment at the expense of higher inflation, this would probably cause the curve to become unstable as peoples' expectations of inflation rose.

This idea was taken up independently in 1967–68 by Friedman and Edmund Phelps. Phelps's papers, in which he sought to develop formal microfoundations for the theory of employment and inflation, are central to our story and are discussed in Chapter 5. Friedman's paper, on the other hand, was prominent by virtue of being his Presidential Address to the American Economic Association, before being published in the *American*

Economic Review (1968). In the course of making his case that policy should involve setting a target for the growth rate of the money supply in order to control inflation, he provided a nontechnical, purely verbal exposition of what rapidly became known as the "expectations-augmented Phillips curve." According to this theory, while demand-management policy might be able to produce short-term changes in output and employment, in the long run, when people had sufficient time to work out what inflation would be, the only consequence of changing the growth rate of the money supply would be to raise inflation: in the long run, the Phillips curve would be vertical, at what Friedman called "the natural rate of unemployment." A lower rate of unemployment could be achieved only at the cost of not just high but also accelerating inflation, a price that would eventually become intolerable.

The stagflation experienced during the 1970s appeared, to many economists, to confirm Friedman's diagnosis. Not only could the expectations-augmented Phillips curve explain how inflation could rise at the same time as unemployment, something not consistent with the simple Phillips curve, but inflation could also be explained in terms of the high rate of growth of the money supply during this period. The proximate cause of the inflation of the mid- and late 1970s might have been rises in the price of oil but, so monetarists argued, behind these price rises lay expansions of the monetary supply. Keynesian macroeconomic models seemed to have broken down, and Keynesianism appeared unable to provide useful guidance for policy. During the 1970s, therefore, the world turned, albeit haltingly, toward macroeconomic policy making that seemed to owe more to Friedman than to the Keynesianism of the golden age. Robert Lucas, who joined Friedman in Chicago, used the idea of rational expectations (the idea that modelers assume that people use all available information as efficiently as it can be used) to develop a critique of any attempt to stabilize the economy through monetary and fiscal policy. Keynesian demand-management policy, Lucas contended during the 1970s, could only destabilize the economy: if policy changes were predictable, private agents would change their behavior to offset their effects. Policy changes would affect output only if they were random and unpredictable, which meant that they would be destabilizing.

By the 1980s, the pendulum had swung against Keynesian demand-management policy toward Friedman's policy of using targets for the growth rate of the money supply to control inflation. Experience was, however, mixed. The Fed under Paul Volcker succeeded in reducing inflation fairly rapidly, and despite the high interest rates needed to achieve this target, U.S. unemployment fell fairly rapidly in the mid-1980s. In contrast, in Europe, unemployment remained high for most of the decade. This experience prompted a noticeable divergence between European and U.S. views on how to model the economy; for example, models of hysteresis – the notion that high unemployment raises the natural rate, perhaps because the longer people are out of work, the harder it becomes for them to find work – fashionable in Europe, never caught on in the United States. In the Third World, high interest rates produced a debt crisis, and the move by the International Monetary Fund (IMF) and the World Bank to argue for structural adjustment programs and market liberalization.

However, while this was happening, moves were also being made to liberalize world financial markets. Remaining foreign exchange controls, were removed, regulations that had confined financial institutions to specific activities were removed, and new financial assets were created, notably in financial derivatives. "Monetarism" had been seen as a conservative "free-market" doctrine, fitting well with deregulation and reducing the role of the state, but by the 1990s, it was clear that deregulation of financial markets was undermining policy based on controlling monetary aggregates. If a monetary aggregate was targeted, banks and private investors could move funds to assets that were not controlled rendering the target less meaningful (called Goodhart's Law, after the Bank of England economist Charles Goodhart). Instead of using interest rates to target monetary aggregates, there was a shift toward using them to target inflation directly. Monetary aggregates were still used, but the idea that a single aggregate represented "the" money supply was abandoned, in favor of a view according to which a range of aggregates provided indicators of how the economy was responding to interest rates and any other interventions the authorities were making in financial markets.

This shift from controlling the money supply to using interest rates to control inflation is represented in the book that is taken as the end-point of our story, Michael Woodford's *Interest and Prices* (2003). In choosing this title, Woodford looked back to the Swedish economist Knut Wicksell, whose book of the same title had been published in 1898. The two books reflected similar perspectives on both monetary theory and monetary policy.[5] The quantity theory might be the only valid theory of the price level (this was explicitly Wicksell's view), but money was a form of credit, the quantity of which was determined within the financial system, and the key

---

[5] Though see Boianovsky and Trautwein (2006) for some significant differences between Wicksell and Woodford, especially concerning the treatment of the banking system.

to controlling it was interest rates. If inflation needed to be reduced, interest rates should be raised, and if it fell too low, interest rates should be lowered. However, in choosing this title, Woodford was also deliberately leaving behind the perspective on monetary economics taken by Don Patinkin in 1956, this being symbolized by dropping the word money from Patinkin's title *Money, Interest and Prices*. He was rejecting both the approach to policy implied by Patinkin's book and the monetary theory on which it was based. Changed attitudes to money and monetary policy were not the only change that lay beneath this change from Patinkin to Woodford, but before turning to other aspects, we turn to the problem of economic growth.

GROWTH THEORY, FROM SOLOW TO LUCAS AND ROMER

The neoclassical synthesis rested on the distinction between a short run in which output was demand-determined and a long run where output was determined by the level of productive capacity – by aggregate supply. The framework in which this was analyzed came to be that laid down by Solow's 1956 model. This was a highly simplified model of the economy, comprising a single sector producing a homogenous "output" that could be either invested to increase productive capacity, or consumed. Given the available stock of capital, determined by what had been invested in the past, and the labor force, the quantity of output that could be produced was determined by a production function that exhibited properties that were both intuitively appealing and mathematically convenient, notably that the marginal product of each factor was positive but diminishing. Technical progress might shift this production function outwards over time, but at any moment it imposed a constraint on what could be produced (see Boianovsky and Hoover 2009).

In itself, the Solow model could do little. It showed how economies should, if full employment could be maintained, converge on a long-run steady state with a constant rate of growth. It could be used to analyze the consequences of changing the proportion of national income that was invested rather than being consumed, but that was pretty much all. However, it provided the framework within which growth theory was discussed for the next two decades. Solow himself, a year later, used this framework to analyze technical progress, providing a method that could be used to decompose the growth of output into the components that could be attributed to increased inputs of capital and labor and the "residual," which was deemed to be technical progress. It also contributed to the intensification of a debate that had begun earlier in the 1950s, about the coherence of the concept, central to the Solow model, of the aggregate production function – the so-called two Cambridges controversy. There were also attempts to extend the model, to make it more "realistic" and to enable it to be used to analyze a greater variety of policy options. Following the example of another paper dating from 1955, by James Tobin, the model was extended to incorporate a government that consumed part of national output and issued debt, with the result that households could use their savings not just to buy real capital (investment) but also to purchase government securities. This permitted the construction of models in which there was a Keynesian short run and a neoclassical long run (e.g., Rose 1973). It was even possible to create a model in which the short run could be represented by an IS-LM model and the long run by a Solow growth model (Backhouse 1981).

However, by the late 1970s, this literature had run out of steam. It had become an overwhelmingly theoretical literature: new models were largely variations on a theme, their evolution being determined by internal theoretical considerations not by their relevance to understanding real-world problems. Furthermore, by the 1970s, the model itself was thoroughly understood. Although textbooks on growth theory continued to appear, growth theory had ceased to be something for specialists and had reached the point where it could be used simply as a tool by economists specializing in other fields.[6] When the 1973–74 crisis hit the world economy, Solow's residual became, under the guise of the growth rate of "total factor productivity," the means for measuring the effect of the oil shock on productivity growth.

The real failing of the Solow framework was that it could not explain the variable that was crucial to policy makers. Economics had tried to endogenize the rate of technical progress, whether by relating it to the share of investment in output or through abandoning the concept of the production function, reflecting the idea that the productivity of capital should depend on when it was installed. But no one had produced a solution to the problem of productivity growth that was considered satisfactory. There was the further problem that though data on national income was increasingly widely available for an ever-increasing range of countries, it was well known that such data was often not comparable across countries. This was the background to the two developments that, in the 1980s, began to revive interest in growth theory: the data set compiled by Alan Heston and Robert Summers (the Penn World Table) that offered consistent time series for national income in a wide range of countries, permitting much more

---

[6] This is exemplified by its use in Anthony Atkinson and Joseph Stiglitz's (1977) *Lectures in Public Economics*.

serious cross-country comparisons than had previously been possible; and the development of so-called endogenous growth theory that sought to explain the rate of technical progress as responding to factors such as investment in human capital or research and development activities.

THE SEARCH FOR RIGOROUS MICROFOUNDATIONS FOR MACROECONOMICS

This book is concerned neither with the new ideas about monetary economics that emerged in the 1960s and 1970s nor with the theory of economic growth, but these developments and the economic events that prompted them constitute important parts of the background to the search that is central to this book – the search for a more rigorous macroeconomic theory based on non-Walrasian foundations. It was taken for granted in virtually all the literature that rigor meant logical rigor and that this involved the construction and formal analysis of the properties of mathematical models, whether the subject was the short-run behavior of the economy, long-run growth, or the theory of economic policy. It was further assumed that these models should relate the behavior of macroeconomic aggregates to the behavior of the individuals, whose behavior was being aggregated. Yet, there was a tension, for whereas the literature on disequilibrium theory was searching for new conceptions of how markets worked that did not involve assuming markets were continuously in equilibrium, theories of money and growth were, to a great extent, moving in the other direction. Some of the new monetary theories involved disequilibrium modeling, but the dominant approach was to explore the implications of rational expectations in market-clearing models; and in growth theory, concerned with the long run, it was even more common to assume short-run equilibrium.

The history of the search for microfoundations of macroeconomics is one in which, as in the history of theories of money and inflation, Patinkin's *Money, Interest and Prices* (1956) and Woodford's *Interest and Prices* (2003) provide useful benchmarks, even if the latter is largely symbolic given that the key components had evolved during the preceding decade or more. It is a story bound up with the interpretation of Keynesian economics, for the dominant question in the literature was whether the new models being created, though undoubtedly more rigorous (as that term was understood) than their predecessors, implied that the Keynesian way of thinking about the economy was fundamentally flawed. Despite the differences between their models, this was the major problem for both Patinkin and for the new neoclassical synthesis represented by Woodford.

Money, Interest and Prices presented what was then the state-of-the-art exposition of monetary economics, and it became the leading advanced graduate textbook in macroeconomics for more than a decade, with a second edition appearing in 1965, till the events of the 1970s rendered its static framework out of date. In this book, Patinkin modified the theory of general equilibrium so as to incorporate money, and from this derived a macroeconomic theory that could produce "classical" or "Keynesian" results under different circumstances. Macroeconomics appeared to have been given "microfoundations," to use the term that later became fashionable. However, during the late 1960s and 1970s, this framework was challenged from two sides.

The most well-known challenge came from Lucas and his fellow "new classical" economists who turned to dynamic models in which households engaged in inter-temporal optimization, often over an infinite time horizon. In conjunction with the assumption of rational expectations this assumption meant that, aside from random errors, economic agents were infinitely far-sighted. The implications of infinitely far-sighted agents emerged dramatically in Robert Barro's (1974a) "Ricardian equivalence theorem," according to which debt-financed government spending had no effect on the budget constraint faced by infinitely lived households and therefore could not affect their consumption. Problems of inter-temporal coordination failure could not arise.

Continuously clearing markets and the implication that there would be full employment focused attention on the supply side, as did neoclassical and subsequently "endogenous" growth theory, which led to an increasing integration of growth models into the macroeconomic models used to analyze monetary and fiscal policy. In the 1980s, the Solow model came into its own for another reason. When introducing the rational-expectations, inter-temporal–optimization framework, Lucas (1972) had explained the business cycle in terms of random shocks to the growth rate of the money supply. By the end of the 1970s, it had become clear that this was empirically a failure: the models did not work. Instead, Fynn Kydland and Edward Prescott (1982) argued that the cycle was driven by real technology shocks, measured by the Solow residual: random variations in the rate of growth of total factor productivity drove the business cycle. This was real business cycle (RBC) theory.

The other challenge to the neoclassical synthesis represented by Patinkin came from those economists, including many Keynesians, who sought a more general, non-Walrasian, or disequilibrium, view of how markets operated. This is the body of work with which this book is concerned. It was very prominent for most of the 1970s, but from around 1980, it became less visible. One reason was that the dynamic modeling of the new classical and real business cycle theorists made its static models seem out of date; another was that it came to be seen, incorrectly, as dealing simply with the consequences of prices being fixed; and it was also partially eclipsed by the large "new Keynesian" literature on models of why the labor market might not clear. It eventually became clear that pure RBC models did not fit the data, and when they were modified, they became more like the models of their Keynesian critics. A new synthesis emerged encompassing the dynamic analysis pioneered by Lucas and the new classical economists and the analysis of market imperfections found in the literature on non-Walrasian models. Economists started talking of the DSGE (Dynamic Stochastic General Equilibrium) models, in which competition might be perfect or imperfect.

Although he was not the first to synthesize these two approaches to microfoundations, Woodford's book summed up the approach that, by the time of the 2008 financial crisis, had become the dominant approach to macroeconomic theory. It represented the perspective on policy that, for all the optimism shown in the 1990s and early 2000s – "the great moderation" or the "NICE (No Inflation, Constant Employment) decade" – was widely perceived to have failed.

The change that had taken place in macroeconomics was profound in the eyes of both its supporters and its critics. The economists who endorsed the new neoclassical synthesis represented by Woodford's *Interest and Prices* believed that macroeconomics had been provided with rigorous microfoundations that were very different from those found in Patinkin's magnum opus. It involved a complete reappraisal of monetary theory and an integration of growth theory into general macroeconomic theory. The transformation of macroeconomics was so profound that in the eyes of many economists, the distinction between macroeconomics and microeconomics, central to economic thinking in the 1950s and 1960s, had simply disappeared. However, not all economists agreed. Some adopted the new methods but constructed models based on different assumptions and reached different conclusions. There were also economists, ranging from Friedman to "old" and "post" Keynesians who were skeptical about the increased use of formal mathematical modeling. For all these economists, whether they endorsed or rejected it, the transformation of macroeconomics that had taken place in the 1970s was profound. The search for disequilibrium microfoundations is only one part of that transformation, but it was, as we hope to show in this book, a very important one.

THREE

Don Patinkin and the Neoclassical Synthesis

DEBATING THE GENERAL THEORY

The Keynesian revolution was the central event in twentieth-century macroeconomics. This is true irrespective of whether one regards Keynes as having broken radically with previous economics or one takes the view, persuasively argued by Laidler (1999), that Keynesian economics, and in particular what came to be known as the IS-LM model, a two equation model of output and the rate of interest that could be manipulated using a simple diagram, was the channel through which ideas about money and the business cycle that had been developed in the inter-war period flowed into modern macroeconomics. Milton Friedman (1956) contended that there was a distinct Chicago tradition that was independent of Keynesian economics, but this claim did not stand up to criticism (Patinkin 1969; Johnson 1971; Laidler 1993). The Keynesian revolution was so important because the theoretical framework that emerged from the Keynesian revolution was the means through which a more technical macroeconomics emerged, centered on the analysis of formal mathematical models. The Keynesian revolution is thus the essential background without which the emergence of disequilibrium macroeconomics cannot be understood: it defined the orthodoxy against which the proponents of disequilibrium macroeconomics were reacting. On top of this, though disequilibrium macroeconomics, as the term is being used in this book, is best dated from the 1960s, its roots lie in the debates about Keynesian economics that took place in the late 1930s and 1940s.

Soon after the publication of J. M. Keynes's (1973[1936]) *General Theory*, economists started to debate the meaning of the book and how it differed from classical economics (see Backhouse 2006). That was done mainly through the formulation of mathematical models of the relationship between saving, investment, the rate of interest, money, wages, and employ-ment (Young 1987). The interpretation of Keynes's macroeconomics in terms of aggregative general equilibrium models would dominate the field until the 1950s, under the strong influence of John Hicks's (1937) formula-tion of the differences between classical and Keynesian macroeconomics in terms of a pair of curves, later labeled IS and LM curves by Alvin Hansen (1953). Hicks was followed by Oskar Lange (1938) – who compared Keynes with Walras, whereas the "classics" in Hicks account were represented by Cambridge Marshallians – and by Franco Modigliani (1944), who, in con-trast with Hicks, explicitly introduced the labor market into his model.

Even before Hicks's (1937) IS-LM model, Keynes's former pupil David Champernowne (1936) put forward a diagrammatic-mathematical inter-pretation, which focused on the distinct assumptions by Keynes and the classics about price expectations in the labor market and the causal rela-tions involved in each approach. Champernowne's analysis, however, was not nearly as influential as Hicks's (see Boianovsky 2005). Price expectations were also important in Hicks's framework, but of a different kind. Hicks identified the assumption that there is a floor to the rate of interest on the left part of the LM curve as the central difference between the *General Theory* and "classical" economics. The notion of a "liquidity trap" – a phrase coined by Dennis Robertson (1936), albeit in a different context – was conspicu-ous in the macroeconomic textbooks from the 1940s to the 1960s, although often interpreted in ways distinct from Hicks's formulation. Hicks's liquid-ity trap was based on the assumption that the short-run nominal interest rate cannot be negative (because of transaction costs) and that the long rate is formed by expectations about the future value of the short rate plus a risk premium. These ideas were fully developed in his 1939 classic *Value and Capital* (Hicks 1946[1939]), which Hicks was writing when he published the IS-LM article (see Boianovsky 2004).

In part 3 of *Value and Capital*, Hicks, strongly influenced by the Swedish economists who formed the so-called Stockholm School – Erik Lindahl, Gunnar Myrdal, Erik Lundberg, and Bertil Ohlin – introduced the method of "temporary equilibrium" in order to discuss economic dynamics. A tem-porary equilibrium was the configuration of the economy that would arise given a set of expectations about the future: it was temporary because as soon as those expectations changed, so too would the equilibrium. It was in that context that Hicks – under the influence of Knut Wicksell's well-known "cumulative process" – put forward the notion of elasticity of price expecta-tions to study the effect of actual prices on price expectations. As pointed out by Hicks (1946[1939]:251), the case of unit elasticity of expectations was at the time implicitly taken for granted by most economists, without realizing its implications for stability analysis. If the expected future price level is given, an excess supply in the market for goods will cause a reduction in current prices, and, by that, a fall in the expected real rate of interest, which will increase aggregate demand for goods and stabilize the price level. However, if the elasticity of expectation is one or higher, the expected future price level changes together with current prices, which precludes stabilization and leads to cumulative falling prices. That was regarded by Hicks (1946[1939]:255) as the "most important proposition in economic dynamics". Under the assumption of unit elasticity of expectations, the floor to the rate of interest implies that downward instability of the price level can be only checked if money-wages are rigid, as in the IS-LM model. In that case, stability is achieved through unemployment and output contraction – under the liquidity trap, the system "does not merely suffer from imperfect stability; it is absolutely unstable" (Hicks 1946:259).

With Modigliani (1944), the Keynes versus "classics" issue changed from the discussion of the specification of the money demand function to the determination of money-wages in the labor market. As mentioned earlier, Champernowne (1936) had already focused on the labor market as the dividing line between macroeconomic schools of thought, but Modigliani's approach was different. Modigliani used the long-period full-employment version of the general classical model with perfectly flexible wages as a benchmark for comparison with Keynes. The floor to the rate of interest is still relevant, but only if the assumption of rigid money-wages is removed from Keynesian theory – as shown by Modigliani (1944:74–75), if the interest rate is at its minimum level, a reduction of money wages will affect only the price level, with no effect on employment and real wages.

The orthodox IS-LM interpretation(s) of the *General Theory* discussed so far has been called "hydraulic" interpretation by Alan Coddington (1976, 1983). Another important contribution to that interpretation was represented by Paul Samuelson's (1948) 45-degree Keynesian-cross diagram illustrating the determination of income by consumption and investment (see Pearce and Hoover 1995:193–97). Coddington (1983:102) choose the term "hydraulic" to describe this approach because it interprets the economy "in terms of disembodied and homogeneous flows between which there exist stable relationships." In the 45-degree line model, the only stable relationship is the expenditure function, equilibrium requiring solely that the aggregate flow of planned expenditure equals the income on which it is based. Even the rudimentary supply side found in the *General Theory*, based on price being equal to marginal cost, is stripped away. When Samuelson (1948:164) introduced the idea that changes in investment determined drove changes in income, he illustrated this with a picture of a water pump, pumping water into a circular flow from which water escaped into savings from a drain at the bottom. A few years later, a machine built by Phillips that was used in several universities for teaching, modelled these flows by pumping colored water through a system of pipes.[1] By the time Coddington used the phrase "hydraulic Keynesianism," this way of explaining macroeconomic equilibrium to beginning students had thus been standard for thirty years.

However, by the early 1960s, in response to this simplified, hydraulic Keynesianism, dissenting interpretations of Keynes and the Keynesian revolution had started to gain acceptance, based on the view that the core of Keynes's conception of the economy was uncertain expectations, deemed incompatible with the notion of equilibrium. Such interpretations were designated "fundamentalist Keynesian" by Coddington (1976, 1983), since they interpreted the *General Theory* as being fundamentally opposed to traditional equilibrium theory, especially in its general equilibrium version (see also Patinkin 1990; Backhouse 2006). Although the first fundamentalist interpretation came from Hugh Townshend's (1937) suggested generalization of liquidity preference to all goods, the furthest-reaching exponent of this view was George Shackle (e.g., 1961, 1967). Shackle claimed that time irreversibility and the ignorance about the future were the main points of Keynes's (1937) reply to the criticism presented by Jacob Viner and others in the 1937 *Quarterly Journal of Economics* symposium.

The interpretation of Keynes with which this book is concerned, however, is what Coddington has called "reconstituted reductionism." It was reductionism in that its method of analysis consisted of "analyzing markets on the basis of the choices made by individual traders." It was "reconstituted" in that it was an attempt to do something that Keynes had already attempted, but to do it on what were considered more secure foundations. Like the fundamentalist interpretation, albeit for different reasons, the reductionists rejected the Keynesian orthodoxy for not dealing adequately with the fact that the Keynesian revolution was about a monetary economy. As explained in detail in the next chapter, this interpretation was effectively started by Robert Clower (1965, 1967), but important elements of it were already present in the work of Don Patinkin (1949a, 1956, ch. 13), whose work formed the most rigorous statement of Keynesian macroeconomics available in the 1950s. He, in turn, had picked up some of the key ideas from his teacher in Chicago, the Polish economist, Oskar Lange.

---

[1] For a photograph, see Backhouse and Giraud (2010).

FROM LANGE TO PATINKIN

The intellectual formation of Don Patinkin (1922–1995; for general information about his life and work, see Boianovsky 2008) at the University of
Chicago in the 1940s may be seen as the result of the tension between the
influence of the economics department of that university, where he stud-
ied under Jacob Viner, Frank Knight, Henry Simons, Lloyd Mints, and,
above all, Oskar Lange, and then at the Cowles Commission for Research
in Economics, where as a graduate student and research fellow, he inter-
acted with Jacob Marschak, Lawrence Klein, Trygve Haavelmo, and others
(see Boianovsky 2002a; Mehrling 2002; Patinkin 1995). Patinkin's doctoral dissertation, "On the Consistency of Economic Models: A Theory of
Involuntary Unemployment," was submitted in the spring of 1947. Its main
theme was overdetermination and inconsistency of systems with homogeneous equations, called the "Patinkin problem" by members of the Cowles
Commission. This dissertation comprised two parts, on the "classical
system" and "involuntary unemployment," respectively. The main results
of the first (microeconomic) part were published in revised form in two
Econometrica articles in 1948 and 1949 (1949b), and the second part came
out, with even more extensive changes, in the *Economic Journal* in 1949
(1949a), after Patinkin had tried unsuccessfully to publish the dissertation.
It was only in 1956 that Patinkin managed to have these two contributions
to classical and Keynesian monetary economics published alongside each
other, in *Money, Interest and Prices*, a book that was soon seen by many
economists as the most important work on the topic since the *General
Theory* (Keynes 1973[1936]).

   Although Patinkin developed the idea with greater rigor and introduced
many important concepts, the idea that Keynesian economics should be
analyzed in terms of an inconsistency, and hence, disequilibrium in a
Walrasian general equilibrium system can be found in the lectures given at
Chicago by Lange, which Patinkin attended in 1945.[2] Lange was an exception to the predominant classical orientation of the Chicago department
of economics in the early 1940s. He taught mathematical economics and
business cycle theory, which included Keynesian economics based on his
1938 *Econometrica* article, his 1942 essay on Say's Law, and his 1944 book
Price Flexibility and Employment. As pointed out by Goulven Rubin (2007),
Lange was a pioneer in the application of Walrasian general equilibrium

---

[2]   Patinkin's lecture notes are in the Don Patinkin Papers, Box 4. David M. Rubenstein Rare
   Book and Manuscript Library, Duke University.

tools to macroeconomic theory. Although published a year later, Lange's (1938) diagrammatic analysis was written independently of Hicks's model. Just like Hicks, Lange focused on the form of the LM curve (called the "isoliquidity curve") in order to discuss under what conditions Keynes's claim that the rate of interest does not react to changes in saving and investment holds. Lange argued that Keynes had in mind the limiting case when the interest-elasticity of the demand for liquidity was infinite and the isoliquidity curve degenerates into a horizontal straight line. The other special case is the traditional quantity theory of money, with a corresponding vertical isoliquidity curve. In contrast with Hicks, in Lange the issue was not the logical existence of a floor to the rate of interest created by a nearly zero short-term rate, but the empirical matter of the value of the interest-elasticity of the demand for money. Lange also used his diagrammatic apparatus to sort out historical issues pertaining to the relation between Keynes's, Walras's and Malthus's respective ideas on money demand and the relation between consumption and the level of activity.

Although the extent of the influence of Lange's (1936–37) restatement of Keynesian economics was second only to Hicks (1937), it was Lange's (1942, 1944) path-breaking formalization of Say's Law and the stability of full-employment equilibrium that really caught Patinkin's attention. Patinkin (1965:537n19) was also attracted to Lange's (1936–37) theoretical treatment of Walrasian tâtonnement as part of the socialist calculation debate. Indeed, the extensive use of the tâtonnement to discuss the equilibration process would become one of the main features of *Money, Interest and Prices*. Lange's (1942, 1944) critique of classical monetary economics and his interpretation of Keynesian involuntary unemployment provided the starting point for Patinkin's double attempt to rescue the quantity theory of money and to reformulate unemployment as a disequilibrium phenomenon (see also Mehrling 2002).

Lange (1942) distinguished Say's Law from Walras's Law (a term created by him), and suggested that the former should be understood as the proposition that the excess demand for money is always zero.[3] Say's Law, accordingly, implied indeterminacy of the price level and was considered incompatible with the quantity theory of money. Moreover, Keynesian "unemployment equilibrium," characterized by equilibrium in the markets

---

[3]   The concept that came, after Keynes, to be known as Say's Law, has a history going back to the early nineteenth century, when it was known as the law or markets or the *loi des debouchés*, the key figures being James Mill, Jean-Baptiste Say, and John Stuart Mill. One of the best discussions of the history of the concept remains in another article dating from this period, Becker and Baumol (1952) (see also Baumol 1977 and 1999).

for money, commodities and bonds, meant, in Lange's (1942:61, 1944:6) interpretation, that Keynes implicitly assumed a supply curve of labor infinitely elastic over an interval with respect to a certain (rigid) level of money-wages. Lange compared with his own definition of underemployment as excess supply of labor, which implied, according to Walras's Law, the existence of excess demand in the other markets of the economy. In Lange's opinion, the choice between the two alternatives was only a matter of convenience, since one is in principle translatable into another.

The overall goal of Lange (1944) was to provide an answer to what he perceived as the main issue between classical and Keynesian economists, that is, the effect of price flexibility (especially money-wages) on unemployment, a key feature of Modigliani's (1944) interpretation discussed earlier. In order to do this, Lange (1944, ch. 3) advanced the concept of a positive "monetary effect", defined as the substitution of goods for money caused by a fall in the price level. This is an income effect that Hicks had overlooked in his analysis of stability and the liquidity trap. However, as pointed out by Lange (1944, ch. 6), the existence of a positive monetary effect does not guarantee that the system is stable, especially in the presence of real price uncertainty caused by Hicksian elastic price expectations that may render the monetary effect rather weak and impose larger fluctuations of prices in order to restore equilibrium.

By incorporating Samuelson's formal dynamic theory into Hicks's general equilibrium, Lange's *Price Flexibility and Employment* represented an attempt to turn macroeconomics into a section of the stability analysis of monetary general equilibrium models (Weintraub 1979, ch. 4; Rubin 2007). Although Patinkin, in Solow's (1991) words, was indeed the single "true heir" of Lange, his macroeconomics was not based on any assumption that there was an inconsistency in the equations for general equilibrium. Patinkin showed how micro- and macroeconomics could be brought together by introducing real money balances as an argument in the utility function of economic agents and, by that, stabilize the economic system in the long run. In the process, Patinkin (1965:175, 625) criticized Lange (as well as Modigliani and others) for assuming that demand functions depend only on relative prices – that is, the so-called homogeneity postulate, (wrongly) supposed to reflect absence of "money illusion." Neither did he accept Lange's claim that there was no essential difference between equilibrium and disequilibrium interpretations of involuntary unemployment. In Patinkin's view, the former was necessarily associated with money-wage rigidity. Instead, he argued that unemployment should be understood as part of an off-curve analysis – workers are off their labor supply curve and firms are off their labor demand curves. However, Patinkin's new macro-economic framework, especially his analysis of the behavior of firms under constrained aggregate demand, would prove problematic.

PATINKIN, INCONSISTENCY, AND UNEMPLOYMENT

Money, Interest and Prices (1956, 1965) is most well known for its integra-tion of monetary theory with the theory of value through the real balance effect. This has nothing specifically to do with disequilibrium macroeco-nomics, because most of the book deals with situations where markets clear. However, in chapter 13, in which Patinkin applied his model to involun-tary unemployment, he derived this by considering a fall in the demand for commodities in a world where prices and wages did not respond immedi-ately (Patinkin 1956:214–24; 1965:318–28). In this case, firms will find that they cannot sell all the commodities they wish to sell, and as a result, they will reduce their demand for labor below the amount given by the labor demand curve, which is constructed on the assumption that they can sell all they wish as the prevailing prices. Reductions in real wages will not cause them to increase their demand for labor, with the result that the classical mechanism for eliminating unemployment will not work: "Both firms and workers are coerced by the same *force majeure* of insufficient demand in the commodity market. Both are thereby being prevented from achieving their optimum mode of behavior.... Not being able to sell all they want, they cannot employ all they want" (Patinkin 1965:322). The argument was illustrated diagrammatically by a change in the usual labor demand curve, which now features a kink at the employment level determined by effective demand, as shown in Figure 3.1.

Although this is only one chapter in Patinkin's book, and was developed less rigorously than the parts dealing with equilibrium, there is strong evi-dence that he considered this the most important part of the book. In con-trast with the real balance effect, introduced only in Patinkin (1948), the discussion of disequilibrium represents the outcome of a research program going back to his doctoral dissertation in Chicago (Patinkin 1947b) reflect-ing the influence of Lange. Although that part of the dissertation had, as has been pointed out, been published in his 1949 *Economic Journal* article (1949a), it was only in the 1956 book that Patinkin developed the argument that firms are off their labor demand curves under unemployment condi-tions (see Boianovsky 2002a, 2006; Rubin 2002). The idea was based on Patinkin's extension to the labor market of the crucial concept of "spillover effects," that is, the notion that an agent's actual demand and supply in one

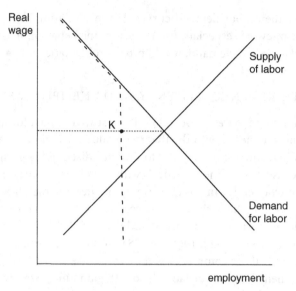

Figure 3.1. Patinkin's labor market
Source: Based on Patinkin (1965, Figure XII-1). Point K has excess supply of labor even though the real wage is at its equilibrium level. The dotted curve is not drawn by Patinkin, though he describes it explicitly in the text (p. 322), as "the kinked curve TAN.1".

market will depend upon the transactions actually performed in other markets: in other words, that a constraint in one market will affect behavior in other markets, an idea that Patinkin had first put forward in 1952 (see Grossman 1969).

Patinkin's program in relation to unemployment was, therefore, to explain it as taking place in a world where prices and wages responded slowly to changes in supply and demand; firms would absorb some of the impact of changes in demand by allowing their inventories to rise or fall, but they would be unable to absorb all changes in this way. He focused on firms' decision making and on spillover effects from commodity markets to the labor market. The formal theory related to the polar cases where prices and wages were either completely flexible or completely rigid; he offered verbal account of the intermediate case but "did not succeed in integrating the intuition with formal economic analysis,"[4] this being the reason why there was no mathematical appendix to the relevant sections (2 and 3) of chapter 13.[5] In a long footnote, Patinkin (1965:323n9) admitted that his suggested solution

[4] Patinkin to Leijonhufvud, February 12, 1974. Don Patinkin Papers, Box 65. David M. Rubenstein Rare Book and Manuscript Library, Duke University.
[5] In 1987 he said he had not known how to write one (see Boianovsky 2006).

to the puzzle of the influence of the firm's output on its labor-input is beset by a "basic analytic problem". Although the kink in the labor demand curve makes sense from the point of view of the economy as a whole, "by definition of perfect competition this kink cannot be taken into account by any individual firm" (see also Boianovsky 2002a, 2006).

It is, however, important to note that, although it is easy to reconstruct such a program from his work, Patinkin's awareness of the significance of his analysis of non-market clearing behavior appears to have grown rather slowly. In the Introduction to the first two editions of *Money, Interest and Prices,* he notes simply that two themes run through the book. The first dealt with "the monetary theory of an economy with full employment" and occupied no fewer than eight chapters. He then noted, "There is a second major theme which deals with the monetary theory of an economy with involuntary unemployment. This is developed in Chapters XIII-XIV" (Patinkin 1956:2–3; 1965:xxv). Terms such as "disequilibrium" or "non-market clearing," which might show that he was aware that his theory of involuntary unemployment might be but part of a more general theory of how markets worked, are conspicuous by their absence. Failure to realize the full significance of what he was doing would be consistent with the fact that during the 1960s and 1970s, he chose to work on other topics, from monetary economics and the history of the Keynesian revolution to the Israeli economy. As is noted in Chapter 4, he failed to see the parallels between his own work on the labor market and Robert Clower's analysis of the consumption function. In contrast, in the Introduction to the third edition, published in 1989, the focus is on the importance of disequilibrium macroeconomics.

THE NEOCLASSICAL SYNTHESIS

Before it was called "hydraulic" by Coddington (1983), the consensus view about Keynesian economics from the 1940s through the 1960s was famously dubbed "neoclassical synthesis" by Samuelson (1955:vi), in the third edition of his influential introductory textbook *Economics.* Samuelson stressed, in a manner that echoed the last chapter of Keynes's (1973[1936]) *General Theory,* the synthesis of Keynesian demand-management policy with the use of the price mechanism to allocate resources, but this position rested on a synthesis of the Keynesian macroeconomic income determination theory with classical or neoclassical microeconomic principles.[6]

---

[6] Pearce and Hoover (1995:202n15) have suggested that Samuelson's coinage was due to his desire to "appear less 'pink'" during the McCarthy era in the 1950s. Samuelson himself has

The post-war consensus was based on the beliefs that microeconomic decisions are rational, but markets are not efficient, in the sense that they are not cleared by quick adjustment of prices and wages. "Cost push" analysis of wage determination, according to which wage rates were, except under conditions of particularly high aggregate demand, determined by factors largely independent of the factors determining the level of employment, was widely held for much of the 1950s and 1960s and was not completely eclipsed in the 1970s. The Phillips curve, computed as an empirical relationship found in nearly a century of British data, was introduced by the LSE economist A. W. H. (Bill) Phillips in 1958. His conclusion was that, except in years when imported inflation was significant, the evidence supported the view that "the rate of change of money wage rates can be explained by the level of unemployment and the rate of change of unemployment" (Phillips 1958:299). Two years later, one of Phillips's younger colleagues at LSE, Richard Lipsey, re-examined the data, quantifying the effects of various factors, including the price level, on wage inflation. Significantly, given subsequent developments, the curvature of the curve found by Phillips, and confirmed by Lipsey's own econometric work, was explained by a rudimentary matching theory: "[t]he larger is the excess demand the easier will it be to find jobs, and the less will be the time taken in moving between jobs" (Lipsey 1960:14). That high aggregate demand could produce high inflation was well known (Forder 2010a, 2010b), but the Phillips curve focused attention on this relationship, coming to be used as the framework around which discussions of inflation increasingly took place. Thus, when they surveyed the problem of anti-inflation policy, Samuelson and Robert Solow (1960) framed their discussion in terms of a Phillips curve, applying it to U.S. data.

As pointed out by Olivier Blanchard (2008), though there was talk of a neoclassical synthesis, research largely developed along two distinct paths. Long-run movements were generally discussed using the Solow-Swan neoclassical growth model that, assuming full employment, focused on the link between factor accumulation and output. In contrast, short-run oscillations around the long-run trend were analyzed using variants of the Hicks-Hansen-Lange-Modigliani IS-LM model and involved research into the demand-side relationships on which it was based (the consumption, investment, and demand-for-money functions). Although there was much

said that, due to attacks on an earlier Keynesian textbook by Lorie Tarshis (1947), his own book had been written, as critics on right and left complained, "carefully, as if a lawyer were at my elbow" (Samuelson 1997:159).

empirical work on wage and price equations, little attention was generally paid to theories of price and wage setting. Structural macroeconometric modeling, developed out of work undertaken at the Cowles Commission in the 1940s by Lawrence Klein and others, being concerned primarily with the short run, was largely based on the Keynesian IS-LM framework. So too was the MPS (Massachusetts Institute of Technology/University of Pennsylvania/Social Science Research Council) model developed in the 1960s by a team led by Franco Modigliani.

Patinkin followed closely the work by Trygve Haavelmo, Klein, and others on structural macroeconometric models at the Cowles Commission in the 1940s, but he did not contribute to that literature. Patinkin had been assigned by Marschak to work on a sectoral econometric model for U.S. manufacturing, but the only outcome of that was a brief report on inventory equations (Patinkin 1946), which contained an embryonic version of his later off-curve analysis (Boianovsky 2002a:252n1; 2006:206–208). The contribution of Patinkin's *Money, Interest and Prices* was purely theoretical, as the outstanding statement of the neoclassical (or neo-Walrasian) synthesis (see, e.g., E. R. Weintraub 1979, ch. 4). Such an assessment is warranted by his rigorous reformulation of the quantity theory of money – even in the presence of liquidity preference and variable velocity of circulation of money – as a long-run proposition about the neutrality of money and convergence to full-employment equilibrium, together with his careful discussion of Keynesian economics as disequilibrium phenomena.

The neoclassical synthesis involved a synthesis of the Keynesian theory of unemployment with "classical" or "neoclassical" ideas about how the economy operated at full employment. However, that term came to stand for the Keynesian orthodoxy represented by the IS-LM interpretation of the *General Theory* as describing an economy in which money-wages were sticky, in the manner of Modigliani (1944) or one in which a liquidity trap or other barriers meant that full employment would not be achieved without government intervention. That was the way the term was used by Axel Leijonhufvud (1968), who called it "Keynesian economics," in contradistinction to "the economics of Keynes." It was a synthesis in which Keynes had not, as he had claimed, created a theory that was more general than the "classical" theory: he had analyzed a special case that, though it might be relevant to the real world, was obtained by imposing some restrictive assumptions on the classical theory. Patinkin's view of Keynesian economics could be interpreted this way, for he wrote that "Keynesian economics is the economics of unemployment *dis*equilibrium" and that it arises when market forces cannot eliminate unemployment "within a socially acceptable period of time" (Patinkin 1965:337–38, 342). However, Patinkin did not see his work as forming part of the neoclassical synthesis – a term he did not use – since he always tried to distance himself from the interpretation of unemployment based on rigid wages and prices. The problem was that his emphasis on the long-run neutrality of money helped to obscure the path-breaking discussion of the connection between the aggregate demand constraint and the demand function for labor put forward in chapter 13 of *Money, Interest and Prices*, which explains why he was seen by a significant part of the profession, much to his disappointment, as an anti-Keynesian economist (see Boianovsky 2011). This accounts for the paradox whereby *Money, Interest and Prices* appears both as the definitive statement of the orthodoxy against which disequilibrium macroeconomics was a reaction and as part of the challenge to this orthodoxy.

The consensus represented by the neoclassical synthesis ended in the 1970s. The conventional account of its demise focuses on both the collapse of confidence in demand-management policies in response to the economic turmoil that followed the 1973–74 oil price rises and growing perception that there was an element of "schizophrenia" involved in treating agents as being rational and at the same time regarding markets as being ineffi-cient (Blanchard 2008). There is truth in both of these points. However, the neoclassical synthesis was also challenged from a completely different perspective. When Robert Clower (1965) attacked the "Keynesian coun-terrevolution," the view that Keynes was not a major theoretical innovator, he was attacking what we have called the neoclassical synthesis. Whereas Patinkin's call for a disequilibrium interpretation of unemployment had had relatively little impact on the profession, Clower's attempt to reinterpret the Keynesian theory of aggregate demand and the foundations of monetary economics, reinforced by the publication, three years later, of a much more comprehensive critique of the Keynesian orthodoxy by Axel Leijonhufvud (1968), caught the attention of macroeconomists. Our contention is that the subsequent history of macroeconomics cannot properly be understood without understanding the fate of the resulting literature on what we are choosing to call disequilibrium macroeconomics.

FOUR

Clower, Leijonhufvud, and the Re-Appraisal
of Keynesian Economics

In the mid-1960s, many economists sought to reappraise Keynesian economics (see, for example, Coddington 1976). Two of the names that are almost universally cited as inspiring this literature were Robert Clower (1926–2011) and Axel Leijonhuvfud (b. 1933), whose names were frequently bracketed together. The paper that was perceived to have started much of this literature was Clower's "The Keynesian Counter-revolution: A Theoretical Appraisal" (1965). As we explain in the following section, this was not his first attempt to reappraise Keynes, but it was the one that drew attention to the need to rethink the microeconomic foundations of Keynesian economics and which provided the theoretical idea, his "dual-decision hypothesis," that is crucial to virtually all of the ensuing literature. His target was the attempt, christened "the Keynesian counter-revolution," to interpret Keynes within the framework of general equilibrium theory, the main examples of which were Hicks and Patinkin. The problem with this literature, Clower argued, was that if one accepted its interpretation of Keynesian economics, it was not at all clear what the novelty of the *General Theory* (Keynes 1973[1936]) was.

Clower's answer was the dual-decision hypothesis. Traditional theory assumed that a household chose its labor supply and consumption to maximize utility subject to the constraint that income earned from selling labor must not be less than the cost of consumption goods purchased. Clower contended that if there is unemployment, households face an additional constraint on the quantity of labor that they can sell. As a result, demand for consumption goods will depend on realized sales of labor, and income will enter as an independent variable in the consumption function. The significance for general equilibrium theory was that it undermined Walras's Law, the law that the sum of excess demands is zero, for if there is excess supply of labor, the additional constraint will bind, and households will not be in a position to express their notional demand for consumption goods – the demand they would express in the absence of any quantity constraints, which means there will be no corresponding excess demand for consumption goods. Virtually all the literature on Keynesian economics drew on this result. It was significant because it suggested that the key to the Keynesian revolution was found at the level of the theory of the individual household.

Clower's work was immediately seen as important, but what caught the imagination of many of the economists was Axel Leijonhufvud's book *On Keynesian Economics and the Economics of Keynes* (1968). Like Clower, Leijonhufvud argued that the theoretical foundations of Keynesian economics needed to be reappraised, but rather than base this claim on a single technical point about household behavior, the dual-decision hypothesis, he offered a much broader vision of what was revolutionary about Keynesian economics. It was about economics without the Walrasian auctioneer. Leijonhufvud thus vindicated Keynes's claim, which had been called into question in the literature from Hicks to Patinkin, that his theory was more general than the classical theory.[1] Keynesian economics was not, as implied by Patinkin's interpretation, concerned with the special case of when there was some barrier to the adjustment of wages so that markets cleared within a socially acceptable period: it was classical economics, with its assumption of an auctioneer who could ensure that markets were always in equilibrium, that was the special case.

These ideas, that markets would not necessarily be in equilibrium (and that Keynesian unemployment implied excess supply of labor) became the foundation of the literature discussed in Chapters 5 and 7 of this book. For this reason alone, it is important to understand where they came from. However, the wide use of these ideas makes careful consideration of the work of Clower and Leijonhufvud important for another reason: their ideas about what happened when markets did not clear were later developed by economists who, as we show, had agendas that were very different from those of Clower and Leijonhufvud, whose work thus needs to be considered separately in order to avoid reading it through the lens of the literature that developed in the 1970s, most of which Clower and Leijonhufvud had little sympathy.

---

[1] Leijonhufvud buttressed this with other arguments that distinguished "Keynes's economics" from "Keynesian economics," notably the argument that the aggregative structure of the general theory did not correspond with that of Keynesian economics. If one were working with a two-asset model, should bonds be aggregated with money or with real capital?

CLOWER AND DISEQUILIBRIUM PRICE DYNAMICS

Robert Clower spent the years from 1949 to 1952 at Oxford, studying toward a doctorate under John Hicks. It was failed by his examiners, Ian Little and Frank Hahn, even though by that point he had published two papers, a short note on consumer theory, and a substantial paper on the consumption function when preferences are inter-dependent (Clower 1952a, 1952b). In 1957, he moved to Northwestern University where he remained, with several periods of leave, till 1972 when he took up a position at UCLA, where he remained till 1986. During the 1950s, he published textbooks on microeconomics and published articles on the theory of investment and on the theory of how a monopolist will behave when faced with an uncertain demand curve (Clower 1954, 1959).

Like Patinkin, Clower was convinced that Keynesian economics had to be understood in terms of disequilibrium, but he placed more emphasis on dynamics. This is consistent with his self-description as having an iconoclastic frame of mind that inclined him toward doubts about orthodox economics. This took the form of a concern with "how markets work," seeing "no special virtue in the excess-demand adjustment rules of established theory," for he "knew too much about economic organization to imagine that the prices of more than a handful of commodities were determined on a day-to-day basis by impersonal market forces" (Clower 1984:260).[2] His first "significant" publication, on his own assessment, (Clower and Bushaw 1954) was on stock-flow analysis, a dynamic problem. His paper on investment in the same year (Clower 1954) also focused on dynamics. As pointed out by E. R. Weintraub (1991:136–37), the Bushaw-Clower article pioneered the Liapunov technique for demonstrating that the addition of stock-adjustment mechanisms could led to asymptotic stability of the competitive equilibrium, which was not recognized in the literature at the time.

Clower continued his work on dynamics during the late 1950s, when he produced a series of papers on the process of price determination, most of which were never published.[3] In a paper prepared for a staff seminar on November 16, 1956, "Toward a Theory of Unified Market Mechanisms,"[4]

---

[2]   It may be significant that much of his early career involved applied work and visiting African countries. See de Antoni (1999) and Costa (2002) for an overview of Clower's life and contributions.

[3]   Robert W. Clower Papers, Box 4. David M. Rubenstein Rare Book and Manuscript Library, Duke University.

[4]   Robert W. Clower Papers, Box 4. David M. Rubenstein Rare Book and Manuscript Library, Duke University.

Clower sought to develop a theory based on the following premises: (1) buyers tend to purchase from the seller who offers the lowest price; (2) each seller in a given market tends to vary his current sale price when actual sales differs from current sales offers; and (3) sales offers vary when either estimated marginal profit is not zero or actual sales are not equal to current sales offers.[5] This paper, which echoes the dynamic processes discussed in his article on monopoly (Clower 1959), was his way of analyzing the microeconomics of how markets work out of equilibrium. It involved trying to find plausible descriptions of how firms might set prices in circumstances where, presumably, the maximization problem could not be defined.[6]

In another unpublished paper dating from this period, "On the Microdynamics of Price Formation in n-Seller Markets,"[7] Clower wrote that there was a common conceptual problem underlying theories of monopoly, oligopoly, and pure competition: "*to formulate self-contained, logically coherent, and intuitively satisfying description of the determination of the output, price and sales of each seller*" (1956/58:1; these words are underlined in the original).[8] He noted that though one might expect, because this was the common problem, to find uniformities in the treatment of these types of market structure, "the most notable feature of this literature is its qualitative diversity" (Clower 1956/58:1). He went on to provide a dynamic, period analysis of how prices and quantities changed.[9] He assumed that sellers set asking prices (p_i) and offered goods for sale on a take-it-or-leave-it basis and that planned sales (x_i) would typically diverge from actual sales (y_i), deriving a model comprising $3n$ first-order difference equations, where n was the number of commodities. Some aspects of this were conventional, such as the n equations relating changes in asking prices to the differences between planned and actual sales. Less conventional was his equation relating the change in actual sales to both "unsatisfied market demand" and "the

---

[5] Robert W. Clower Papers, Box 4. Rubenstein Rare Book and Manuscript Library, Duke University.
[6] It is worth noting that this work pre-dates the work of George Stigler on markets with imperfect information.
[7] Robert W. Clower Papers, Box 4. David M. Rubenstein Rare Book and Manuscript Library, Duke University. The typescript is undated apart from a pencil annotation, presumably by Clower though this is not certain, "1956 – draft 1958" on the first page.
[8] Clower's problem can be contrasted with the much simpler problem represented by the tâtonnement process.
[9] It is tempting to speculate that his analysis of market periods was influenced by his former supervisor, John Hicks. This would, however, be no more than speculation.

differences prevailing among individual asking prices at the beginning of period t" (Clower 1956/58:5):

$$y_i(t) = y_i(t-1) = A_i\{D[P(t)] - S(t-1)\} + \Sigma_j B_{ij}\{p_j(t) - p_i(t)\}$$

$$\text{where } P(t) \equiv \text{Min } [p_1(t), \ldots, p_n(t)].$$

This equation is useful, not for the details, but because it shows the way Clower was searching for an alternative to the tâtonnement process.

Although there are parallels with his earlier paper on monopoly, the first publication resulting from this research program was "Keynes and the Classics: A Dynamical Perspective" (Clower 1960), which argued that unemployment had to be considered as a disequilibrium phenomenon in which the short side of the market dominated. Two aspects of this paper are worth noting. The first is that he argued that positions to the left of both supply and demand curves, though attainable (unlike positions to the right of either curve) "cannot be maintained more than momentarily because households and firms share a *mutual* desire to increase employment and output under these circumstances" (Clower 1984:22). Such positions amounted to frictional unemployment and could be ignored. When the paper was submitted to the *Journal of Political Economy*, it made use of "various mechanical price and quantity adjustment rules" (Clower 1984:260). Clower thought these plausible, but he could provide little justification for them. The *Journal of Political Economy* found the paper "intriguing but unpersuasive" and rejected it. Clower then removed these price-adjustment rules and sent "an appropriately expurgated version" to the *Quarterly Journal of Economics*, which accepted it.

This is the background to his most-cited paper, "The Keynesian Counter-Revolution" (Clower 1965). This was written in 1962, for a conference on the role of money in general equilibrium theory organized by the International Economic Association near Paris. Unable to think of anything new to say on the topic, recalling an earlier exchange between Hicks (1957) and Patinkin (1959) he turned his attention to Keynes and general equilibrium, and wrote the paper in ten days. That exchange had begun with Hicks's review of *Money, Interest and Prices*, in which he claimed that Patinkin denied that there had been a Keynesian revolution, for "The theory which Patinkin sets out, though it owes much to Keynes, is not Keynesian; it is a modernised version of the theory which Keynes called 'classical'" (Hicks 1957:278). The reason was that, in Patinkin's theory, full employment could be restored, provided that wages were sufficiently flexible. Hicks sought to recover Keynesian economics by providing arguments why the necessary interest rate adjustments might not be possible. In reply, Patinkin was able to point out that Hicks had not understood that his real-balance effect meant that changes in wages and prices could affect demand independently of the rate of interest. He summed up their disagreement by arguing that Hicks had missed the point because he was still thinking in terms of equilibrium, whereas to understand the Keynesian revolution, one needed to think in terms of disequilibrium:

> We now come to a related question: If the real-balance effect can – in principle – restore the economy to a full-employment position, what happens to the Keynesian Revolution? The answer – as I see it – is that the Revolution goes on – though on a somewhat different plane. In particular, the interest of Keynesian economics shifts from "unemployment equilibrium" (which is the concern of the Hicks 1937 article) to unemployment *dis*equilibrium. And the main message of Keynesian economics becomes that the automatic adjustment process of the market (even with the real-balance effect – and even when supplemented by monetary policy) is too unreliable to serve as a practical basis of a full-employment policy. In other words, though the real-balance effect must be taken account of in our theoretical analysis, it is too weak – and, in some cases (due to adverse expectations) too perverse – to fulfil a significant role in our policy considerations. (Patinkin 1959:586)

This may have been a reiteration of what we described as the essence of the neoclassical synthesis, but it stated explicitly that it was necessary to turn to disequilibrium.

In his paper, Clower took Patinkin's observation about disequilibrium more seriously, arguing that if there were disequilibrium, the model of consumer choice used by Patinkin would need to be modified, and posited the dual-decision hypothesis to explain why demands for commodities would differ from those give by the Walrasian equations. Walrasian demand functions, the basis for Patinkin's theory, were what Clower termed "notional" demands, distinguished from the "effective" demands of Keynesian theory.

Clower's paper can clearly be seen as a contribution to the literature in which Patinkin was involved. In correspondence of March 3, 1962, with Patinkin, Clower referred to

> the ideas adumbrated in the second half of your book on disequilibrium systems. [That is] still the weakest part of your entire structure, and the weaknesses arise from undue concentration on the equilibrium properties of household models in Part I. I will say no more on that here, since your concentration on consumer equilibrium saves me all kinds of time to concentrate on consumer disequilibrium – an area in which I am currently specializing, with what I think are interesting results.[10]

---

[10] Clower to Patinkin, March 3, 1962. Don Patinkin papers, Box 25. David M. Rubenstein Rare Book and Manuscript Library, Duke University.

The rest of the letter makes clear that Clower's contribution to the 1962 conference was prompted by what he perceived as some analytical problems of Patinkin's macroeconomic model, although he did not refer to Patinkin's treatment of demand for labor either in the correspondence or in the paper. In particular, Clower pointed out that "you cannot legitimately put income into your demand functions in Part II ["Macroeconomics"] of your book, if you suppose that individuals earn income from inside the system – for then income is not an independent variable." That was the heart of the matter, for "you do not in fact have income coming from heaven in Part II, nor could you and still talk about employment and unemployment. But if you want to stick to utility analysis so be it." In the published version of the paper, Clower (1965:111–12) repeated that criticism. Like the published version of his previous paper, the 1962 piece contains no discussion of Clower's theories about price dynamics. However, to understand Clower's subsequent intellectual trajectory, it is important to locate it against the background of his earlier work on disequilibrium dynamics.

Frank Hahn, one of the conference organizers, has claimed that, recognizing the importance of Clower's paper, he assigned Patinkin, as the most eminent economist present, as the discussant.[11] In that role, Patinkin agreed with what he saw as the "basic message" of the paper, that is, the interpretation of the Keynesian system in terms of a "disequilibrium model" (Brechling 1965:301). Yet, in the same way that Clower did not see the parallel between his own analysis of the demand for commodities and the analysis of the labor market in chapter 13 or *Money, Interest and Prices* (discussed in Chapter 3 of this book), neither did Patinkin make the connection. Patinkin did not see that the two demand curves shown in Figure 3.1 in Chapter 3 corresponded to Clower's concepts of notional and effective demand.

At the time, Patinkin did not dispute Clower's rejection of Walras's Law in disequilibrium, even though this differed from his own formulation (see Patinkin 1987). The significant difference between the two approaches is that, for Clower, unemployment does not imply any pressure to reduce prices, for the constrained demand for goods is equal to planned supply of goods at prevailing price and income levels. In contrast with Patinkin, Clower could accept Keynes's assumption that the goods market always cleared (see Brechling 1965:304). The main question investigated by Clower (1965) was which excess demands drive prices – notional or effective excess demands. If prices respond to effective excess demands instead of notional

---

[11] E-mail from Hahn to the authors, February 25, 2005.

demands, as claimed by Clower (1965:123), the dynamic behavior of the economy will differ from that predicted by the Walrasian tâtonnement. In particular, under the assumption that effective demand depends on realized rather than notional income, there would be no pressure on wages and prices to move in opposite directions and hence for real wages to fall when there was unemployment, since Walras's Law does not hold for the demand functions described by the dual decision hypothesis. Clower's greater interest in dynamics is consistent with his later remark that Hahn and Patinkin "completely missed" the main point of his paper, which was that "When you introduce transactions you have a non-linearity and create a terrible problem for the logistics of exchange that is never looked at" and that "you lose all help from linear dynamic systems" (Clower interviewed in Snowdon and Vane 1999:185). However, it is important to note that, at least in criticizing Hahn, he is criticizing one of the external examiners responsible for his failing his doctorate a decade earlier (Snowdon and Vane 1999:178).

Clower, however, left open the question of whether his dual-decision hypothesis could provide a new concept of (non-Walrasian) equilibrium or was just a modification of the stability analysis of classical full-employment equilibrium. Some passages suggest that he was inclined to the latter interpretation, especially his remark that "*when income appears as an independent variable in the market excess demand functions ... traditional price theory ceases to shed any light on the dynamic stability of a market economy*" (1965:123, italics in the original). Convergence to full employment through changes in real wages was still possible, but the mechanism could not be illuminated by classical theory. Clower's model illustrated Keynes (1973[1936], ch. 19) concern that money-wage cuts have a direct negative impact on aggregate demand via reduced realized income. The model, however, could not account for the indirect effect through interest rates (discussed by Keynes) or real balance effects (discussed by Patinkin), because money is not introduced. Money was mentioned by Clower in the debate that followed his presentation, when he discussed the possibility that the reduction in demand resulting from excess supply of labor could bring about higher prices to the extent that it resulted in lessened demand for an asset rather than a reduction in demand for commodities (Brechling 1965:305).

The rationale for the dual-decision hypothesis was that agents are operating in a monetary economy in which they have to obtain money before they can buy goods. Although he did locate his argument in the literature on stock-flow models and in the foundations of monetary economics, to which

Bushaw and Clower (1960) had contributed,[12] in "The Keynesian Counter-revolution," Clower insisted that the essential characteristics of the dual-decision hypothesis would come out more clearly if money demand was not introduced at the outset. However, he soon changed his mind, for in a paper published two years later, still focusing on general equilibrium as expressed in Patinkin's *Money, Interest and Prices*, Clower (1967) proposed a model of monetary transactions featuring the so-called Clower (or cash-in-advance) constraint, noting in words that were set in italics that "the total value of goods demanded cannot in any circumstances exceed the amount of money held by the transactor at the outset of the period."[13] The way he reached this conclusion was through assuming that money was a commodity that could be traded for any other commodity, whereas goods other than money could be traded only for money: they could not be traded directly with each other. There is a clear parallel with what Patinkin had done twenty years earlier when he had argued that consumption would depend on holdings of real balances, but Clower took it in a different direction.[14] Although it rested on money having unique properties, it was a characterization of a monetary economy that he later found unsatisfactory, on the grounds that it implied that the use of money reduced the opportunities open to people, whereas it would natural to assume that the use of money enabled people to achieve things that could not be achieved under barter, for why would people use money if it restricted the activities they could undertake?

LEIJONHUFVUD AND COORDINATION FAILURES

On Keynesian Economics and the Economics of Keynes (1968), arguably the most important book in the literature on the search for microfoundations, was based on Axel Leijonhufvud's doctoral dissertation, presented to Northwestern University in 1967. He had been an undergraduate in Sweden where, for one semester in 1957–58, he was taught macroeconomics by Erik Lundberg. Leijonhufvud recalls that Lundberg provided a conventional reading of Keynesian economics, based on the "Keynesian cross," and that though ideas of viewing this as a coordination failure were no doubt always in the background (Lundberg's 1937 doctoral thesis was one of the important works from the Stockholm school), it was not something

[12] See Clower (1965, note 16).
[13] See also Boianovsky (2002b).
[14] Clower's 1967 reconsideration of the monetary structure of transactions later had a significant influence on Leijonhufvud's (1973a) notion of "effective demand failures," discussed later.

that was discussed explicitly.[15] From Sweden, he went to the University of Pittsburgh, where, due to the influence of Edwin Witte, he read everything written by Modigliani. So when he came to choose a school in which to take his Ph.D., he considered MIT. When he arrived for interview, he spoke to Modigliani, who said that he was about to leave for Northwestern, but that if Leijonhufvud would apply there, Modigliani would advise the department to give him a fellowship. Leijonhufvud thus spent three years, from 1960–63, at Northwestern.

The University of Pittsburgh was also important, Leijonhufvud recalls, because of the influence there of Herbert Simon, then at Carnegie Tech, also in Pittsburgh. Thus, his master's thesis was on the "Formal and Substantive Problems in the Theory of the Firm," and in 1961–62, when he was still working out what his doctoral thesis would be on, he wrote papers titled "Autonomous and Instrumental Organizations" and "Concepts of Goal and Function in Administrative Theory" and on topics that included the aggregation of interests, profit maximization, and decision making.[16]

At Northwestern, he was taught macroeconomics by Modigliani, but was also influenced by Meyer Burstein, who became his dissertation supervisor and chaired his dissertation committee. Leijonhufvud has written that it took him a long time to settle on a topic; and that by 1963, he had independently worked out a debt-deflation theory of the Great Depression; and that his intention was to explain why it developed as it did. Burstein, who was later to write an idiosyncratic book on monetary economics (Burstein 1986), had interests in stock-flow interactions and was an enthusiast for Keynesian economics, despite his training having been at Chicago where he had been taught as an undergraduate by Henry Simons and, twelve years later, as a graduate student, by Milton Friedman. Despite a year (1963–64) at the Brookings Institution, where Leijonhufvud discussed his thesis with James Tobin, he did not discover Irving Fisher's work till the end of the year, when David Meiselman told him to look in the early issues of *Econometrica*. He then had to find a new thesis topic.

The process of writing what became his dissertation, therefore, took place between 1964 and 1967, after Leijonhufvud left Northwestern to become an assistant professor at UCLA. Just before he left Northwestern, he met Robert Clower, who had been on leave working in Africa on development problems, from whom he received advice and with whom he remained in

[15]   E-mail from Leijonhufvud, June 1, 2011
[16]   Axel Leijonhufvud papers, Box 1. Rubenstein Manuscripts and Rare Books Room, Duke University.

close touch. However, though he had read the German version of Clower (1965), the thesis made little use of Clower's dual-decision hypothesis, the more extensive discussion of this being introduced only when the thesis was rewritten into the book, the stage at which he was most strongly influenced by Clower and by one of his colleagues at UCLA, Armen Alchian.

Armen Alchian, who had come to UCLA in 1946 and been a consultant at RAND since its foundation in the same year, had a background in statistics, in particular in their application to biology, as found in the work of R. A. Fisher.[17] Alchian's most important work had been on evolution and biological analogies in relation to the theory of the firm (Alchian 1950), and with problems of information. When Leijonhufvud arrived at UCLA, Alchian had recently published his paper on the way costs fell during production processes, work that stemmed from a RAND discussion paper in 1949, on costs in airframe production, which he had not previously been allowed to place in the public domain (Alchian 1963: 679). He also had an unpublished working paper on "Unemployment and the Cost of Information," that had been circulating for several years and was eventually published as Alchian (1969) and in the Phelps volume (Alchian 1970; discussed in Chapter 6 of this book), from which Leijonhufvud was to draw important ideas for his thesis.[18]

Despite the earlier efforts by Patinkin (1956) and Clower (1965), it was Leijonhufvud's 1968 book that succeeded in stimulating interest in macroeconomic analysis under nonmarket clearing conditions (see, for example, Barro and Grossman 1976:xi; Bliss 1975). Harry Johnson, Canadian but Cambridge and Harvard trained, who at this time was at the height of his influence, simultaneously Professor at Chicago and LSE, and one of the profession's most prolific authors, was important in promoting the book. He put it on his LSE reading list as "a critical study of modern trends in macroeconomics" and a "stimulating complement" to more orthodox approaches; he arranged for Leijonhufvud to give two lectures on the book that were then published in a pamphlet by the Institute of Economic Affairs (Leijonhufvud 1969) and he reviewed it in *Encounter* (Moggridge 2008). Johnson also cited Leijonhufvud's work very favorably in his widely read Ely Lecture "The Keynesian Revolution and the Monetarist Counter-Revolution" (Johnson 1971) and in other writings on the Keynesian revolution (e.g., Johnson 1976).

---

[17] See Levallois (2009).
[18] See Leijonhufvud (1968:69n3, 78, 390) and Levine (undated).

The book's key claim, made in its paradoxical title, in arousing interest in Leijonhufvud's arguments, was that "Keynesian economics" as it existed in the 1960s had failed to do justice to the concerns of Keynes, who was concerned not with wage stickiness but with a much deeper problem of system-wide coordination failure. Part of Leijonhufvud's concern was, of course, with doctrinal history: with demonstrating that economists had gotten Keynes systematically wrong. However, he wanted to contribute to economics, not just engage in doctrinal history. He recognized that he was reading between the lines of Keynes's (1973[1936]) *General Theory* (though nowhere near to the extent that some commentators suggested)[19] and that in places he knowingly sought to extend Keynes ideas. In part, this was because Keynes had not fully articulated his vision of the problems with capitalism that he was diagnosing.

Leijonhufvud made his approach very clear in a letter to Patinkin on June 15, 1974, after Patinkin had promised to read *On Keynesian Economics and the Economics of Keynes*:

I thought I was discussing contemporary theory issues ("contemporary" meaning early '60's – when I did my graduate work and not doctrine-history). In theory I had been taught general equilibrium models on the one hand and Keynesian models (by Modigliani) on the other; I was struck mostly by the incompatibilities, offended by the "Neoclassical synthesis", and saw no palatable way out. It was in searching for a way out from this cul-de-sac that I eventually started to "backtrack" into doctrine-history, trying to identify, as it were, the forks in the road where the major decisions on what conceptual experiment to pursue were made.[20]

The big point made by Leijonhufvud in his book was that Keynesian economics was about how an economy would behave if there were no Walrasian auctioneer to bring markets into equilibrium. An important part of that story was Clower's dual-decision hypothesis: in the absence of an auctioneer prices will fail to clear markets, trade will take place at disequilibrium prices, commodity demands will diverge from Walrasian demands, and as a result, activities may fail to be coordinated.

For quantity constraints to come into effect, it was not necessary, Leijonhufvud claimed, to introduce institutional price rigidities, merely the assumption that prices (including wages) did not adjust as fast as quantities. He conceptualized this by talking in terms of the ranking of adjustment speeds. The classical assumption was that prices adjusted more quickly than

---

[19] Grossman (1972b) and Coddington (1976); see Leijonhufvud (2000:24–27) for comments on their criticisms.

[20] Leijonhufvud to Patinkin, June 15, 1974. Don Patinkin Papers, Box 65. David M. Rubenstein Rare Book and Manuscript Library, Duke University.

quantities, but Keynes reversed this ranking and the consequence was that the system behaved in a completely different way due to the quantity constraints that would arise.[21] All that was needed was that price changes took place in real time and were therefore not instantaneous.

However, there was much more to Leijonhufvud's book than this. Reflecting a long-standing interest in aggregation problems, on which he had written working papers in 1961–62,[22] before he had started his Ph.D. dissertation work, Leijonhufvud argued that economists had missed much of what Keynes was trying to say through failing to see that the way he aggregated financial and real assets was different from the conventional way. Keynes, he claimed, treated bonds and capital goods as a single aggregate, and he did not aggregate consumer goods and capital goods (Leijonhufvud 1968:135ff). The result was that, for Keynes, the rate of interest was a long-term rate and was the relative price of real assets as much as the relative price of two financial assets.[23]

This opened the way for Leijonhufvud to argue that the heart of the *General Theory* lay in an inter-temporal coordination failure.[24] The rate of interest is the relative price of current and future consumption and Leijonhufvud claimed that Keynes's theory of liquidity preference amounted to a theory of why the rate of interest would fail to coordinate economic activities. If, because of speculative activity, the rate of interest were too high, the result would be a level of investment that was lower than the amount that consumers wished to save. In other words, consumers were trying to transfer resources to the future but, because of speculative effects on the rate of interest, the investment needed to achieve this was not forthcoming.

In summarizing his argument, in the first of what he called "two post-scripts," Leijonhufvud argued that Keynesian economics should be viewed through the lens of cybernetics, for it was concerned with communication

---

[21] One of the authors once tried to sort out, using a framework close to that of Solow and Stiglitz (1968) and Barro and Grossman (1971), what such a reversal might mean; see Backhouse (1980, 1982). Even the "Marshallian" case is not so simple as is sometimes assumed. For reasons that should become clear, such an approach did not appeal to Leijonhufvud.

[22] Box 1 of the Axel Leijonhufvud Papers, Rubenstein Rare Book and Manuscript Library, Duke University, contains working papers on the aggregation of interests (September 1961) and "Coalitions and the Aggregation Problem" (January 1962).

[23] Box 1 of the Axel Leijonhufvud Papers, Rubenstein Rare Book and Manuscript Library, Duke University, contains early discussions of the rate of interest with Burstein and William Jaffe. This included a paper on Böhm-Bawerk.

[24] Given the importance of inter-temporal optimization to the subsequent literature (see Chapter 8), it is interesting to note that Leijonhufvud was arguing in these terms in the 1960s.

and control in dynamic systems (1968:387–401). This pointed to the importance of information, to which Alchian had drawn his attention, for, as Norbert Wiener, who introduced the term cybernetics, stated when distinguishing between cybernetics and traditional physics,

> Here there emerges a very interesting distinction between the physics of our grandfathers and that of the present day. *In nineteenth century physics, it seemed to cost nothing to get information.* (quoted in Leijonhufvud 1968:397; italics added by Leijonhufvud)

Leijonhufvud drew an analogy between Maxwell's demon and Walras's auctioneer, arguing that the latter was a demon that needed to be exorcized. Although it is tempting to see this as an afterthought, perhaps linking the discussion of cybernetics to the remark, which appears a few pages later, that we should "go back to Hayek" (Leijonhufvud 1968:401), it is perhaps best seen, as in Howitt's (2002) appraisal, as the theme crucial to understanding Leijonhufvud's book. Clower's dual-decision hypothesis was important because it showed the complexity of the information flows that needed to be analyzed when considering macroeconomic systems. It was arguably Alchian's work, and perhaps even ideas going back to Simon, who does not even appear in the book's index, that framed Leijonhufvud's thinking.

Thus, although Clower's influence was important, it should not be overemphasized. As pointed by Leijonhufvud in a letter to Patinkin dated June 15, 1974, "although my degree was from Northwestern, Clower was in Liberia and England during my stay there and I only got to lay emphasis on his work after I came to UCLA – so there was not the direct connection there that most people tend to assume." Indeed, Clower wrote to Leijonhufvud on October 4, 1964,[25] that

> I am returning the copy of Chapter III with some marginal comments. I found the discussion as a whole very rewarding. I must say that I had never thought particularly about the possibility of connecting the Keynesian type of adjustment with the sort of short-run quantity adjustments discussed by Marshall – but your discussion of the matter convinces me that there is something in that way.

Clower was referring, of course, to Leijonhufvud's well-known claim about the reversal of the velocity of Marshallian price and quantity adjustments in the short run. According to Leijonhufvud, this could be explained

---

[25] Axel Leijonhufvud Papers, Box 1. David M. Rubenstein Rare Book and Manuscript Library, Duke University.

by informational problems and liquidity constraints. As indicated by the correspondence, Clower disagreed with Leijonhufvud's emphasis on the inter-temporal coordination issue (see Leijonhufvud 1998:175). The matter was discussed in a letter dated October 18, 1965 (emphasis in the original), when Leijonhufvud explained, "I am assuming ... that all the disturbances of major interest to someone concerned with the possibility of the *emergence* of an income constrained process ... bring about ex ante hoarding (or ex ante excess of S over I)."[26]

Leijonhufvud's message, therefore, was that in the absence of an auctioneer to ensure that appropriate prices prevail, there will be systematic coordination failures, involving goods, labor, and asset markets. These coordination failures arise not from rigidities, or any simple barrier to price adjustments, but from features that are inherent in any decentralized, dynamic economy in which decisions are made in real time – in other words, in any economy in which there is no auctioneer to bring about the equality of supply and demand. In an interview given to Brian Snowdon on May 17, 2002, Leijonhufvud explained that his 1968 book "is essentially about the kind of information questions that do not occur in neoclassical Walrasian general equilibrium models. The issues I was dealing with had to do with how information and communication flow in the system so as to enable a coordinated solution to be achieved."

Perhaps part of the reason why readers were not more aware of the perspective from which the book was written and, instead, saw it as dealing with the economics of price-rigidity rather than as concerned with the consequences of costly information, is that he failed to distinguish his approach sufficiently clearly from the work of his teacher, Modigliani, who, after his 1944 article, was for the rest of his career, one of the key supporters of the idea that the Keynesian economics was about the consequences of wage rigidity. When, during an interview in 2002, not published till after Modigliani's death, he was asked about his disagreement with Modigliani, he replied,

Yes, and this was a great embarrassment to me because I have so much respect and affection for Franco Modigliani (I felt the same about John Hicks whom I met later). My conclusion was indeed that Modigliani's 1944 paper was fundamentally wrong. Every generation of young researchers is supposed to challenge the older generation, but I felt very badly about it. My book is not quite honest about this because it avoids challenging Modigliani directly. (Snowdon 2004:124)

---

[26] Robert W. Clower Papers, Box 2. Rubenstein Rare Book and Manuscript Library, Duke University.

He went on to say that he was very reticent about contacting Modigliani to discuss their differences.

REPAIRING TO MARSHALL

From 1971, Clower and Leijonhufvud, whose careers had previously been separate, were together at UCLA, and their research converged.[27] They wrote a number of joint articles, and in 1972, they planned to write a textbook together, to be titled *The Coordination of Economic Activities*, though it was never written. This was at exactly the time that their work was receiving great publicity through Barro and Grossman's much-cited "A General Disequilibrium Model of Income and Employment" (1971). However, though they were routinely cited as having laid the foundations of this literature (discussed in Chapter 5 of this book), Clower and Leijonhufvud had little sympathy with it and their own work took them in a different direction: they paid more attention to money, and they decided that, in contrast with what most other economists were doing, their theory was built on a Marshallian framework, not a Walrasian one. This distinction, between Marshall and Walras, was not one to which either had previously paid much attention.

Leijonhufvud suggests that by the time Barro and Grossman (1971) was published, they had already moved on. In a letter to Erroll Glustoff, he wrote that he and Clower had stopped talking about sales constraints, in favor of cash constraints.[28] This was in recognition of the fact that, in a monetary economy people hold stocks of cash and need not respond to sales constraints by immediately reducing their purchases. In the same letter, Leijonhufvud criticized Grossman for neglecting stocks. These ideas were incorporated by Leijonhufvud (1973a), which may be regarded as his last contribution to the field of disequilibrium macroeconomics per se. The 1973 article introduced the notion that the economic system is stable within a certain range of normal circumstances, called a "corridor." Within the corridor, a decline in aggregate demand is dampened by wage and price adjustment. This happens because the presence of buffer stocks of liquid assets, the inelasticity of permanent income expectations and the accumulation of inventories contribute to smooth out the potential deviation-amplifying multiplier process. Things are different, however, if the initial downfall of

---

[27] They diverged later as Leijonhufvud, younger than Clower, moved into new fields, but that would take us beyond the current story.

[28] Leijonhufvud to Glustoff, January 22, 1972, Axel Leijonhufvud Papers, Box 1. Rubenstein Rare Book and Manuscript Library, Duke University.

aggregate demand is large and persistent. Effective demand failures will become prominent, with sellers reacting to the low effective demands constrained by current incomes in a monetary economy instead of notional demands (see also Howitt 1990:35). As Leijonhufvud (2000:25) would put it years later, in a belated reaction to Barro (1977b), "although there are no obstacles to price movements, the price system may ... fail to communicate all the information required to enable agents to exhaust potential gains from trade." Grossman (1974) rejected the corridor concept and criticized Leijonhufvud for viewing quantity and price adjustments always as alternatives. In a long, undated letter to Grossman, Clower tried to persuade him not to submit the paper for publication, for it "may suggest to readers that there is a skirmish going on within the ranks of disequilibrium theorists which, in turn, may induce a feeling amongst people presently moving into this area that the whole field is so confused as to be hardly worth bothering about."

At the same time, Clower had realized that his earlier (1967) characterization of a monetary economy did not make sense (in it, money was more constraining than barter, because it ruled out possible transactions) and was trying to develop a better theory of how transactions took place (cf. Clower 1984:267). He wrote that some years after the counter-revolution paper, he introduced the dual-decision hypothesis into an otherwise conventional model of price dynamics, only to discover that it yielded implausible results (Clower 1984:265–66). The result was that he had given up the original formulation of the dual-decision hypothesis even before the "counter-revolution" was published (cf. Leijonhufvud 1968:74ff). He was thus surprised when Barro, Grossman, and others used it, together with Patinkin's model of constrained supply, which he thought "even less coherent" (Clower 1984:266).

More important than this, both Clower and Leijonhufvud came to the conclusion that Keynes's theory was built on a Marshallian framework, not the Walrasian one in which they had been working in the 1960s.[29] This had the merit of making their ideas accessible to the profession, which shared a Walrasian perspective, but it was not the way they wished to go. Thus, although Leijonhufvud conceded that he had been in part responsible for the disequilibrium macroeconomics literature, constructing "Keynesian" models on "neo-Walrasian optimizing foundations ... did not seem a promising way to go and [he] took no part in this development" (Leijonhufvud 1998:175). By 1974, he was arguing that Keynesian economics had to be

---

[29] For a recent analysis of Keynes's Marshallianism, see Leijonhufvud (2006).

understood in a Marshallian framework.[30] This involved rejecting some of his 1968 arguments, most notably that concerning Keynes's reversal of Marshall's ranking of price and quantity adjustment speeds. He blamed this error on his having been misled into adopting a Walrasian perspective (Leijonhufvud 1974a:169; cf. 1968:20–25; see also the discussion in Harcourt 1977:91).

Clower (1975:7) took the same view, drawing a distinction between the Walrasian general equilibrium analysis that underlay disequilibrium macroeconomics and what he chose to call Marshallian partial process analysis:

In the Marshallian scheme of thought … the central task of economic science is to provide an intellectually satisfying account of the coordination of economic activities in an ongoing economic system comprised of business firms and households whose informational links with each other are provided by markets in which dealers of various kinds … stand ready continuously to trade goods for money or money for goods on terms that each trader varies independently in response to forces that impinge directly upon his own working stocks of money and commodity inventories.

CONCLUSION

What the work of Clower and Leijonhufvud shows is that, well before there had developed any sense of crisis in Keynesian economics, they were re-examining the conceptual basis of macroeconomics because they believed that conventional theories of how markets worked, as represented by Patinkin's *Money, Interest and Prices*, were flawed. This belief went deeper than simply concern with Keynesian economics, for there was a belief that the Walrasian tâtonnement model could not explain real-world markets: to understand how markets worked it was necessary to understand how prices changed. In Clower's case, this meant the dynamics of price changes, and in Leijonhufvud's, paying attention to the ranking of adjustment speeds. They both reached the conclusion that once attention was paid to how real-world markets, where price adjustments necessarily took time, Walrasian excess demand functions and adjustment mechanisms needed to be replaced with something that was much more Keynesian. Just as their ideas were becoming widely discussed, in the early 1970s, they were moving on toward different ways of understanding the distinguishing features of a monetary economy.

---

[30] Leijonhufvud (1974) and his unpublished Marshall Lectures in the same year. See Leijonhufvud (1998:175).

Clower never thought in terms of Walrasian general equilibrium, his earliest models being attempts to provide alternative dynamic adjustment mechanisms. Leijonhufvud thought more in general equilibrium terms, though he was never a general equilibrium theorist in the way that this term was coming to be understood. Although they recognized that prices were not completely flexible, neither of them was simply examining the consequences of prices being sticky: both were motivated by the prospect of providing a more general theory of market processes than was found in standard models. When other economists did start constructing models of equilibria with inflexible prices, they kept their distance. It is to these models that we now turn.

FIVE

Macroeconomics with Slow Price Adjustment

During the 1970s, there developed a substantial literature on macro-economic models in which prices were inflexible. Although, as we have explained in Chapter 4, they distanced themselves from it, virtually all of this literature owed something, directly or indirectly to Clower, and many writers cited Leijonhufvud. The central work was by Robert Barro and Herschel Grossman, but the appropriate starting point in this literature is a much-less-cited article by Robert Solow and Joseph Stiglitz that was published a few years earlier. Not only was this the first model in this tradition, acknowledged by Barro and Grossman, but its authors also became key players in the debates that followed.

SOLOW, STIGLITZ, AND THE DYNAMICS OF INCOME DISTRIBUTION

Joseph Stiglitz was a graduate student at MIT at the time when interest in growth theory was at its peak, the "two Cambridges controversy," in which Robert Solow was one of the major participants, arguably reaching its climax in 1966 (see Harcourt 1972).[1] It involved disputes about the measurement of capital and about income distribution: whether the distribution of income was determined by marginal productivity (the neoclassical view held at MIT) or by the rate of capital accumulation and the capitalists' propensity to save (the view of Joan Robinson and Nicholas Kaldor at the University of Cambridge, in England).[2] While he was a student at MIT, which included an important summer with Hirofumi Uzawa in Chicago,

---

[1] See Stiglitz (1993, 2002).
[2] The precise formulation of the theory was the subject of controversy. This formulation is Pasinetti's. See Harcourt (1972) for more detail. In the remainder of this paragraph, Cambridge refers to the English university.

and during a year at Cambridge,[3] Stiglitz worked on the problems of economic growth, capital accumulation and the dynamics of the distribution of income, that formed the basis for his doctoral thesis. Solow (for whom Stiglitz had once worked as a research assistant at MIT) had also been working on economic growth, capital theory and distribution, and starting with a visit to Cambridge in 1963–64, had been arguing with Kaldor about income distribution. He wanted to work out the difference between the two theories of distribution.[4] This was the background to their jointly written paper "Output, Employment and Wages in the Short Run" (Solow and Stiglitz 1968).

The two theories of income distribution that were being debated were the marginal-productivity theory and the "Cambridge" theory according to which the distribution of income between profits and wages was determined by the the growth rate and the savings behavior of capitalists and workers (Solow and Stiglitz 1968:537; Stiglitz 1993:151). Believing that the notion of an aggregate production function in which aggregate output was a function of the capital stock and the quantity of labor employed was logically flawed,[5] they started from the idea that in marginal-productivity theory, the real wage adjusted to clear the labor market, but that in the Cambridge theory its function was to clear the commodity market. Most of the literature on distribution analyzed steady state growth but, perhaps influenced by Frank Hahn, who, according to Stiglitz (1993:149), was the only Cambridge economist who did not do this, they tackled the problem through exploring the short run dynamics of wages, output, and employment. Their conclusion was that "There is a sense in which the marginal-productivity theory can be said to hold at any supply-limited equilibrium, and the Cambridge theory can be said to hold at any demand limited equilibrium" (Solow and Stiglitz 1968:558).

The model had several characteristics that marked it out as disequilibrium macroeconomics. The change in employment, $\dot{N} = dN/dt$, was given by

$$\dot{N} = \theta \left(F^{-1}(Y^S, Y^D) \right) - N.$$

---

[3] Unless otherwise stated, "Cambridge" will be taken to mean the University of Cambridge.

[4] Letter from Solow to the authors, July 12, 2004.

[5] It was, so they argued, impossible for the same aggregate simultaneously to measure the physical capital stock that formed an input into the production process and the value of the capital stock on which calculations of the rate of profit was based. The reasons are not relevant here, but suffice it to note that the problem was that whenever income distribution changed, relative prices would change, which aside from special cases, would move the two measures of capital in different ways. See Harcourt (1972) for a widely read survey.

Y^S is the output that maximizes profit given the real wage. Y^D is investment plus consumption out of wages and profits, a higher propensity to save being associated with the latter than the former (the hallmark of the Cambridge theory). Output was also associated with a short-side condition, though without the lag structure, they associated with employment:

$$Y = min(Y^*, Y^D),$$

where Y^* was the momentary supply of output given by $F(N)$. The other key component of the model was price and wage-adjustment equations:

$$\frac{\dot{p}}{p} = h\left(\frac{Y^D}{Y^S}\right) + j\frac{\dot{w}}{w}, \qquad j \leq 1$$

and

$$\frac{\dot{w}}{w} = h\left(\frac{N}{N^S}\right) + k\frac{\dot{p}}{p}, \qquad k \leq 1$$

They solved the model by working out stationary loci for employment and showed that there could be a wide variety of stable equilibria (as well as unstable equilibria), depending on the parameter values. From this, their conclusions about theories of income distribution followed.

Their concern with dynamics is obvious, throughout the paper. As recalled by Stiglitz in his Nobel Prize "Memoir" (2001:8), "the problem was not that [wages and prices] were absolutely fixed, but with the dynamics of adjustment. With Robert Solow I explored these dynamics to explain the persistence of unemployment." Solow and Stiglitz (1968:542–43) were fully aware of the impossibility of reconciling excess supply and perfect competition in the goods market (closely related to the "Patinkin problem" discussed in Chapter 3). Under those conditions, price exceeds marginal cost, which encourages each producer to attempt to "increase his profits by selling more at the going price and, as a perfect competitor, he ought to succeed. But all producers together can sell no more than Y^D for the going real wage." Solow and Stiglitz's way out of the difficulty was to "assume like Patinkin that, despite the excess of price over marginal cost, producers in the aggregate are restrained from increasing output beyond $Y = Y^D$ by the *force majeure* of effective demand. Under conditions of aggregate excess supply, however, there may be downward pressure on prices." As pointed out by Leijonhufvud (1998:187n13), the notion that quantities adjust faster than prices was an assumption shared by both his and Solow-Stiglitz's 1968 models – but Leijonhufvud failed to notice that there was a common ancestor in Patinkin's discussion of labor demand.

The nature of their implicit research program is made clear by the ways in which they suggest extending the model. It needed an explicit monetary mechanism, something they saw as posing no technical problems: "the model could easily be extended to include the standard IS-LM apparatus" (Solow and Stiglitz 1968:539). To do this would, however, involve a loss of transparency, for the model would become three-dimensional (ibid.:559). They also wanted to extend the model to the long run, and they sketched how this might be done. The influence of the Cambridge capital controversy is shown by their offering ways in which this might be done without running afoul of Robinson's critique of the production function. Output dynamics needed to be modified to take proper account of inventories, which become important when supply and demand diverge.[6] Finally, they suggested modifying the price and wage-adjustment equations to remove the element of money illusion that they implied. In view of subsequent developments in the theory of inflation, it is worth noting that they proposed modifying the wage-adjustment equation so that any prolonged period of inflation would come to be expected, with the result that k would be unity in the long run and less than unity in the short run, consistent with empirical studies of wage behavior (Solow and Stiglitz 1968:560).

BARRO AND GROSSMAN AND THE SEARCH FOR MICROFOUNDATIONS

Although Solow and Stiglitz's (1968) came first, the paper that was responsible for leading economists to take disequilibrium macroeconomics seriously was Barro and Grossman's (1971). In graduate school, at Harvard, Robert Barro (b. 1944) became influenced by Clower (1965) and Patinkin (1965, ch. 13), noting that they seemed complementary "in terms of how excess supply spills over from one market to another" (Snowdon and Vane 1994:269–70). (He had asked Christopher Sims, for whom he was working as a teaching fellow on an intermediate macroeconomics course, how all markets could simultaneously be in excess supply, only to be answered with "I don't know."[7]) Together with Herschel Grossman (1939–2004), a colleague at Brown University, he used this to provide a choice-theoretic foundation for Keynesian economics to replace the "embarassingly weak choice-theoretic" basis that he found in "post-Keynesian" macroeconomics (Barro and Grossman 1971:82). Barro recalls that he thought about Patinkin's chapter 13, and Grossman about Clower's paper, before they put

---

[6] Inventories were later taken into account by Muellbauer and Portes (1978), See Chapter 8 of this book.

[7] E-mail from Barro to the authors, April 1, 2005.

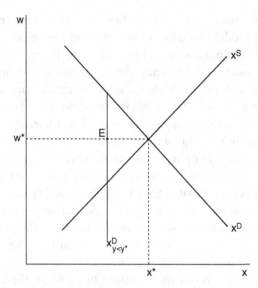

Figure 5.1. Barro and Grossman's representation of the labor market

them together.[8] Barro's reason for tackling Keynesian economics was not that he considered himself a Keynesian, but that at the time, "it seemed to be the only game in town in terms of macroeconomics" and he wanted to understand it (Snowdon and Vane 1994:269).

They started their model by outlining Patinkin's analysis of the labor market, though augmenting his diagram by actually drawing a labor demand curve that was constrained by realized sales of output when output was less than the quantity that firms wished to sell. They then developed a parallel analysis of demand for commodities, based on utility maximization and Clower's dual-decision hypothesis. The result was a pair of diagrams in which demand curves for labor and commodities were truncated, each constrained by realized sales in the other market shown as Figures 5.1 and 5.2.

The conventionally sloped supply and demand curves (noting that w is the real wage rate, W/P, the inverse of the P/W) are, using Clower's terminology, the notional demands and supplies that determine the Walrasian equilibrium at wage rate w^*. If there is a constraint on the output that can be sold, the demand for labor curve will become vertical at some point, and if there is a constraint on sales of labor, demand for commodities will become vertical at some point. Thus, if the economy gets stuck, for some reason, at a low level of output and employment, such as at point

[8]   E-mail from Barro to the authors, April 1, 2005.

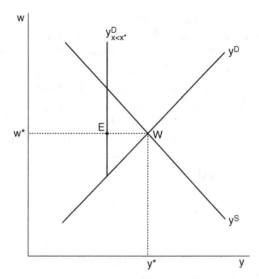

Figure 5.2. Barro and Grossman's representation of the goods market

E, it is possible for there to be excess supply in *both* markets, even at the Walrasian wage rate, w^*.[9] In addition, making the assumption that realized sales are the minimum of supply and effective demand (the vertical demand functions), there is a range of values within which changing the real wage rate will have no effect on employment and output. The economy has become stuck in a low-level equilibrium from which changes in the real wage cannot move it. From there, they went on to analyze the various configurations of the economy that could arise, taking the wage rate and the price level as parameters. Depending on the parameters, it was possible to have excess supply of labor co-existing with excess supply of goods, or with excess demand for goods, leading to the conclusion that "This classical type of involuntary unemployment should be clearly distinguished from the type of unemployment discussed above, which arises, with the real wage at or below w^*, from a deficiency of demand for commodities" (Barro and Grossman 1971:87). A further diagram offered a version of the "Keynesian cross," in which a demand function intersected a supply function. This diagram was clearly a generalization of the conventional 45-degree line diagram of elementary textbooks. They appeared to have demonstrated how their more rigorous choice-theoretic model could explain Keynesian economics.

---

9   See Barro and Grossman (1971), figures 1 and 2.

However, that was not all, for they had shown that excess supply might occur simultaneously in both labor and commodity markets: it was not just the labor market that was out of equilibrium. They had answered the question that Sims had not been able to answer when he and Barro had been teaching intermediate macroeconomics. The phrase "general disequilibrium" was appropriate, indicating that Keynesian economics was, as Keynes and Leijonhufvud had argued so forcefully, not simply the result of labor market imperfections. In addition, Barro and Grossman extended the analysis to generalized excess supply – the phenomenon that later came to be described as repressed inflation. Although this was not central to their account, they suggested that it might be important if there were rationing or price controls (Barro and Grossman 1971:91). General disequilibrium theory encompassed more than simply Keynesian economics.

It was Barro and Grossman who, in 1971, saw the parallels between the models of Patinkin and Clower, though the point that Patinkin and Clower were both addressing trading at non-market clearing prices was articulated by Grossman (1969). This was something that Clower and Patinkin had missed. Barro and Grossman also cited Leijonhufvud (1968) as having pointed out the inadequacy of Keynesian economics to represent the economics of Keynes – an inadequacy that their model was intended to put right – although, as pointed out in Grossman 1972 as a criticism of Leijonhufvud 1968, it was incorrect to suggest that disequilibrium macroeconomics could be found in Keynes (1973[1936]). In a footnote, Barro and Grossman (1971:84n6) acknowledged that Solow and Stiglitz had presented a "somewhat similar" analysis, though emphasizing different questions. They pointed to three differences, the first (and arguably most important) being that they did not discuss the choice-theoretic basis of their theory. Given Barro's and Grossman's aims, this was a significant difference. They also noted that the model of Solow and Stiglitz did not determine the absolute price level, whereas theirs did, and that the lagged adjustment of employment was a complication that "obscure[d] what would seem to be essential in the inter-market effects of disequilibrium" (1974:84n6). These comments are significant because they point to the difference between the two approaches. Unlike Barro and Grossman, Solow and Stiglitz approached the problem from the standpoint of growth and dynamics. Explaining the price level was not their goal and in any case, rather than simply postulate, with Barro and Grossman, that household utility depend on real money balances, they had decided to postpone treatment of the monetary sector to a subsequent paper (Solow and Stiglitz 1968:559–60). Solow and Stiglitz did not bother writing down explicit choice-theoretic foundations for the model, believing that to do so would not reveal anything of interest. Moreover, as Solow later pointed out, providing formal microfoundations might involve working with unsatisfactory assumptions.[10]

Although Barro and Grossman presented their model as bringing together the approaches of Patinkin, Clower, Leijonhufvud, and Solow and Stiglitz in a way that built on their contributions, the reactions of these economists to each other suggest that they did not necessarily see it that way. Perhaps the most remarkable evidence, given that the parallel between Patinkin's analysis of the labor market and Clower's dual-decision hypothesis is now generally accepted, is that when Clower had presented his dual-decision hypothesis in 1962, Patinkin was his discussant, but failed to see the connection with his own chapter 13. Neither did Clower appreciate Patinkin's work on this. In an article addressing the problem of Walras's Law, he clearly had to discuss Patinkin, whose book provided the most advanced treatment of the subject, but he did not see the full significance of chapter 13 at the time. This may reflect Clower's (1965:113–14) notion that his model was an alternative, rather than a complement, to Patinkin's spillover model (cf. Grossman 1969). It was only after Barro and Grossman (1971) that Patinkin understood the connection between his and Clower's model (see Patinkin 1995). This perhaps vindicates their approach in relation to Solow and Stiglitz, for though the latter's model was arguably more general, points such as this could get lost in its richness. As Patinkin implied in correspondence of February 12, 1974 with Leijonhufvud, he felt vindicated by Barro and Grossman (1971) and especially Grossman (1972b), who gave his chapter 13 the acknowledgment he had never got before. Leijonhufvud (1968) cited Patinkin, but referred to his treatment of real balance effect and his price-theoretic approach, not to chapter 13. On June 15, 1974, he wrote to Patinkin, "I read your book, very thoroughly, as a graduate student & could not, then, understand or appreciate Chapter 13." He went on to offer an explanation for why he did not pay more attention to it: "As you note the message of 13 did not 'fit the modl' and at the time I was trying very hard exactly to learn the 'modl.'"[11] In the same letter, he explained that he did

---

[10] In a letter to the authors (February 3, 2005) Solow wrote "if you insist on formal microfoundations, you have to go with the microfoundations you have, not the ones you wish you had. The fallacy, of course, is to believe that you have to go." Solow (2004) developed this point in the context of James Tobin's work which, he argued, was based on microfoundations, even if these were less formal than the representative-agent microfoundations commonly used in modern monetary economics.

[11] The use of the word "modl" is an allusion to Leijonhufvud (1973b).

not see the link between Patinkin's work and his own, even after Barro and Grossman. "The full story is even more odd: Even when Barro & Grossman linked your Chapter 13 with Clower's paper, I refused to see a connection (and wrote G. to that effect)."[12]

Leijonhufvud's attitude to Barro and Grossman's article was explained in an exchange of letters with Errol Glustoff. Glustoff, on January 14, 1972[13] had asked him, "I do not see what is original about this paper. That is, what is it that they have done which you didn't do, aside from giving Patinkin more credit?" Leijonhuvud, on January 22, 1972, wrote in reply, "I agree that there is nothing very original about the Barro-Grossman paper." The paper's appeal lay in its suitability for teaching: "there are numerous macro-teachers around the country who have expressed some interest in our stuff but find it (esp. my book) pretty 'unteachable'. They basically want a curve-shifting apparatus and may, perhaps, find themselves served by Barro and Grossman." Leijonhufvud took the view that though the paper was not original, he and Clower had nothing against others using their work and "the more it is spread about the better". Leijonhufvud's printed reaction to Barro-Grossman came out in his 1973 piece on "Effective Demand Failures". As he explained to James Witte in a letter of January 26, 1973, the 1973 paper "also takes exception to the Barro-Grossman interpretation – although rather diplomatically and discretely since we don't have allies to waste, exactly." Clower felt at the time that the Barro-Grossman article could play a role in spreading the ideas of disequilibrium theorists and, as editor for Basic Books, Clower was responsible for commissioning an extension of the 1971 article into a book that extended the model to include, amongst other dimensions, price and wage dynamics, eventually published as *Money, Employment and Inflation* (Barro and Grossman 1976), and he was in close contact with Grossman in the late 1960s and early 1970s:

I commissioned the Barro and Grossman book for Basic Books. Grossman came to Essex for six months and we had many long conversations before he started working on his papers. He always seemed to have his feet on the ground and was very quick. Barro's background was in physics so he had a very inductive approach to economics. I think they collaborated very well but somehow or other the book became too mechanical. It was turned down by basic books and had to be published by Cambridge. Although it did well its main contribution seems to have been its influence on the work of Malinvaud. (Clower 1999:186)

---

[12] Presumably "G" stands for Grossman.
[13] Axel Leijonhufvud Papers, Boxes 2 and 1 respectively. David M. Rubenstein Rare Book and Manuscript Library, Duke University.

Although this statement clearly expresses Clower's difference from the approach adopted by Barro and Grossman – that the approach was too mechanical and missed out important problems – the reason why Basic Books turned the book down was that it was intended to be part of a series, and when they failed to commission any other textbooks, they abandoned the whole series.[14]

BÉNASSY'S MODEL OF THREE REGIMES

In 1973, a student from Paris, Jean-Pascal Bénassy, submitted a dissertation, *Disequilibrium Theory*, to Berkeley. This was initially supervised by Gérard Debreu, but when another student drew Bénassy's attention to the similarity between the model he was developing and Bent Hansen's (1951) model of inflation, Hansen (also a professor at Berkeley) became involved as well.[15] As well as two articles on general equilibrium, one of which focused on Keynesian economics (Bénassy 1975) and the other on linking disequilibrium to monopoly (Bénassy 1976b), that are discussed in Chapter 7, Bénassy provided a simple aggregative macroeconomic model that he discussed in a paper delivered to a conference in Vienna in 1974, published as Bénassy (1978).

This model assumed a single aggregated consumer and a single aggregated firm. A key simplification was assuming utility to be linear in the logarithms of consumption, money balances, and leisure, causing the households demand for commodities and supply of labor to be linear. Following Barro and Grossman, Clower-Patinkin effective demand functions were then derived. These formed the basis for distinguishing between three regimes, "stagflation" (excess supply of labor and excess demand for goods), "deflation" (excess supply in both markets), and "inflation" (excess demand in both markets). There was theoretically a fourth case (excess supply of commodities and excess demand for labor) in which households would be unconstrained and firms constrained in both markets, but Bénassy showed that this was a degenerate case, corresponding to the boundary between the inflation and deflation regimes. The various regimes were depicted graphically as shown in Figure 5.3.

The traditional conception of a Keynesian equilibrium was a point such as K, where the goods market was in equilibrium but where there was excess supply in the labor market.

---

[14] E-mail from Barro to the authors, April 1, 2005.
[15] Hansen's model was the so-called "two-gap" model in which inflation depended on excess demands in both labor and goods markets.

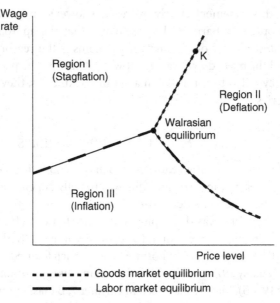

Figure 5.3. Bénassy's three-regime diagram
Source: Bénassy (1978, Figure 3, p. 536). Compare Bénassy (1973, Figure 4, p. 56).

Although more elegant, the diagram was close to one used by Barro and Grossman. However, Bénassy then took the argument further in two ways. The first was that he superimposed on it price dynamics, assuming that the price level and the wage rate changed in response to excess demands. This resulted in the scenario shown in Figure 5.4. In region I, wages are falling but prices rising; in region II, both are falling; and in region III, both are rising. At a Keynesian "equilibrium" along the line WK, prices will be constant because excess demand for goods is zero, but wages will be falling and the arrows will be vertical. What is of note is that the economy will end up somewhere on the line WZ, where both markets clear. However, there is a possibly large set of initial prices from which the economy will not converge to the Walrasian equilibrium.

Perhaps of more significance is that Bénassy then extended the model to discuss monopolistic price setting in both labor and commodity markets. The Keynesian case, along the line WK, corresponded to monopoly in the labor market but to competition in the goods market. Double monopoly, with firms setting prices and workers setting wages, would imply region II. If the firm were a monopolist in the goods market and monopsonist in the labor market, the result would be a position on the line WZ. Other combinations of monopoly, monopsony, and competition

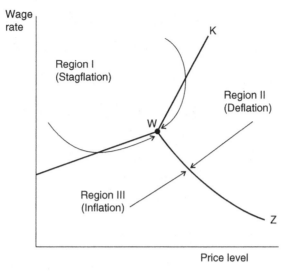

Figure 5.4. Bénassy on wage-price dynamics
Source: Bénassy (1978, Figure 2, p. 530; 1973, Figure 3, p. 49).

would correspond with other regions of the graph. The significance of this introduction of imperfect competition, however, is more conveniently discussed in Chapter 7.

DEVELOPING THE FIXED-PRICE MODEL

During the 1970s, due to the dramatic macroeconomic events outlined in Chapter 2, and the theoretical challenges coming from Phelps, Lucas, and the new classical macroeconomics, discussed in Chapter 6, interest in fixed-price models declined. However, they still attracted significant attention, particularly in Europe, where there remained a desire to develop a macroeconomics that was not based on the assumption that markets cleared. Richard Quandt, a Princeton econometrician, put the difference between the two continents very starkly.[16]

In the late 1970s I had written a paper on how one might test the hypothesis that a set of data was generated by an equilibrium rather than a disequilibrium model. I would give this paper in various seminars and I remember that in the US my introduction to the paper was usually greeted with a remark such as, "What you are doing is silly, because everyone knows that prices clear markets and hence there is

---

[16] Quandt's work on disequilibrium estimation is discussed later in the chapter.

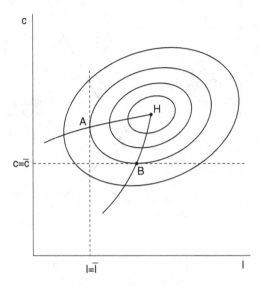

Figure 5.5. Consumers' equilibrium under rationing

nothing to test." Giving the same paper in Europe, I would usually be greeted with the remark, "Everybody knows that prices never clear markets, hence there is nothing to test." (Quandt 1992:xxii)

So, despite the success of market-clearing macroeconomics, there were attempts to develop the fixed-price model and to provide new graphical expositions throughout the decade.[17] The most significant of these was "Macroeconomic Models with Quantity Rationing," by Muellbauer and Portes (1978), who proposed a "two-wedge" diagram to depict the various regimes that could be generated by the model and with which comparative-statics exercises could be performed. The principle behind this is illustrated in Figure 5.5, which shows the consumers optimization problem. Ideally, the consumer would be at point H, and the indifference curves around H denote successively lower utility levels. If consumers face a constraint on their labor supply ($l \leq \bar{l}$), they choose a point such as A, where utility is maximized subject to the given demand for their labor. In contrast, if consumer goods are rationed ($c \leq \bar{c}$), they choose a point such as B, where a horizontal line is tangential to an indifference curve. Quantity-constrained equilibria will therefore be on one of the branches of the wedge shown in Figure 5.5.

---

[17] An example not considered here is Stoneman (1979). One of the authors worked on developing these models, in 1975–77, though the results were not published till later (Backhouse 1980, 1982).

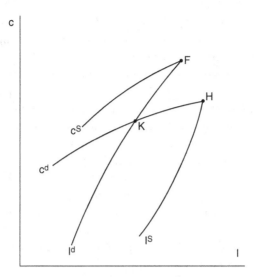

Figure 5.6. Keynesian unemployment

A similar exercise can be undertaken for firms, who will have concentric iso-profit curves surrounding their optimal combination of output and employment (point F), from which another wedge can be derived. The curves making up the two wedges correspond to demands and supplies for consumer goods and labor when agents are faced with quantity constraints using self-explanatory notation. The wedges for households and firms can be put together to show the configuration of the economy. In Figure 5.6, the situation is one of Keynesian unemployment, for at K, firms face a constraint on their sales of goods, and are hence on the lower branch of their wedge, and households face a constraint on their sales of labor, placing them on the upper branch of theirs. Of course, if F and H were in the same position, this would be the full "Walrasian" market-clearing equilibrium, and there would be no rationing.

Comparative statics results can be generated by working out how changes in the exogenous variables shift the two wedges. This model achieved greater prominence when a version of the paper was included, under the title "Macroeconomics When Markets Do Not Clear," as an appendix in the second edition of one of the leading macro textbooks of the period, *Macroeconomic Theory and Policy* (1979) by Princeton economist William Branson.

However, what was arguably most significant feature of this model theoretically was not its pedagogic value but the fact that it extended the Barro-Grossman model to make it more dynamic. Barro and Grossman had themselves, in their textbook, extended their model to encompass dynamics, but this was through adding a "tâtonnement" process, but with effective rather than notional excess demands driving changes in price.[18] However, whereas most fix-price models were essentially static, albeit with dynamics added on, Muellbauer and Portes modeled consumers and firms as making optimal inter-temporal choices.[19] As part of this process, consistent with the literature's focus on disequilibrium and quantity adjustments, they introduced explicit modeling of inventories, something lacking up to that point, and arguably essential in a model in which agents do not necessarily achieve their desired sales and purchases of goods.

The process of making the model more dynamic was taken a stage further by Peter Neary and Joseph Stiglitz, in a paper first presented to the Econometric Society in 1979, though not published till four years later, in 1983. They argued that decisions would be influenced not simply by quantity constraints faced in the current period, but also on expectations concerning such constraints in the future:

we show that if individuals expect there to be unemployment next period, it is more likely ... that there will be unemployment this period; whereas if individuals expect there to be excess demand for goods next period, then it is more likely that there will be excess demand for goods this period. As a result, for any particular set of current wages and prices, there may exist multiple expectational equilibria that exhibit "bootstraps" properties; e.g. households expect that they will be unable to sell all their labor both this period and next, then it will turn out that they will be unable to sell all their labor; but had they expected there to be inflationary pressures this period and next, then that would have turned out to be the case instead. (Neary and Stiglitz 1983:200)

They went on to analyze equilibria in which individuals held rational expectations about future constraints, showing that the introduction of rational expectations, contrary to what was widely claimed, was not sufficient to undermine Keynesian results: the key assumption in undermining Keynesian results was the assumption that prices adjusted instantaneously to clear markets. They used these results, which they claimed captured Keynesian insights better than did the static model, to argue that the key innovation in the new classical macroeconomics was not the rational expectations concept:

These results suggest that the critique of the effectiveness of government policy presented by "new classical macroeconomists" ... rests primarily on their assumption

---

[18] Quotation marks are used here because a tâtonnement in effective demands might be seen as an oxymoron.

[19] In other parts of macroeconomics, inspired by the new classical macroeconomics, discussed in Chapter 6, this was rapidly becoming a standard assumption.

that prices and wages adjust instantaneously to clear markets, and *not* on their use of the rational expectations hypothesis. (Neary and Stiglitz 1983:225)

Neary and Stiglitz concluded by arguing that achieving equilibrium through price adjustments might be slow and difficult. Shifts in expectations might cause significant changes in the prices needed to achieve market-clearing equilibrium and disequilibria might arise in markets other than the ones in which prices were sticky. They therefore conjectured what they called a "dynamic second-best theorem," according to which "with limited flexibility of some prices, increasing the flexibility of other prices may reduce rather than increase the ability of the system to return to Walrasian equilibrium" (Neary and Stigltiz 1983:225).[20]

In this paper, Neary and Stiglitz were clearly still developing disequilibrium macroeconomics into what could, potentially, be a general theory, for a major component of their thesis was that the assumption of rational expectations did not, as was widely believed, lead to "new classical" conclusions.

FROM NEW PARADIGM TO SPECIALIST TECHNIQUE

By the end of the 1970s, models of macroeconomic disequilibrium had been extended to encompass inherently dynamic phenomena, something that was clearly important if such models were to explain the turbulence of the 1970s. However, it was still necessary to rationalize the use of such models. One way to do this was to view models of equilibrium with rationing not as general models of how markets behaved, but as models applicable to certain specific circumstances.[21] Disequilibrium theory became one more set of models in the economist's toolkit.

An early example of the use of disequilibrium theory as a specialist technique is a paper by John Flemming (1973) that showed that income constraints could be used to explain otherwise puzzling features of consumption behavior and that it offered an alternative to the dominant permanent-income theory. The basis for assuming that disequilibrium was relevant to the problem of consumption was the observation that, in reality, households faced clear constraints on their ability to borrow. On top of this

---

[20] It is interesting to note that, though this was not the basis for their argument, their stress on the importance of dynamic complications as the cause of unemployment echoes Keynes (see Backhouse and Laidler 2004).

[21] The distinction between regarding disequilibrium models as a specialist technique and as general explanations of how markets work is not clear-cut, but it is serviceable as a way to distinguish the approaches to justifying disequilibrium models discussed in this section and the next.

was the observation that when aggregate income fell, the result was not that all households experienced the same fall in income but that some households moved from earning a wage to receiving unemployment benefits: for such households, there was typically no prospect of being able to borrow against the earnings they expected to receive once their spell of unemployment had finished. Flemming showed that it was easy to construct a model in which the aggregate marginal propensity to consume was a weighted average of the marginal propensities to consume of households that were and were not experiencing unemployment. Whilst the latter might be close to zero, or even positive (they might not have experienced any fall in income), the latter would be income-constrained and would have a marginal propensity to consume that was close to, if not equal to, one. The aggregate consumption function would thus reflect not the behavior of a representative household, but the distribution of unemployment across the population.

Another illustration of disequilibrium models being used in this way, as a technique applicable in specific circumstances, was Avinash Dixit's "The Balance of Trade in a Model of Temporary Equilibrium with Rationing" (1978). Dixit's starting point was the observation that the conventional approach to balance of payments adjustment involved using simple income-expenditure model, with no underlying choice theory. The monetary approach to the balance of payments, represented by Harry Johnson, did allow for price changes, but only by assuming instantaneous adjustment in both commodity and labor markets, an assumption Dixit found unsatisfactory. His aim was to improve on this state of affairs by turning to the methods developed for closed economies in the literature on disequilibrium macroeconomics. Disequilibrium was justified by arguing, fairly conventionally, that wages did not instantaneously adjust to clear the labor market and that the exchange rate was either sticky or fixed by government policy. Although disequilibrium in the labor market would manifest itself as unemployment, the distinctive feature of his model was that disequilibrium in the goods market would produce balance of payments disequilibria, something clearly observed in the real world. Dixit's conclusion clearly illustrates the way he conceives the model, not as an alternative paradigm, but as a technique that will sometimes be useful:

Even after all these refinements, it could not be claimed that quantity-adjusted temporary equilibria will always depict reality better than price-adjusting ones. However, the opposite is not universally true, either. We should take models of both kinds seriously, and learn appropriate quantitative lessons from both, *while paying attention to the particular combination of flexibilities and rigidities that occurs when thinking about any particular application*, and applying these lessons accordingly. (Dixit 1978:404, emphasis added)

Disequilibrium models were applied to a number of other fields,[22] but the one that best illustrates the way it became seen as a specialized technique is perhaps its application to the problems of centrally planned economies. Here, one of the two key figures is arguably Richard Portes, one of the authors of "Macroeconomic Models with Quantity Rationing" (1978), discussed earlier. His co-author, John Muellbauer, had taken a Ph.D. at Berkeley, had by then published extensively on the microeconomics and empirics of consumer behavior, a literature in which heterogeneity of agents was very important (he was also at Oxford, with Flemming, when the latter published his article on the consumption function). Portes, on the other hand, came to this subject from the study of the centrally planned economies of Eastern Europe, in particular Hungary.

It had long been realized that these economies did not have freely adjusting markets – it was enough to observe the chronic shortages faced by consumers and stories of economic irrationality abounded amongst students of these countries. This idea had been summed up by the Hungarian economist Janos Kornai in *Anti-Equilibrium: On Economic Systems Theory and the Tasks of Research* (1971). This book offered a methodological critique of general equilibrium theory from the perspective of an economist involved in the Hungarian economic reforms of 1968, which had introduced a degree of decentralization in resource allocation and increased the role of the profit motive. The economists who planned these reforms had much experience of how economic systems worked, but were without any economic theory on which they could draw:

No scientifically established theorems were available to guide them in their work. It would certainly have caused great amusement if, at some committee meeting, a mathematical economist had claimed on scientific grounds that an atomized market with perfect competition was needed to ensure that prices would become the sole regulator of the economy and that an optimum equilibrium would be achieved. (Kornai 1971:xv)

The main problem with general equilibrium theory, he contended, was "the supposition that optimality characterizes the actual behavior of economic organizations," for that assumption forced the theorist to make other departures from the real world, such as assuming convexity and neglecting uncertainty. General equilibrium theory was in no sense a general theory, describing only a small part of the world. It could not even bear to a new theory the relationship that Newtonian physics bore to modern physics: that of a practically useful special case.

---

[22] For example, the problem of credit rationing.

Kornai proceeded, therefore, to develop a new language for discussing economic problems, more general than that of conventional economics, focused on the notion of an economic system. The market, which he considered an imprecisely defined notion, was merely one device for controlling an economic system. In criticizing general equilibrium theory, Kornai tackled many issues, such as the existence of signals other than prices, and what in the disequilibrium macroeconomics literature were known as spillover effects, but his perspective was very different. His perspective was more general, encompassing processes operating outside markets, and, as has been noted, he rejected the notion that Walrasian equilibrium could even serve as a useful reference point for a general theory.

Anti-Equilibrium focused exclusively on mathematical theory, somewhat narrowly conceived. Even Herbert Simon's behaviorism was described as "economic sociology, or political sociology" (Kornai 1971:371). Keynes's *General Theory* was mentioned briefly, alongside Simon's work, under the heading of "non-mathematical works", "not employing (or making little use of) formal models" (ibid.). More significantly, he noted that though his concepts of "pressure" and "suction" were related to "macroeconomic disproportion," "the macroeconomic relations between income, employment, investments and savings … belong largely outside the scope of economic systems theory" (ibid.). Furthermore, though he recognized that Keynes had been influential, "there has been no organic integration between Keynesian macroeconomics and the traditional Western microeconomics (*nor could there be*)" (ibid., emphasis added). There was, therefore, no mention of the work of Patinkin, Clower, or Leijonhufvud, even though they were arguably addressing themes that overlapped with Kornai's. It is tempting to attribute this to isolation arising from working behind the Iron Curtain (he cited Alvin Hansen's *A Guide to Keynes* [1953], then eighteen years old, as the most important commentary on Keynes, suggesting an out-of-date view of the macroeconomic literature), but this failure to mention their work was presumably deliberate, as the book had been completed during a stay in the Cowles Commission, and he acknowledged the advice of several eminent Western economists.

Portes had embarked on the study of such economies before *Anti-Equilibrium* was published. His D.Phil. thesis, submitted at Oxford in 1969, was on the "Economic Decentralization and the Industrial Enterprise in Hungary, 1957–1968," after which he continued to write on the behavior of enterprises in centrally planned economies and he presented a papers on the Hungarian economic reforms with which Kornai had been involved, and on planning procedures in centrally planned economies to the 1970 and 1971 American Economic Association meetings (Portes 1969, 1970, 1971). Then, in the mid-1970s, he tackled the problem of macroeconomic equilibrium in such economies, focusing on the questions of inflation and, crucially, whether these economies were, as was commonly believed, characterized by chronic, repressed inflation. Repressed inflation would arise when shortages of goods prevented consumers from purchasing what they wanted to purchase, causing them to accumulate money balances. Had prices not been fixed by the planners, these excess money holdings would have been spent, raising the prices of the goods that were in short supply. In that it involved excess demand in both commodity and labor markets, repressed inflation was the mirror image of Keynesian unemployment in disequilibrium models such as that of Barro and Grossman. Portes, however, argued that, paradoxically, there was no evidence for generalized excess demand in centrally planned economies: to the contrary, there was excess supply. The reason was that the system was structured to cause firms to accumulate more stocks than were needed to cover what was needed for production.

Although Portes supported his arguments with close analysis of the institutional structures of centrally planned economies, his work was significant in that he sought to bring econometric evidence to bear on the problem of disequilibrium. With David Winter, he sought to estimate supply and demand functions for commodities in such economies (Portes and Winter 1977, 1978). Shortly afterward, starting from the assumption that markets were in disequilibrium, they were able to test the hypothesis that supply and demand were equal, a special case of their more general model; they concluded that the hypothesis that the countries they considered were characterized by sustained excess demand should be rejected (Portes and Winter 1980). The theoretical framework underlying their work was that described in Muellbauer and Portes (1978), but they also drew on research into the econometrics of disequilibrium that had been developing since the early 1970s.

By the mid-1970s, econometricians had developed techniques for estimating demand and supply functions in markets that did not clear (Fair and Jaffee 1972; Maddala and Nelson 1974; Goldfeld and Quandt 1975). One of the key figures here was Richard Quandt, since 1956 a professor at Princeton, where Portes had been an assistant professor from 1969–72. During the period 1975 to 1990, on the eve of the demise of communism, he produced a long series of articles, with a series of co-authors, notably Stephen Goldfield, but also including Portes and Winter, developing the theory of disequilibrium estimation and applying it to centrally planned economies. By 1985, Quandt was so impressed with the amount of work that had been done on disequilibrium methodology that he brought it together in *The Econometrics of Disequilibrium* (1988). His attention was, however, not confined to centrally planned economies, but extended to the U.S. labor market, with Princeton colleague Harvey Rosen (Quandt and Rosen 1978, 1986, 1988). In the last of these, he concluded that, despite considerable uncertainties involved in testing competing models, "the disequilibrium model does a better job of characterizing the U.S. labor market than its equilibrium counterpart," going on to observe that "The disequilibrium research agenda is rich and varied" (Quandt and Rosen 1988:92)

RATIONALIZING PRICE STICKINESS

Leaving aside work on centrally planned economies, where the reasons for price rigidity were clear, models of macroeconomic disequilibrium took prices as given. However, during this period, economists were increasingly reluctant to assume individual behavior that was inconsistent with rationality. The consequence was that it became increasingly necessary to explain why, if individuals were rational, they would not take advantage of the opportunities presented by disequilibrium and the presence of rationed individuals. Why, for example, would firms not reduce their wage rates if they knew that there was a pool of unemployed labor that they would be willing to work at wages lower than were currently being paid. Similarly, if firms failed to sell all their output, why would they not cut their prices, and why would unemployed workers not offer to work for lower wages than those currently working? During the 1970s, economists developed a number of answers.

For Stiglitz, his paper with Solow (1968) had been one element in a much broader research program centered on dynamic modeling and increasingly, from the late 1960s, centered on problems related to information and market imperfections. For example, in a series of papers around 1970, he worked out the implications of bankruptcy for the Modigliani-Miller theorems, which, in the late 1960s, had become the standard framework for thinking about the value of the firm. Uncertainty and problems of information were critical, for managers, whose payoffs would typically differ from those of shareholders, might deliberately undertake policies that gave a higher probability of bankruptcy than shareholders or other creditors would choose. This posed a problem for corporate control, for shareholders would typically know less than managers about the precise policies being pursued. In the mid-1970s, such ideas were applied to the labor market explaining wages and labor turnover. This led, later, into models of commodity, labor, and financial markets, the common feature of which was that, in the presence of information problems, markets would not behave like the perfectly competitive markets of economic theory. Situations might easily arise in which, for example, firms set wages higher than was necessary to clear the labor market, resulting in unemployment, or banks set interest rates sufficiently high that they had to ration credit amongst those who wished to borrow. However, despite developing what can legitimately be described as a general theory of equilibrium with asymmetric information, and applying his ideas to wage determination in developing countries, he did not make the connection with macroeconomic disequilibrium models until the early 1980s.[23]

Other economists, on the other hand, did begin to develop a literature explaining why prices might be inflexible. This was in large part a reaction to the rational expectations revolution brought about by Robert Lucas and others, discussed in Chapter 6. Jo Anne Gray (1976), Stanley Fischer (1977), Edmund Phelps and John Taylor (1977), Phelps (1978) and Taylor (1980) showed how nominal inertia is caused by wage indexation and staggered long-term wage contracts. The introduction of nominal wage rigidity into rational expectations models indicated that the assumption of continuous market clearing was essential for the validity of the new classical monetary policy ineffectiveness proposition. As pointed out by Snowdon and Vane (2005:367), those models were not based on rigorous microfoundations, but on the assumption that long-term contracts represented a device to avoid the transactions costs involved in frequent changes of prices and wages. These models of nominal wage rigidity could account for the real effects of aggregate demand fluctuations in the business cycle, but economists were also searching in the 1970s for an explanation of persistently high unemployment rates, which led them to formulate models of real wage rigidity. The earliest work, including Baily (1974), D. F. Gordon (1974) and Azariadis (1975) postulated implicit labor contracts between risk-neutral firms and risk-averse unions in which a relatively stable real wage rate provided workers with insurance against income fluctuations.

A more radical approach to the problem of explaining prices and wages was offered by the group of economists that were, in the 1970s, appropriating the label "Post Keynesian," previously used by figures such as Paul Samuelson in what had by then become the Keynesian establishment. The most prominent statement of the case for this approach to economics was

---

[23] This work is discussed in Chapter 9.

provided by Alfred Eichner and Jan Kregel (1975).[24] Their main aim was to integrate the Keynesian theory of the short run with the theory of growth developed by Joan Robinson (1956) and the elaboration of the Ricardian theory of pricing by Piero Sraffa (1960). However, the mechanism through which they achieved this was postulating that markets were imperfectly competitive and that firms set prices as a mark up on cost designed to raise the funds they needed to finance their planned level of investment, an idea developed by Eichner in his *Megacorp and Oligopoly* (1976).

This group of economists, which owed much to Sidney Weintraub, the creator of the term "microfoundations," and Paul Davidson, who founded the *Journal of Post Keynesian Economics* in 1978, increasingly went its own way, believing that the main journals of the profession, such as the *American Economic Review*, were not open to their work (see Lee 2000, 2010; King 2009). The most visible engagement between these Post Keynesians and their counterparts was a session at the December 1979 meeting of the American Economic Association, titled "Appraisals of Post-Keynesian Economics." Janet Yellen, a Yale-trained economist who had worked on problems of monopoly, argued that though mark-up pricing was far from new, having been used by much more traditional Keynesians, the argument that prices were set to finance investment was novel and had the potential to generate new results. However, she argued that if money were introduced into the Post-Keynesian model, the results might no longer differ from conventional ones. She was also critical of the Post-Keynesian refusal to specify the dynamic structure of their models in sufficient detail for it to be possible to tell whether they generated different behavior out of equilibrium. Lorie Tarshis (1980), whose Keynesianism dates from the 1930s, criticized Eichner's microfoundations for overlooking the role of debt financing in the investment decision as stressed by Hyman Minsky's (1975) financial fragility hypothesis. However, most economists would probably have agreed with Tarshis that Post-Keynesian economics was "a promise that bounced", with the result that, though many economists did turn, in the 1980s, to theories of monopolistic competition, they ignored the approach represented by Eichner and Kregel. To understand these developments, we need to look in more detail at what became the dominant approach to microfoundations in the 1970s, the "equilibrium" theories of Phelps and Lucas.

---

[24] Two years earlier, Kregel (1973) had argued that Post-Keynesian economics constituted a new paradigm for economics.

SIX

"Equilibrium" Microfoundations

EDMUND PHELPS AND THE "PHELPS VOLUME"

Although it was far from universally accepted, by the end of the 1970s, the most prominent approach to the problem of microfoundations was the new classical macroeconomics, associated with Robert Lucas (1972, 1976). Lucas, together with Thomas Sargent, dramatically sounded the death knell of Keynesian economics in their provocatively titled "After Keynesian Macroeconomics":

> That these predictions [of Keynesian economics] were wildly incorrect and that the doctrine on which they were based is fundamentally flawed are now simple matters of fact, involving no novelties in economic theory. The task now facing contemporary students of the business cycle is to sort through the wreckage, determining which features of that remarkable intellectual event called the Keynesian Revolution can be salvaged and put to good use and which others must be discarded. (Lucas and Sargent 1978:49–50)

Lucas's approach, reliant on the concepts of continuous market-clearing and rational expectations is often perceived as a development of the position taken by Milton Friedman (1968) in his much-cited Presidential Address to the American Economic Association in which he argued that governments could not control unemployment for more than a limited period. It has been called "Monetarism, Mark II." However, though this approach to microfoundations did pose a challenge to Keynesian economics and to the attempts to evaluate the microeconomic foundations of macroeconomics discussed earlier in the Chapters 2 through 4, its origins lie not in Friedman, but in the simultaneous attempt by Edmund Phelps to provide a new microeconomic basis for Keynesian economics.

In the autobiography written for the occasion of his award of the Nobel Memorial Prize, Phelps (2006) described how he got into this problem:

By the middle of the 1960s, I began to be aware that neither I nor anyone else was addressing what I felt ever since college was the most important challenge in economics: to integrate microeconomics and macroeconomics. Finally I decided to try to do it myself! I had already concluded that textbook micro, which was based on the classical model of perfect competition, truly was irreconcilable with anything like the prevailing macro. I suspected that any macro that we might find recognizable would have to be based on some different kind of micro – a micro in which, say, individual firms with their employees or customers were in imperfect communication with other firms and, more generally, the rest of the economy.... I immersed myself, with a few breaks to do other things, in a project to rewrite the Keynesian economics of employment determination from the first half of 1966, when I started work on the project at London School of Economics (LSE) and Cambridge during a sabbatical leave from Yale, through 1971.

Whereas most of the literature on the reinterpretation of Keynesian economics, from Lange and Patinkin to Clower and Leijonhufvud, was motivated by a concern to explain how unemployment could arise, Phelps, in contrast, linked unemployment with inflation from the beginning.[1] This is no doubt linked to the fact that his graduate work had been undertaken at Yale, with Keynesians James Tobin and Arthur Okun (Samuelson had failed to recruit him for MIT; Samuelson 2003:1; Phelps 2006) and that he was visiting Britain, going to Cambridge and LSE, the latter taking him to the department where Phillips had discovered his curve and where Lipsey had developed its theoretical foundations. As Phelps (1995:17) later recalled, "my efforts at a theoretical understanding of the Phillips curve began in earnest over the summer of 1966 in the Sidgwick Avenue building at Cambridge." This may explain his taking Joan Robinson's (1937) criticism of Keynes's (1973[1936]) discussion of money-wage dynamics as one of his starting-points (Phelps 1968:679; see also Boianovsky 2005).

However, Phelps's first paper on the subject, "Phillips Curves, Expectations of Inflation and Optimal Unemployment over Time" (1967), written at LSE in the spring of 1966, the paper that forms the basis for his claim to be considered a co-inventor of the expectations-augmented Phillips curve, was not about the problem of microfoundations. Focusing on the optimal time path of aggregate employment, it was a continuation of his previous work on optimal capital accumulation (such as Phelps 1961). Previously, he claimed,

---

[1] The literature on market disequilibrium did not completely ignore inflation (see, for example, Bent Hansen's *A Theory of Inflation* [1951]), but it was ignored in much of the literature and was secondary to issues of aggregate demand and output.

the problem of the optimal level of employment had been approached only in a static way, whereas it was an inherently dynamic problem. The main reason why employment policy should be modeled as a dynamic problem was that the level of employment in one period would affect inflation (via the Phillips curve), and this would in turn, through affecting expected infla-tion, affect the position of the Phillips curve in the following period.[2] What he called "the 'equilibrium' unemployment ratio" was the unemployment rate at which expected inflation and actual inflation were equal: it was pre-sented as a by-product of the search for an optimal policy.[3]

Phelps's first paper on the Phillips curve went only part of the way toward his goal of integrating microeconomics and macroeconomics. It demon-strated the importance of expectations, clearly relating employment to the beliefs of economic agents, yet there was nothing in this paper about agents as individuals. Steps in this direction were taken in "Money-Wage Dynamics and Labor-Market Equilibrium," the first version of which was distributed as a University of Pennsylvania Discussion Paper in February 1967, before being published in the *Journal of Political Economy* (1968a).[4] In this paper, Phelps explored the relationship between wage changes (not discussed in the earlier paper, which modeled price inflation), labor turnover, unem-ployment, and vacancies. Firms had to recruit workers who were suited to the jobs they had to offer, meaning that it was necessary to engage in search, an idea that had been explored by his one-time colleague at LSE, Richard Lipsey (1960), who had "brilliantly" deduced a relationship between the vacancy rate and the equilibrium unemployment rate (Phelps 1968a:685).

The main thrust of this paper was to counter the notion, widespread in the literature, that cost inflation at high levels of aggregate demand was linked to the existence of trade union monopolies in the labor market. Phelps could find no reason why cost inflation was more likely with monop-oly. Moreover, such explanations seemed inappropriate for a labor market,

---

[2] It is worth noting that Phelps did not present the dependence of inflation on expected inflation as being novel. Neither did he see the idea of an equilibrium rate of unemploy-ment as novel. The novelty of his argument lay in providing a dynamic model of the opti-mal level of employment.

[3] Note that we have not claimed that Phelps was original in claiming that inflation depended on expectations of inflation (see Forder 2010a, 2010b). Indeed, the way he introduces it implies that he did not think of this as novel (see Forder 2010b:503). It was Phelps who drew the diagram with a series of downward sloping short-run Phillips curves and a verti-cal long-run curve, though he did not use this terminology (the short-run Phillips curves were labeled "quasi Phillips curves" and the long-run curve was simply a locus of points where inflation expectations were correct).

[4] The third incarnation of this paper was as Phelps (1970b) in a volume discussed later in this chapter.

such as that of the United States, in which no more than 25 percent of the labor force was unionized. However, Phelps did not assume labor markets were perfectly competitive, for firms would, he argued, have what he called "dynamic monopsony power." In a subsequent version of the paper, he explained this at length:

But the labor market here is not perfectly competitive. I exclude any Walrasian auctioneer who, by collecting information on everyone's supply and demand data, might be capable of keeping the labor market in a full information, full employment equilibrium. Lacking anyone else to do so, each firm must set its own wage rates. Because suppliers of labor lack detailed information about each firm's wage rates, the individual firm has *dynamic monopsony power*: Given its other recruitment efforts, such as help-wanted advertising, the higher the wage rates it sets relative to other firms' wage rates, the faster will it attract labor. The effect of such a wage differential is "dynamic" and gradual because the diffusion of the wage information through the market takes time. (Phelps 1970b:131, emphasis in original)

Thus, unlike Friedman (1968), who emphasized real wages, Phelps was focusing on the perspective of personnel managers who, in order to recruit and retain labor, had to form and base their decisions on expectations of the wage rates that other firms were offering. Although heterogeneity of the labor force was not necessary for his model, Phelps claimed that these information problems would be greatly reduced in a world where labor was homogeneous, for it would become much easier to disseminate information.

A significant reason why Phelps's work attracted so much attention was that, in addition to writing on the subject himself, he organized a conference at the University of Pennsylvania, on January 25–26, 1969, that brought together more than a dozen people working on these problems relating to information and labor markets, the papers from which, including a significantly revised version of Phelps's paper in the *Journal of Political Economy*, were published as *Microeconomic Foundations of Employment and Inflation Theory* (Phelps et al. 1970). This created a community of economists working on the problem. To quote from the Preface that Phelps wrote two months after the conference, "Last year several of us were excited to learn that we were not alone. Similar life existed on other campuses" (Phelps 1970a:vii). The book, very widely known simply as "the Phelps volume," also did much to popularize the idea of microfoundations, though it was not yet "the microfoundations of macroeconomics."[5] About a month before

---

[5]   These terms are discussed in Chapter 8.

the University of Pennsylvania Conference, Phelps (1969) presented a paper titled "The New Microeconomics of Inflation and Employment Theory" at a session on "Wage-Price Dynamics, Inflation and Unemployment" held in Chicago as part of the 1968 American Economics Association meetings. That session, which may be regarded as a preview of the 1969 University of Pennsylvania Conference, included also papers by G. C. Archibald and Charles Holt. Indeed, Phelps (1969) referred to and discussed some of the papers forthcoming in the *Microeconomic Foundations* book. Moreover, Phelps (1969:149) suggested that Leijonhufvud's (1968) notions of money-wage stickiness and unemployment were close to Alchian's (1970) idea that search unemployment is a function of aggregate demand. Indeed, the notion that unemployment was essentially a search phenomenon can be traced back to J.A. Schumpeter, albeit in a different theoretical context (see Boianovsky and Trautwein 2010).

Given subsequent developments, it is important to note that the Phelps volume was conceived as an economics of *disequilibrium*. Phelps (1970a:vii) wrote in his preface that "An economics of disequilibrium seemed to be forming." His "The New Microeconomics in Employment and Inflation Theory" (1970c), based on the eponymous paper (Phelps 1969) presented to the American Economic Association in December 1968, made it clear that this work was conceived as departing from the world of Walrasian market-clearing equilibrium. In such a world, it was not possible to explain why changes in aggregate demand should affect wages, or why it should be possible to "buy" increased output and employment at the cost of higher inflation (Phelps 1970c:2). In contrast, many of the papers in the volume showed how such phenomena would arise. They key assumption was "the removal of the Walrasian postulate of complete information"; once this step was taken, "the way is at last open to the formal study of general disequilibrium" (Phelps 1970c:6).

In this Introduction, Phelps introduced a metaphor that was widely taken up to explain the approach being taken: he wrote of the economy as a group of islands.

I have found it instructive to picture the economy as a group of islands between which information flows are costly: To learn the wage paid on an adjacent island, the worker must spend the day traveling to that island to sample its wage instead of spending the day at work. (Phelps 1970c:6)[6]

---

[6] This idea is in Phelps (1969), though not so fully developed. Given his earlier discussion of dynamic monopsony, he might have noted that it was also necessary for firms to communicate with other islands to know what wage to set.

If it is believed, without sampling having taken place, that wages on other islands are the same as on one's own island, non-Walrasian equilibrium can be established. However, if there were a fall in aggregate demand affecting all islands uniformly, workers would not initially realize that all islands were affected, and would assume that the fall was, at least in part, specific to their own island. Rather than accept a proportionate fall in money-wages, they would decide to invest in searching for jobs on other islands, and employment would fall. Eventually, of course, they would learn about conditions on other islands and wages would come down. Given developments discussed in the next section, it is also worth noting that, at least as far as Phelps was concerned, his model did not rule out involuntary unemployment: in the short-run dynamic monopsony, power might raise wage rates above the market-clearing rate – firms would have an incentive to raise wages to reduce the costs associated with labor turnover – and even in equilibrium there would be involuntary unemployment, for there might be unemployment in some sectors categories of skill (Phelps 1967:266). As pointed out by Phelps (1969:157n31), the macroeconomic consequences of the confusion between absolute and relative prices had been discussed by Dennis Robertson in his 1922 classic *Money*, which might have been a source of inspiration for Phelps's "islands" metaphor (the idea may be found also in other writings by Robertson; see Boianovsky and Presley 2009).

FROM PHELPS TO THE NEW CLASSICAL MACROECONOMICS

One of the contributors to the Phelps volume was Robert E. Lucas, a graduate from Chicago, who was in his first teaching position at Carnegie Mellon University. His first serious exposure to economic theory had been when, preparing himself for Chicago's graduate economics program, he had taught himself economics by studying, on his own, Paul Samuelson's *Foundations of Economic Analysis* (1947), which he had been told was the best book on the subject. Thus, when he came to Friedman's price theory course, he translated Friedman's ideas into the more rigorous mathematics:

> After every class, I tried to translate what Friedman had done into the mathematics I had learned from Samuelson. I knew I would never be able to think as fast as Friedman, but I also knew that if I developed a reliable, systematic way for approaching economic problems I would end up at the right place. (Lucas 1995)

Not having attended Friedman's money and banking workshop, he had not been exposed to Friedman's views on macroeconomics, and, for him, macroeconomics was Keynesian macroeconomics as understood by his teacher Martin Bailey in a course based on a draft of his textbook (1962).[7] At Carnegie Mellon, the dominant influence was Herbert Simon, whose work on the interfaces between management, political science, economics, and psychology centered on information processing. However, Lucas (1995) pointed out that there was a large group of economists "interested in dynamics and the formation of expectations": not just John Muth, but Morton Kamien and Nancy Schwartz (industrial organization using dynamic optimization methods, on which they were later to write a textbook), Richard Roll (efficient markets theory), Thomas Sargent (Lucas's later collaborator), Morris DeGroot (statistical decision theory, who taught a course taken by Lucas and Edward Prescott), and John Bossons and Michael Lovell (studying direct evidence on expectations). Although Lucas was still Keynesian in his outlook (Lucas 2004), he was approaching economics in an environment where expectations and techniques for dynamic optimization under uncertainty were being discussed. It is thus not surprising that Lucas's first publications, leaving aside a very early paper on which he had collaborated with some of his Chicago teachers, were on the theories of investment and supply, exploring the implications of dynamic optimization in the presence of uncertainty and adjustment costs (Lucas 1967a, 1967b).

When Lucas had to teach macroeconomics, he taught a Keynesian course similar to that of his Chicago teacher, Bailey. In the course of this teaching, Lucas and Leonard Rapping, who had joined Carnegie Mellon a year earlier and became a close friend of Lucas's, concluded that the Keynesian macroeconomic models they were teaching lacked an adequate supply side, so they proceeded to develop one. Friedman's Presidential Address was, according to Lucas (Snowdon and Vane 1998:124) crucially important, because it was inconsistent with the Phillips curves that they were estimating, forcing them to rethink. The resulting paper was published both in the *Journal of Political Economy* (1969) and in the Phelps 1970 volume

Crucial to their model was a labor supply function that, following Friedman's *Theory of the Consumption Function* (1957), a book Lucas admired because of the way it integrated theory and data, was based on households maximizing utility over two periods, with the result that labor supply depended on current and expected real wages. Expected real wages were determined, using adaptive expectations (they responded to observed real wages with a lag), an assumption used in many other papers in the

---

[7]   See Lucas (1995) and the interviews in Snowdon, Vane, and Wynarczyk (1994) and Klamer (1984). Lucas (2004) defends his Keynesian credentials during this period.

Phelps volume, resulting in a function in which labor supply depended on current and past real wages and the inflation rate. Combining this with a standard marginal productivity theory of the demand for labor they produced a model that could be estimated using standard labor market data. The paper showed that it was possible to reconcile short-run fluctuations in employment and apparent "money illusion" in labor supply with rational household behavior (Lucas and Rapping 1969:748; 1970:285).

Hoover (1988:27) argues that this paper by Lucas and Rapping was "surely the first paper to deserve to be called 'new classical'" on the grounds that the center piece of their analysis was that unemployment was voluntary. Thus, Lucas and Rapping (1969:748; 1970:285) explain that a corollary of their analysis is that

> Measured unemployment (more exactly, its nonfrictional component) is then viewed as consisting of persons who regard the wage rates at which they could currently be employed as temporarily low, and who therefore choose to wait or search for improved conditions rather than to invest in moving or occupational change.

This is followed by the remark that "nonfrictional unemployment is, in this sense, 'voluntary.'"

But, although the shift to accepting Friedman's view of unemployment as voluntary is without any doubt important (see de Vroey 2004), key aspects of what was to become the new classical view were absent.[8] The most obvious of these is the assumption of rational expectations, an idea that Lucas had encountered before he wrote the paper with Rapping, but had not used it. "I did not understand then how fundamental a difference it made econometrically. I didn't realize that if you took it seriously you had to rethink the whole question of testing and estimation. I guess no one else did either, except for Muth" (interview with Lucas in Klamer 1984:38). Another significant feature was that it was a model of just part of the economy – the labor market was taken in isolation. The methodology on which it was based involved constructing econometric models of different components of the economy (consumption, investment, and so on) and then using these to build a model of the economy as a whole.[9] Later in the 1970s, it would be argued that consistency required that models of the economy as a whole be estimated.

---

[8]   Hoover (1991) recognizes this in a paper, the aim of which is to argue that it is impossible to find a Lakatosian hard core of propositions underlying the new classical macroeconomics.

[9]   In Klamer (1984:36), Lucas argues that their model could have been written anywhere and was not a "Chicago" one. Backhouse (1995) has described this process as the piecemeal removal of free parameters, the terminology Lucas later adopted for parameters that were not grounded in individual optimizing behavior.

Lucas (1995) has pointed to three influences that lay behind the transition to the position he had reached by the early 1970s. Phelps convinced him that he and Rapping needed to develop their ideas into a general equilibrium model. David Cass, a specialist in optimal growth theory, who moved from Yale to Carnegie Mellon in 1970, aroused an interest in Paul Samuelson's (1958) overlapping-generations model. But rational expectations came in through work on investment with Edward Prescott, whom Lucas had known when he was a Ph.D. student at Carnegie Mellon, but who had moved to the University of Pennsylvania in 1966. Lucas had, in 1966, written a paper on the "Optimal Investment with Rational Expectations" that remained unpublished till included in Lucas and Sargent (1981), but this did not allow for uncertainty.[10] In a paper with Prescott (1971), Lucas extended the analysis to the problem of investing when returns were uncertain due to fluctuations in the demand curve. They noted that the conventional approach to modeling expectations – assuming them to be a fixed function of past values, an assumption inappropriately called "adaptive expectations" – would generate errors that would generally "be persistent, costly to forecasters and readily correctible" (Lucas and Prescott 1971:660). Implying that the ideal solution, to model the process by which expectations were formed, was not feasible, they chose instead to go to what they described as the opposite extreme: "To avoid this difficulty [the errors generated by the assumption of adaptive expectations] we shall, in this paper, go to the opposite extreme, assuming that actual and anticipated prices have the same probability distribution, or that price expectations are rational."[11] The importance of this to their results was made clear in their conclusions, the first of which was that they had shown that anticipated and actual prices were determined simultaneously, which "radically alters the nature of the problem" (Lucas and Prescott 1971:680).

These ideas – a general equilibrium model based on an overlapping generations model of the household, market-clearing prices and rational expectations – were brought together in "Expectations and the Neutrality of Money" (Lucas 1972), a paper that had been rejected by the editor of the *American Economic Review* in 1970, who found it too difficult to understand

[10] As Fischer (1996) points out, that volume provided no explanation of why the paper had not previously been published. Given the problems Lucas had with his later paper (discussed in the following), it is tempting to conjecture that this might not have been unconnected with the problem of finding an audience, in the mid-1960s, for the level of mathematics used.

[11] A footnote acknowledged that the term rational expectations was taken from Muth (1961), though they were using it slightly differently.

and pitched at "a distressingly arid level" (Gans and Shepherd 1994:172). Given the importance of this paper, it is worth quoting Lucas's (1972:103) account of what he was trying to achieve:

This paper provides a simple example of an economy in which equilibrium prices and quantities exhibit what may be the central feature of the modern business cycle: a systematic relation between the rate of change in nominal prices and the level of real output. The relationship, essentially a variant of the well-known Phillips curve, is derived within a framework from which all forms of "money illusion" are rigorously excluded: all prices are market clearing, all agents behave optimally in light of their objectives, and expectations are formed optimally.

This was doing more rigorously what he and Rapping had tried to do in their earlier paper – to explain the Phillips curve. Thus, Lucas's (1972:122) concluding words were "most of the interesting features of the observed business cycle have been abstracted from, with one notable exception: the Phillips curve emerges not as an unexplained empirical fact, but as a central feature of the solution to a general equilibrium system."

LUCAS'S CONCEPTION OF EQUILIBRIUM

Given that this paper and the literature it inspired are so well known (see Hoover 1988, 1999), the paper does not need to be reviewed in detail. It is, however, necessary to make clear what happened to the notion of equilibrium. In it, he states explicitly that he is adopting a new notion of equilibrium:

The substantive results developed below are based on a concept of equilibrium which is, I believe, new (although closely related to the principles underlying dynamic programming) and which may be of independent interest. In this paper, equilibrium prices and quantities will be characterized mathematically as functions defined on the space of possible states of the economy, which are in turn characterized as finite dimensional vectors. This characterization permits a treatment of the relation of information to expectations which is in some ways much more satisfactory than is possible with conventional adaptive expectations hypotheses. (Lucas 1972:104)

Prices are in equilibrium not in the sense that they are fixed but that they are functions of the set of states of the world. This "new" concept of equilibrium – as a stochastic equilibrium equilibrium made the new classical theory of the business cycle possible. It made it possible have an economy that was in equilibrium and yet exhibited a business cycle driven by random shocks (money supply shocks in Lucas's early models and real, productivity shocks in the later literature inspired by Kydland and Prescott [1982], discussed in Chapter 9). But the adjective *equilibrium* came to have another meaning. In "An Equilibrium Model of the Business Cycle" (Lucas 1975), equilibrium clearly meant "competitive equilibrium", augmented by the assumptions of rational expectations. Immediately after explaining what he intended to do in the paper, he devoted a paragraph to defending this by claiming, in tones that echo the "Lucas critique" that was to be published a year later (Lucas 1976), that this was the only way to avoid constructing models that "rely on arbitrary mechanical rules of thumb, adjustment rules, illusions, and unspecified institutional barriers" (Lucas 1975:1114). If there were, for example, a change in policy, one could not predict how an "illusion" or "rule of thumb" would change. The business cycle arose from unsystematic monetary shocks and an accelerator effect.

If the objective of this chapter was to explain the effect Lucas had on the evolution of macroeconomics, there is much other work that would need to be discussed, notably his extensive empirical work on output-inflation trade-offs, the so-called Lucas critique, and his work on the time-consistency of macroeconomic policy. However, the significance of the research program that he represents for the literature on disequilibrium macroeconomics with which this book is concerned is best seen in a methodological paper, "Methods and Problems in Business Cycle Theory" (Lucas 1980). In this, he places his own work in the context of the development of twentieth-century business cycle analysis.

How should one approach the problem of the business cycle? Lucas argues that, although the importance of work such as that of Wesley Clair Mitchell (1927; Burns and Mitchell 1945) in uncovering empirical regularities should not be underestimated, the aim of the economic theorist should not be to describe the economy. Instead, it should be to build "fully articulated, artificial economic systems that can serve as laboratories in which policies that would be prohibitively expensive to experiment with in actual economies can be tested out at much lower cost" (Lucas 1980:696). To play this role, it was important that, in discussion, these should be distinguished "as sharply as possible" from real-world economies. In his view, "a 'theory' is not a collection of assertions about the behavior of the actual economy but rather an explicit set of instructions for building a parallel or analogue system a mechanical, imitation economy" (Lucas 1980:697). This analogue system would comprise FORTRAN programs to which the inputs would be policy rules and the outputs would be values of the time series in which the economist was concerned (Lucas 1980:709).[12] Such analogue systems are tested by comparing the way they behave when subjected to shocks with the way real-world economies behave when subjected to the same shocks. They can then be used to ascertain the effects of shocks about whose consequences we have no knowledge. The question then is how these artificial economies should be constructed.

Lucas takes the book from which he first learned how to do rigorous economics, Samuelson's (1947) *Foundations of Economic Analysis*, as having laid out the conventional way to construct these artificial systems. He argues that Samuelson put forward "the main ingredients for a mathematically explicit theory of general equilibrium: an artificial system in which households and firms jointly solve explicit, 'static,' maximum problems, taking prices as parametrically given" (Lucas 1980:701). However, such static equilibria, even though they could be modified to take account of slow and predictable long-term trends, could not account for the business cycle, which clearly implied a system that was not at rest. The way Samuelson introduced dynamics was to postulate a model of price adjustment in which prices responded to "excess demands" in the system.[13] Doing this "introduced sufficient additional (to those needed to describe tastes and technology) parameters to the equilibrium system so that, given an initial shock to the system, a wide variety of paths were consistent with its eventual return to equilibrium" (Lucas 1980:702). This program, represented by Don Patinkin's *Money, Interest and Prices* (1956), another book that had impressed Lucas in his youth, made it possible to unify static economic theory with Keynesian econometric models and produced a "vast amount of useful economics" (Lucas 1980:702). This neoclassical synthesis became so successful that theoretical propositions that made sense only within the context of the theory became confused with the facts.

The problem was that the introduction of what Lucas, in this account of economic theory, called "free parameters" allowed economic theory to explain an enormous variety of phenomena: indeed, the problem was that, though free-parameter models might do better than ones without, they were both too flexible and potentially misleading because the free parameters would reflect past behavior and might not remain stable when the

---

[12] FORTRAN was the the general computer programming language most commonly used for this type of work at the time Lucas was writing. Specialist applications for economic applications were much less developed then than they are today.

[13] Lucas puts the term "excess demands" in quotation marks. Recall that his earlier papers had questioned the idea that excess demand for labor was a useful notion for explaining wage movements.

system experienced new shocks. The remedy, Lucas argued, was to move away from the static view of competitive equilibrium, prevalent when Samuelson wrote *Foundations*, and to move toward a dynamic, competitive, contingent-claim equilibrium, presaged in John Hicks's *Value and Capital* (1939) and rigorously developed by Kenneth Arrow (1964) and Gerard Debreu (1959).

Thus, Lucas argued that economists such as Leijonhufvud (1968) missed the point that "progress in economic thinking means getting better and better abstract, analogue economic models, not better verbal observations about the world" (Lucas 1980:700). He observed that while it is possible to synthesize the new equilibrium models with Samuelsonian models of price adjustment, as in the literature we have labeled "disequilibrium macroeconomics,"[14] he saw no point in doing so.[15] This is a strategy that leads to an enormous class of models in which anything can happen.

BARRO AND GROSSMAN

Even if its importance is largely symbolic, the turning point in the history of disequilibrium macroeconomics in the United States may be represented by the session "An Appraisal of the Non-Market Clearing Paradigm" that took place at the 1979 meetings of the American Economic Association and was published in the *American Economic Review* (May 1979, Papers and Proceedings). The participants, who all announced the end of the disequilibrium approach, were Barro, Grossman, and Peter Howitt. Howitt was then working very closely with Clower and with Leijonhufvud, who, as we have seen, were never supporters of the fix-price approach, despite the widespread perception that they were its creators. But how did the authors of what was one of the most successful articles in macroeconomics, Barro and Grossman (1971), come to renounce their earlier work?

For Barro, disequilibrium macroeconomics was primarily about providing a microeconomic foundation for Keynesian economics. Until the mid-1970s, he worked on disequilibrium macroeconomics, doing further work with Grossman on Keynesian economics and the theory of consumption (Barro and Grossman 1974, written in 1972–73, and 1977, initially presented at a conference in 1974) and publishing the graduate textbook *Money, Employment and Inflation* that Clower had first commissioned.

---

[14] He cites Malinvaud (1977) and Drazen (1980), both of which are discussed later.
[15] Although this is conjectural, it is tempting to see a parallel with Friedman's reasons for rejecting the theory of imperfect competition (a synthesis of the theories of monopoly and perfect competition).

However, Barro has recalled that by this time he had lost interest in the disequilibrium approach:

I went to Chicago in 1972. Was not too interested in the disequilibrium macro approach at that time, and neither were my Chicago colleagues. It was painful finishing the book with Herschel, but I agreed that it was useful to have the whole model in published form.[16]

In the book, Barro and Grossman extended their original model to encompass price dynamics and expectations. However, unlike Clower's work in the 1950s, their price-adjustment equations were in a sense not micro-based in that they did not specify what individual firms would do. When they moved beyond the tâtonnement, they retained the idea that prices would respond to market signals, but assumed that nominal prices and wages would respond to differences between effective demands and supplies, for it would be these demands that price-setting agents would observe (Barro and Grossman 1976:95). It is possible to discern similarities with the work on inflation discussed earlier in Chapter 4 of their book, in that they argued that because, by assumption, they did not hold money and because there were no transactions costs, firm behavior would be independent of expected inflation, whereas households would be affected, creating an asymmetry, in a manner loosely reminiscent of that in the Phelps-Lucas models of the labor market. When they came to endogenize inflation expectations they postulated adaptive expectations noting, citing Muth (1961), Lucas (1972), and Sargent and Wallace (1973) in support of their claim, that though this "will represent an optimal predictor of the rate of inflation only under very special conditions" the precise formulation was not essential for their results (Barro and Grossman 1976:178). They clearly understood the arguments of Lucas, Sargent, and Wallace but had not drawn the same conclusions, continuing to assume that expectations lagged actual inflation, in a way that was without precise microfoundations.

However, alongside this work, Barro began to work on other problems, using different types of model. His most influential paper from this period, "Are Government Bonds Net Wealth?" (1974a), owed nothing to the disequilibrium approach. In "Rational Expectations and the Role of Monetary Policy" (1976), he built on the work of Friedman, Lucas, Sargent, and Wallace (see Barro 1976:1–2). The appearance of this work alongside his continuing work on disequilibrium macroeconomics with Grossman suggests that he was simply using different models for different problems. This is consistent with the approach adopted in his intermediate textbook, *Macroeconomics*

---

[16] E-mail from Barro, April 1, 2005.

(1987), which, although designed as an exposition of New Classical economics, included a chapter on the "Keynesian Theory of Business Cycles Fluctuations" (Barro 1987, ch. 18). In that chapter, Barro argued that Keynesian macroeconomics, as far as it goes (and it does not go very far), must be interpreted in terms of the fixed-price approach put forward in his 1971 article with Grossman. In particular, he rejected the "new Keynesian" formulation of macroeconomics through contracting and imperfect competition models discussed later in this chapter. Moreover, Barro (1994b) criticized the usual textbook aggregate supply/aggregate demand model for assuming that the adjustment of the price level eliminated the excess supply of goods. According to Barro, this was inconsistent with the Keynesian notion that firms are constrained by aggregate demand.

The change in his approach, in terms of his published output, appears to have come in 1976. In his survey of monetary theory, written jointly with Stanley Fischer (1976: 149), it was argued that the role of money generating disequilibrium could not be explained by models in which prices were exogenous. They observed that the outstanding problem in disequilibrium theory was the working out of a joint theory of price and quantity determination. They looked forward to a "synthesis" in which "the large information and search-theory literature on price determination will undoubtedly play a role" (ibid.), ending with an agnostic view of the role for disequilibrium analysis: "While disequilibrium analysis has succeeded in presenting models in which many Keynesian notions – notably that of effective demand – are clarified, it remains to be seen whether the same analytical structure will prove useful when applied to situations in which price determination is endogenous." By the time Barro wrote "Long-Term Contracting, Sticky Prices, and Monetary Policy" (1977b), he had come to a different view. His target was the long-term contracting models that sought to explain why wages would be rigid, leading to disequilibrium in the labor market, reaching the conclusion that

When optimal contractual arrangements are specified for determining employment [as well as wages], the output and employment effects of currently perceived monetary disturbances disappear. In other words, the link between contracting theory and sticky prices does not produce a reconciliation between the standard Keynesian model and rational behavior. (Barro 1977:306)

Shortly afterwards, he moved even further away from disequilibrium theory toward equilibrium modeling:

Basically, efficient contracts would allow output and employment to be determined as if prices had been flexible....It is possible that more mileage will come out of analyses that account for limitations on contractual contingencies, enforcement costs, and so on ... At present, contracting analysis seems mostly to suggest that continuous market clearing would be a useful *as if* device for analysing the determination of output and employment. (Barro 1981:61; see also 1979:54)

With this, Barro's move away from disequilibrium macroeconomics was complete. In short, he identified fix-price models with long term contracts, with the result that when he realized that long term contracts were efficient, it became possible to argue that markets would behave as if prices were flexible. Wage/price stickiness per se, according to Barro (1977:315), was not the fundamental feature of Keynesian models. The crucial element – which marks Keynesian economics as non-market clearing analysis – "is the nonexecution of some *perceived* mutually advantageous trades." Keynesian economics does not explain why agents should be constrained to trade at a wage-price vector that does not equate quantities supplied and demanded, which is related to the "Patinkin problem" discussed earlier. Barro suggested that the distinction between the non-market clearing (e.g., Barro-Grossman 1971) and the market-clearing (e.g., Lucas 1972) models is that while the former focuses on changes in the amount of perceived mutually advantageous trades that are not executed, the latter investigates fluctuations in the size of the gap between perceived and actual mutually advantageous trades as influenced by imperfect information. Interestingly enough, he concluded from this that "the two approaches are not mutually exclusive," which explains why the disequilibrium approach continued to play a role in Barro's macroeconomics, even if a minor one.

Likewise, Grossman (1979) understood the non-market clearing and the incomplete information paradigms discussed in Chapter 5 as alternative formulations of non-Walrasian fluctuations in aggregate employment. The inability of disequilibrium macro to provide a convincing rationale for persistent restriction on transactions (a problem already noticed in Barro and Grossman [1976:6]) prompted Grossman to move toward the assumption that business cycles are caused instead by the effect of incomplete information on the incorrect perception of potential gains from trade in market-clearing models. Grossman found necessary to augment Lucas's misperception model with a theory of implicit contracts for shifting risk in labor markets (see Grossman 1978). Implicit contract models are consistent with market clearing (since layoffs do not imply a failure to realize perceived gains of trade) and, moreover, are able to account for the predicted effect of aggregate demand on employment and the observed stickness of real wages without imposing unrealistic restrictions on worker utility functions as in the original Lucas's model (Grossman 1979:66–67). However, Grossman's econometric testing of equilibrium macroeconomics would soon lead to second thoughts about the empirical validity of market-clearing models of economic fluctuations (see Boschen and Grossman 1982). The inability of Lucas's model to explain the data was, according to Grossman (1983, 1987) the main factor behind the "remarkable survival of non-market clearing assumptions". The phrase "non-market clearing" was not restricted to dis-equilibrium macro à la Barro and Grossman (1971, 1976), but included any theory that assumed widespread failure of economic agents to realize per-ceived opportunities to gain from trade, such as the rational expectation model with money-wage stickiness advanced by Fischer (1977). Although such models – like the early disequilibrium models – violate the postulate of maximization, they were seen by Grossman (1983: 237) as potentially reconcilable with neoclassical analysis in that they assume that the objective of wage and price-setting agents is to satisfy market-clearing conditions. In the 1990s, Grossman changed his research agenda and moved away from macroeconomic theory.

CONCLUSION

Armen Alchian drew attention to the problem of information, applying this to factor markets in a paper that circulated unpublished for much of the 1960s. As explained in Chapter 4, Leijonhufvud took up these ideas, showing how they could be used to argue that market economies, lack-ing any central coordination mechanism, would typically be out of equi-librium, with the result that agents would face quantity constraints of the type identified by Clower. The economics of Keynes could, therefore, be rationalized as an economics of disequilibrium. Alchian's insight about the importance of information was also taken up by Phelps, in whose volume Alchian's paper was eventually published, but it was developed in a very different way. Instead of developing a vision of the economy as a whole, Phelps and his co-authors focused on the labor market, developing formal models of how limited information could solve puzzles that conventional models could not solve. In particular, Phelps gained credit for what came to be called the expectations-augmented Phillips curve, also developed, with much greater publicity and on very different theoretical foundations, by Milton Friedman (1968).

The most prominent development of the Phelps approach to modeling the labor market was that of Lucas and the new classical macroeconomists who used it to argue for the explicit modeling of expectations: when they com-bined rational expectations with a Walrasian view of markets, their market-clearing models produced anti-Keynesian conclusions, seemingly justifying the rhetoric of Lucas and Sargent, quoted at the start of this chapter. After being one of the most prominent creators of disequilibrium macroeconomics, Barro almost immediately moved away from it, embracing, instead, equilibrium modeling and arguing as strongly as Lucas against Keynesian policies. Within the space of a few years, he became one of the leading new classical macroeconomists. However, this is not the only direction in which the search for what might be called "equilibrium" foundations went. Phelps did not go in that direction and neither did many other economists, even amongst those who wanted a rigorous integration of macro and microeconomics. Phelps, as became increasingly clear after the 1980s, clearly wanted to place his own work into a school that was fundamentally different from the new classical macroeconomics. Other economists, many of them adopting the label "New Keynesians," took up the arguments that individuals must be making optimal intertemporal choices and that opportunities for profitable trade would not be ignored, but constructed models of why the labor market (and sometimes other markets) would not clear. These models included the explanations of why price stickiness might occur even in otherwise perfectly competitive markets, discussed previously in Chapter 5, and the models of imperfect competition discussed in Chapter 7. The result was that in the 1970s, what might be called "equilibrium" macroeconomics (macroeconomics based on the assumption that agents were choosing the best options they could from those that they were able to choose) was being developed both by economists who believed Keynesian economics to be mistaken and also by economists who believed that their theories could be used to vindicate some of Keynes's insights.

SEVEN

General Equilibrium and Imperfect Competition

The models discussed in Chapters 5 and 6 are macroeconomic in the sense that, although they all discuss the behavior of individual agents, analysis of the economy as a whole is conducted in terms of aggregates – national income, employment, and the price level. However, there were also attempts to build non-Walrasian models of general equilibrium: these models contained arbitrary numbers of individuals and of commodities, but they embodied the constraints on behavior that were crucial to the results contained in the macroeconomic literature. If one market did not clear, this had spillover effects on other markets. Given that this literature is almost universally given the label "general equilibrium," to distinguish it from the literature on aggregative models, but that it deals with "disequilibrium" in the sense that there is no automatic tendency for markets to clear, terminology is particularly treacherous (see the earlier discussion in Chapter 1). Wherever the terms *equilibrium* and *disequilibrium* are used, the meaning has to be inferred from the context.

Adopting a general equilibrium framework requires analysis of individual agents in a way that macroeconomic modeling does not, for individuals are modeled explicitly. This focuses attention on individual decision making and leads naturally to the problem of price setting. However, if agents have the power to set prices, markets cannot be perfectly competitive, which leads naturally into a discussion of imperfect, or monopolistic competition.

This chapter considers the origins of that literature, tracing it back to within a few years of the time when the Arrow-Debreu model was first formulated in the early 1950s. Although this literature came to be seen as part of the attempt to provide microfoundations for Keynesian macroeconomics, and was indeed aimed at doing this, its origins lie deeper, in questions that arose within general equilibrium analysis itself. The earliest work, centered

105

on Arrow and Stanford, around 1960, is covered in the next section. This led into the attempts by Hahn and Negishi to model equilibrium with imperfect competition. It then turns to the work of Drèze, Bénassy, and others. These francophone economists had direct links with U.S. general equilibrium theory in that two of the senior figures, as we will see, engaged with Arrow and Debreu at the Cowles Commission around 1950, and two of the younger ones took their Ph.D.s at Berkeley, supervised by Gérard Debreu. The chapter then turns back to the attempts of Hahn, Negishi, and some younger theorists to take further the analysis of imperfect competition in the second half of the 1970s. In this chapter, the story is taken up to the late 1970s when there appeared a number of widely read surveys, discussed in Chapter 8, that sought to bring together different approaches to the problem of microfoundations.

ARROW, NON-TÂTONNEMENT, AND
IMPERFECT COMPETITION

Interest in general equilibrium theory revived in the 1930s and 1940s, with John Hicks's *Value and Capital* (1939), Paul Samuelson's *Foundations of Economic Analysis* (1947), and independent work on the problem of existence of equilibrium by mathematicians whose work began in Vienna before they immigrated to the United States, notably Abraham Wald (1933–34) and John von Neumann (1945). A more general existence proof was worked out by Lionel McKenzie (1954) and Kenneth Arrow and Gérard Debreu (1954), all with connections to the Cowles Commission during the period when these papers were written.[1] In this work, the general equilibrium model was extended to deal with problems of time and uncertainty through the introduction of markets for dated, contingent commodities (effectively assuming a full set of futures markets and that it was possible to ensure against any eventuality), and the analysis was conducted in terms of the properties of convex sets, permitting a more general representation of consumer preferences and technology than was found in the earlier literature. By the end of the 1950s, this had become the standard model of competitive equilibrium, widely seen as the most rigorous way to do economic theory. It received its canonical statement in Gerard Debreu's *The Theory of Value* (1959).

---

[1]   The history of these papers is discussed in E. R. Weintraub and Gayer (2001) and E. R. Weintraub (2002, 2011).

These developments were part of the background to Patinkin's *Money, Interest and Prices* (1956), discussed earlier in Chapter 3. Although his style was more traditional in that, like Hicks, he placed his mathematics in appendices and he did not use the mathematics of convex sets, he cited the work of Wald, von Neumann, Arrow, and Debreu.[2] However, whereas Patinkin, writing in the late 1940s and early 1950s, could simply take general equilibrium as the starting point in his attempt to sort out monetary economics, by the 1960s, the state of general equilibrium theory was very different. The problem facing the theory was that although very general proofs of existence were available, the problem of stability had not been solved: there was not, so Weintraub (1991) has argued, even any agreement on what it meant. There were some results (e.g. Arrow, Block, and Hurwicz 1959), but none at the same level of generality as that of existence proofs. Moreover, it soon became clear that completely general proofs of stability might not be possible. Scarf (1960) offered some counter-examples, of systems that ought, given conventional beliefs, to have been stable, but were not.

There were two main reasons for this apparent impasse. One was problems caused by the relationship between income distribution and aggregate demand, which meant that aggregate excess demands need not have the same properties as individual excess demands. Indeed, it was proved rigorously by Hugo Sonnenschein (1972), R. Mantel (1974) and Debreu (1974), that even if individuals' preferences were well behaved, market excess demand functions could have almost any shape. Given that price changes were assumed to depend on market excess demands, this meant that the project of finding restrictions on preferences that would ensure stability was doomed. However, an even more fundamental problem was the absence of a satisfactory theory of what should happen out of equilibrium – when demand and supply were not unequal in one or more markets. Out of equilibrium, by definition, there was an inconsistency in that not all demands and supplies could be satisfied.[3] If there were excess demand for a good, there must be at least one potential buyer who could not buy all that he or she wanted; correspondingly, if there was excess supply, at least one seller must be disappointed. The route of assuming that such inconsistencies were resolved before trade took place (re-contracting or tâtonnement) was

---

[2] Although not McKenzie, presumably because, if he was aware of that paper, he was concerned neither with the problem of international trade nor with proving existence of equilibrium.

[3] This was of course the problem that had exercised Patinkin, in a different context, in the late 1940s.

clearly unrealistic; the alternative, non-tâtonnement, was difficult because there was no clear theory of what should happen and it was no longer possible to assume that the equilibrium would be independent of the process whereby equilibrium was reached.

This was the context in which Kenneth Arrow (1959), in the same year that Debreu's definitive statement of the theory was published, identified what he called three scandals in general equilibrium theory: (1) there was no integration of macroeconomics and microeconomics; (2) general equilibrium theory did not incorporate imperfect competition; and (3) general equilibrium theory did not take account of the costs of making transactions. This posed a challenge that was taken up by Takashi Negishi and Frank Hahn. Negishi was a research student from Tokyo, who from 1958–60 held a research post working for Arrow at Stanford. Hahn had completed a Ph.D. on income distribution and economic growth under Nicholas Kaldor in the 1940s, and had since been working on various aspects of general equilibrium theory, earlier in the fifties producing a series of papers on dynamics and market stability (Hahn 1952, 1955). He visited Berkeley for the academic year 1959–60, where he was in contact with Arrow and Negishi at Stanford, and for many years in the 1960s was a summer visitor to Stanford. Their backgrounds overlapped significantly in that, in 1958, Hahn, Negishi, and Arrow (with Hurwicz) had independently proved a theorem on local stability of general equilibrium.

In his work on general equilibrium in Stanford, one of the themes Negishi (1961) took up was responding to Arrow's challenge to incorporate imperfect competition by proving existence and stability of equilibrium in a model where some markets were imperfectly competitive. An important feature of his model was that though prices changed in response to excess demands in competitive markets, excess demands would, so he argued, necessarily be zero in imperfectly competitive markets, and prices were set by a price-adjustment rule, according to which firms continuously moved their prices toward their profit-maximizing levels. Because monopolistically competitive firms distributed profits to shareholders but not losses, he claimed that Walras's Law would hold only in equilibrium.

Another theme in this literature was the analysis of stability when transactions took place out of equilibrium. Here, the technical problem was working out what trades would take place when not all demands could be satisfied. Various assumptions could be made, for example the one made by Hahn and Negishi (1962) that if a good is in excess demand, no agent will hold more than his or her desired quantity, and vice versa for goods in excess supply. Negishi postulated a world in which prices changed, but in each period, trading took place according to this rule. Even though endowments would change in response to realized trades, they were able to show that the system approached equilibrium.

These two problems, of imperfect competition and non-tâtonnement, were related. As Arrow (1959) had pointed out, whenever markets are out of equilibrium, agents, by definition, are unable to sell as much as they like at the prevailing price. Non-market clearing and imperfect competition thus go together. Following a suggestion made by Edmond Malinvaud in response to his presenting his survey of stability theory to the Econometric Society in 1960, Negishi (1961:61; 1994:99) explored the idea that non-tâtonnement processes could be modeled as bargaining between economic agents, opening parallels with game theory.

Given these concerns with adjustment processes taking place out of equilibrium, it is perhaps not surprising that Hahn saw the importance of Clower (1965) when it was offered to an International Economic Association Conference in 1962 that he was organizing.[4] When Arrow and Hahn wrote their *General Competitive Analysis* (1971), they drew on Clower's distinction between target and active excess demands.[5] It underlay their discussion of out-of-equilibrium (non-tâtonnement) dynamics in a monetary economy, and it was central to their discussion of the Keynesian model. Keynesian economics followed on from their discussion of trading out of equilibrium: the problem was not that there were no prices at equilibrium could take place, but that the price mechanism fails to bring about equilibrium with full employment – a dynamic problem. However, their focus was on Keynesian economics as illustrating what might happen in a monetary economy: there was no explicit discussion of imperfect competition, even when markets did not clear.

GENERAL EQUILIBRIUM WITH PRICE RIGIDITIES

Jacques Drèze has described the two themes linking his research as being the allocation of resources under uncertainty and the desire to integrate different theories into the unified approach provided by general equilibrium theory (Licandro and Dehez 2007).[6] He has attributed this interest to practical experiences of coping with uncertainty in his father's business, while also studying business at the University of Liège, where he graduated

---

4   Hahn's choice of Patinkin as discussant was discussed in Chapter 4 above.
5   Clower had, of course used different labels: notional and effective demands.
6   This section draws heavily on this interview.

in 1951. His interest was stimulated by several developments during his period as a graduate student in the United States in the 1950s, when, on George Stigler's advice, he did not remain all the time at Columbia, but spent time at MIT, Harvard, and the Cowles Commission, then in Chicago. While there, he met Gérard Debreu, trained as a mathematician, and was introduced to economics by Maurice Allais, who had moved to the United States and who had become a research associate at the Cowles Commission shortly before. One of these developments was the work of Arrow (1964[1953]) and Savage (1954) on decision making under uncertainty: in his dissertation, in 1958, Drèze sought to extend Savage's theory to encompass state-dependent preferences and moral hazard. He also began, during the same period, to be interested in the relationship between uncertainty and savings, having learned the life-cycle theory from Franco Modigliani, with whom he worked on the problem, starting in 1953. His first academic post was at the Carnegie Institute of Technology in 1957–58, after which he spent over thirty years at Louvain, helping to build up its economics department.

During the 1960s, Drèze turned to the problem of how subjective probabilities affected the prices for contingent claims, aware that markets are generally incomplete. The assumption of complete markets was clearly unrealistic. Firms engage in activities designed to improve their assessments of future events; differences of opinion over future events are common (takeover battles); and investment decisions need to be reconsidered in the light of new information (Drèze 1974: 263). He thus worked out a model with a stock market but no insurance markets, leading to his proof that if markets were incomplete, stock market equilibria need not be efficient. Although the paper was strongly influenced by Diamond (1967), and related to Stiglitz (1972), Drèze reports having conceived the idea in 1963–64, during a visit to Chicago.[7] During this time, he was turning to public economics, through surveying the contributions of French economists to this topic (Drèze 1964). He has said that it was in the course of this work, extending inverse-elasticity pricing rules to the case when private goods are allocated in part by quantity constraints, that he noticed a formula that could be interpreted as a multiplier: "Lightning struck, and I foresaw the possibility of doing general equilibrium macroeconomics" (Licandro and Dehez 2007:289).

These distinct but related lines of inquiry, relating to the allocation of resources under conditions of uncertainty and incomplete markets, formed

---

[7]   He held a position at Chicago till 1968.

the background to "Existence of an Exchange Equilibrium under Price Rigidities" (Drèze 1975), written in 1971.[8] This explored the implications of nominal and real price rigidities, where these were expressed as inequality constraints on prices. Although in the text he illustrated this with examples of institutional rigidities – minimum wages, rent and price controls, usury laws, and the condition that prices be uniform over time or place – a foot-note suggested a broader interpretation of the theory. This was that "wage rigidities" might be "viewed as a form of income insurance for which mar-ket opportunities offer no substitute" (Drèze 1991[1975]:34). His work on risk-sharing and second-best efficiency when markets were incomplete made him realize "that price flexibility, geared to continuous clearing of spot markets, could be less efficient than suitable forms of price stability, commonly labeled 'price rigidities'" (Drèze 1991a:xviii).

This paper established what came to be known as the "Drèze equilib-rium" – widely taken to mean equilibrium with fixed prices and certain assumptions about how goods would be rationed when prices did not equate supply and demand. It had been written in 1971, but had been rejected as a CORE discussion paper. In the autumn of 1972, Jean-Michel Grandmont, who had gained a Ph.D. on the integration of money in general temporary equilibrium and the microeconomic foundations of macroeconomics at Berkeley in 1971, supervised by Debreu, was a visitor at CORE and a col-league told him of its existence. Drèze showed him the paper, explaining its history and Grandmont was able to suggest some minor technical improve-ments, and it appeared as a CORE discussion paper in August 1973. It was then submitted to the *International Economic Review* in 1974.

Grandmont recalls that, during 1972–73, he tried to persuade Drèze that his work was important for the microeconomic foundations of Keynesian macroeconomics, but this was not how Drèze thought of his paper.[9] For him, it related to general equilibrium theory. Perhaps part of the reason for this was that, whereas Barro and Grossman (1971) presented a fixed-price model, Drèze did not see his work as involving fixed prices:

It came as a surprise to me that more macroeconomically oriented colleagues con-centrated their attention on the special case of fixed prices – so that their work was labelled "fixed-price equilibrium macroeconomics", and was eventually discounted on grounds of insufficient rationale for the fixed-price assumption. I still feel that income insurance, in a dynamic incomplete markets set-up, is a convincing ratio-nale for downward wage rigidities. (Drèze 1991:xix)

---

[8] This date is given in Grandmont (1977:537).
[9] E-mail from Grandmont to the authors, December 13, 2011.

It was thus significant that he specified *inequality* constraints on prices, not fixed-prices.

Although Drèze was the senior figure, and though his work can be traced back to his visit to the Cowles Commission in 1951, he had not been the first to construct a disequilibrium model. He was closely involved with a group centered on the research center, CEPREMAP, based in Paris, where a young Tunisian economist, Yves Younès, had presented a paper in 1970. Edmond Malinvaud, one of the organizers of the Malinvaud-Roy seminar in which it was presented, later recalled that

> In the first half of the 1970s, a small group French economic theorists, in which Jacques Drèze also needs to be included, was very interested in the development of a theory of general equilibrium under fixed prices with rationing. The first publications of this group date from 1975: but mimeographed papers had been circulated previously. It may well be that the first of these was the one that Yves Younès presented at a seminar in January 1970, under the title, "On a notion of equilibrium that can be used in the case where economic agents cannot be assured that their plans are not consistent." (Malinvaud 1999:13)[10]

However, although Younès, like many others, had the idea of developing a concept of equilibrium, he was not successful, because he could not prove a key proposition on the existence of equilibrium. His 1970 French paper was revised when he visited Debreu at Berkeley in the spring of 1973 and had access to Bénassy's Ph.D. dissertation (discussed in the following section) and when Debreu introduced him to a type of proof that was appropriate for his problem (Younès 1975:493). A revised English version was circulated as a Berkeley working paper in July 1973 under a new title and finally was published in 1975 in the *Review of Economic Studies*, in the same issue as Bénassy (1975), though placed first, possibly in recognition of Younès's priority.[11] Younès also worked with Grandmont on proving the existence of equilibrium in a monetary economy.[12] Their early work (Grandmont and Younès 1972), modeled money as a store of value in a world where trade had to take place through spot markets – markets were thus incomplete. This was not presented as an exercise in non-Walrasian modelling

---

[10] Younès (1975:489) gives the title of this paper as "sure une notion d'équilibre utilisable dans le cas ou les agents économiques ne sont pas assurés de la compatibilité de leurs plans."

[11] Grandmont recalls that he may have recommended this, having been a referee for both papers.

[12] This was also a problem on which Hahn (1965) had also been involved. Grandmont has said that when he started on this topic, Debreu had told him he would be on his own, because it was a subject that he had not previously thought about.

but they believed that there was a clear link in that they were addressing the problem that there is no essential role for money, in a Walrasian world. However, in the world analyzed by Drèze, Grandmont, and Younès, there was a clear role for money. In his 1975 paper, which Younès described as co-authored with Edmond Malinvaud, a senior figure in this group,[13] he drew on Drèze's work to prove that "The existence of a non-Walrasian equilibrium requires that there be a good, called money, which has to appear in each transaction or which simply has to be the measuring rod of the profitability of each transaction" (Younès 1975: 489).[14] Although following on from Drèze's work, Younès changed the interpretation of the equilibrium in that he focused on what he called "p-equilibrium" – equilibrium given the price vector, p. Drèze's equilibrium was being re-interpreted as fixed-price equilibrium.

In addition to his work with Younès, Grandmont also worked on the problem of Keynesian equilibrium during 1972–73 when he was having discussions with Drèze at CORE, the paper eventually appearing as Grandmont and Laroque (1976). This was written in 1973, and they tried to get it included as the first of the discussion-paper series that CEPREMAP was setting up. However, it was written in English, and at that time, some politicians were protesting about French publicly funded research institutes publishing work in English (and for some, using mathematics was also a problem). So it had to be translated into French, with the result that it was the sixth to appear, in 1974. Although their model was, they conceded, unsatisfactory in that prices were set by sellers, it was a model in which prices were set by monopolistically competitive agents and in which short-run adjustments took place through quantities.

BÉNASSY AND MACROECONOMIC DISEQUILIBRIUM

Bénassy's doctoral thesis, *Disequilibrium Theory*, the result of work that he undertook independently of what was being done in Louvain and Paris, and submitted to Berkeley in June 1973, sought to provide a general analysis of disequilibrium states. He opened by remarking that, though Marx and Keynes had seen the importance of disequilibrium, it was Clower and Leojonhufvud who had opened the way to develop the tools that were needed for analyzing such states. By taking account of the additional

---

[13] The paper was published under Younès's name, but in footnote 2 he wrote that Malinvaud "can be regarded as a co-author of this study." Malinvaud's own contribution to the literature is discussed in Chapter 9.

[14] Younès (1972) had also tackled problems of planning.

constraints that arise outside equilibrium, he sought to develop a broader concept of demand and, hence, of the types of equilibrium that could arise, of which both Walrasian and Keynesian equilibria would be special cases.

The argument was developed in stages. He started by analyzing effective demands in a monetary economy, including the concept that was crucial to his work, of "perceived constraints". Decisions did not depend on actual constraints but on agents' perceptions. From here, he constructed a general model of short-run Keynesian equilibrium before presenting the simplified Keynesian model discussed earlier in Chapter 5. From here, reverting to the more general model, he turned to long-run dynamics, monopolistic competition, and temporary Keynesian equilibrium.[15] In 1974, he produced three discussion papers from the thesis, later published as Bénassy (1975, 1976a, and 1978).

In the first of these papers, Bénassy (1975) noted that macroeconomists such as Barro and Grossman had successfully used simple models and that they had used new concepts such as effective demand and quantity constraints to explain theories such as the multiplier and the accelerator as income-constrained processes. However, a limitation of such models was that they could handle only one or two goods, and Bénassy sought to improve on them by reformulating these ideas "in the usual framework of General Equilibrium analysis" (Bénassy 1975:503). He adopted a framework in which prices were fixed to keep the analysis simple, though citing his dissertation and his later (1976b) paper as evidence that the same analysis would hold where prices were allowed to vary.[16]

Given fixed prices, markets would not always clear, and traders would not necessarily be able to trade as much as they wished. To model this, Bénassy made the assumption that each agent would perceive a constraint on his or her trades; he then assumed that this would be a function of the demand expressed by all other agents. His reasoning was not that agents knew all other agents' demands, but that their demands would be based on information, and that this information would reflect the demands expressed by other agents. Using such perceived constraints, he was able to derive Clower's consumption function and Grossman's accelerator.

In the text of his paper, he proved the existence of a "neo-Keynesian" K-equilibrium, in which agents were maximizing utility subject to the constraints they perceived themselves to face. To do this, he had to assume a type of tâtonnement, for he could not explain how the economy got into

[15] These topics correspond to his chapter titles. There was a final chapter relating the theory to previous work, including Hansen (1951), Kornai (1971), and Marx.
[16] This was also the strategy followed by Keynes (1973[1936]).

equilibrium. The result was an equilibrium that bore a formal similarity to those of Drèze (1975) and Grandmont and Laroque (1976).[17] There was, however, a difference in that Bénassy's K-equilibrium allowed for a greater variety of rationing schemes, which were not necessarily efficient. However, even in the context of fixed-price equilibrium, he sought to go beyond this, by sketching, in an appendix to the paper, a non-tâtonnement model. To keep it manageable he assumed that an agent visited markets in a particular order. This meant that when trading in a particular market (say, market i), the agent would face four constraints: realized sales in markets visited before i, his perceived constraint in market i, constraints that were expected to hold in markets to be visited after market i, and a "transactions constraint" that money balances be non-negative. Making simple assumptions about expectations, Bénassy was able to derive results such as the dynamic Keynesian multiplier.

The second article based on the thesis, Bénassy (1976a) started instead from Negishi (1961) He took from Negishi the idea of perceived demand curves, seeking to extend the model into one where transactions took place outside equilibrium. He analyzed this in terms of a sequence of events: (1) there is a vector of prices that have been set by firms; (2) given these prices, a K-equilibrium is established and trade takes place; (3) each firm observes some prices and quantities and re-estimates its perceived demand curve; and (4) prices are changed on the basis of these perceived demand curves. The process then repeats itself, equilibrium occurring when no firm wishes to change its price. As in Bénassy's previous paper, Clower-type constraints operated out of equilibrium. Bénassy then proposed extending the model by having households as well as firms set prices (setting the prices at which they were prepared to supply labor) and bringing in more elaborate rules for estimating perceived demand curves (for example, taking account of past prices and quantities over a longer period).

Bénassy justified his theory by arguing that it got away from the tâtonnement involved in most previous models of monopolistic behavior. In his theory, it was important that firms did not know their demand curves but had to estimate them based on observed prices and past sales. He postponed for a future paper, analysis of the "general" case where prices and quantities were determined simultaneously, and he noted the invalidity of his methods to situations of oligopoly.[18] However, it was clear that the long-

---

[17] He cited the 1973 discussion-paper versions of both papers.

[18] Bénassy's procedure involved accepting what Leijonhufvud had called the Keynesian ranking of adjustment speeds. This was a simplification but many of the same principles would apply in the more general case.

term goal should be a general theory of how prices were established out of equilibrium.[19]

IMPERFECT COMPETITION AS A THEORY
OF PRICE ADJUSTMENT

In the late 1970s, considerable progress was made in constructing models of imperfect competition. Imperfect competition was being used in macroeconomics as an explanation of why the labor market was not in equilibrium. Given that trade unions were still strong, especially in Western Europe, it made sense to assume that union power might be important. However, in the general equilibrium literature, theorists worked on models of imperfect competition because it offered a theory of how prices adjusted, something that models of perfect competition, in which no agent had the power to change prices, could not provide. Many authors worked on this problem, identifying and solving some of the technical problems involved.[20]

One of these was the form of the demand function. Negishi (1961) had assumed that the demand curves facing firms were linear, but in the early 1970s, he reached the conclusion that this was not correct and that where there was a shortage of demand, demand curves must be kinked – horizontal up to current sales, and downward sloping after that. However, the position of the kink, because products were not differentiated, depended on the starting point – the price and the quantity determined by macroeconomic conditions. In addition, Negishi observed that the output of individual firms was indeterminate, for firms' products were not differentiated, meaning that there was no reason for any particular distribution of output amongst firms to prevail: the only way a determinate macroeconomic equilibrium could be derived was through assuming all firms were identical: "The microeconomics of the firm is not only dependent on the result of macroeconomics ... but also indeterminate except in the sense of the representative firm" (Negishi 1976:35). The point here is that Negishi was not simply postulating imperfect competition (for example, on the grounds that there is competition between many producers of differentiated products) but that he was also trying to model the imperfections of competition that were inherent in any trading outside equilibrium.

---

[19] Some of his subsequent work toward this goal is discussed later in Chapter 8.
[20] A further reason for interest in imperfect competition, not discussed here because it is tangential to the argument being made, is that models of imperfect competition can accommodate increasing returns to scale, a characteristic of the real world, but incompatible with perfect competition.

This goal is even clearer in Hahn (1977, 1978), whose rationale for considering non-Walrasian equilibria merits close attention. He wanted to be able to explain Keynesian phenomena; these, he claimed, make no sense without Clower's distinction between notional and effective demands (Hahn 1978:1). However, this was not his only rationale, for he linked his concern with non-Walrasian equilibria to one of the logical problems with Walrasian theory identified by Arrow (1959) – that, in a perfectly competitive world, there is no one to change prices. Non-Walrasian theory both solves this logical problem and the empirical problem of explaining Keynesian phenomena as well as other empirical problems with the theory. In developing a non-Walrasian theory, he started with a model with fixed prices, pointing out its similarity to those of Drèze (1975) and Grandmont and Laroque (1976),[21] but the significant part of the paper was where he generalized this to a model in which prices were not fixed.

Hahn's more-general model built on Negishi's in that he observed that in a non-Walrasian world, firms have to make decisions on the basis of conjectures about the demand curves that they face.[22] As with Negishi, he was not postulating exogenous market imperfections, but was describing imperfections of competition that were inherent in disequilibrium trading. Equilibrium required that firms' conjectures led to actions that confirmed those conjectures. This is what Hahn (1977) termed a "conjectural equilibrium." The Walrasian equilibrium was always, by construction, one possible outcome: the point of the paper was to show that, in addition to this, non-Walrasian equilibria were also possible. This led to the conclusion that "Once agents change prices (and not the auctioneer), an economy, which with given conjectures has a competitive equilibrium, may 'get stuck' in a non-Walrasian one" (Hahn 1978: 2). Although Hahn observed that this was a novel result, even though his model was related to those of Bénassy (1976a) and Malinvaud and Younès (1975), it is worth noting that Bénassy's simplified macroeconomic model, discussed previously in Chapter 5, also showed that, if it did not start from suitable prices, an economy might converge on a non-Walrasian equilibrium, even if a Walrasian equilibrium existed. A significant objection to the type of model Hahn used was that it started with given conjectures. He addressed this by drawing an analogy with preferences: we do not take preferences as given because

---

[21] Although note that Drèze had made a distinction between his model in which prices were inflexible downwards, and a fixed-price model.

[22] He defined as non-Walrasian any economy in which agents trading possibilities cannot be defined simply by the constraint that the value of their purchases be less than the value of their sales.

we believe preferences are fixed at birth, but because we have no suitable theory for an economy in which they are endogenous. Taking conjectures as given was but a first step, because in any application, it would be necessary to consider what those conjectures were. The option of going down the "rational expectations" route was neither possible nor appropriate. It was not clear that it would always be possible even to define the meaning of rational conjectures, for even if market behavior were such as to confirm agents' conjectures, this would not imply that those conjectures were correct. There were also classes of conjectures in which it was possible to show that rational conjectural equilibrium would not exist. Hence, the only realistic strategy was the more modest one of taking them as given and working out their implications.

The way economists concerned with the problem of price setting were led to imperfect competition is illustrated by Guy Laroque and Jean-Michel Grandmont, who were at CEPREMAP in the early 1970s working on monetary economics and on dynamic models of temporary equilibrium. They sought to provide a model that could reconcile what they saw as the "polar cases" of flexible and fixed-price systems. They acknowledged (Grandmont and Laroque 1977:42) that Drèze had allowed for price movements and did not fall into the latter category, though they argued that his equilibrium concept was similar to those of Younès and Bénassy. They made the important claim that the fixed-price was not a limited, special case of the Walrasian model: to the contrary, it was far *richer* than the Walrasian model, for it allowed agents to respond to quantity as well as price signals. It was, of course, necessary to explain how prices changed. In the Walrasian model, in which prices are determined by supply and demand, there was a sense in which it was not necessary to explain how prices changed (so long as there was equilibrium), but in fixed-price models, "the mere logical consistency of the model requires that one specifies how prices move from one period to the next" (Grandmont and Laroque 1976:53–54, 1977:42). They rejected the route of assuming that prices responded to excess demands (following Hansen [1951] or Grossman [1972] or, we might add, Barro and Grossman [1976]), for to do this would be effectively to introduce an auctioneer. It was, they argued, better to assume that prices were quoted by agents and that they were revised each period in response to information received.

The 1976 issue of the *Review of Economic Studies*, in which Bénassy's article came out, also contained Grandmont and Laroque's "On Temporary Keynesian Equilibria" (1976). Although this article cited a 1973 discussion-paper version of Benassy's article, describing it as an earlier work on the same subject, using different techniques, the first version of their paper was written independently of Benassy's doctoral dissertation in the fall of 1973, when Grandmont was visiting CORE. A French version was circulated as a CEPREMAP discussion paper in November 1973.[23] They described their task as being to analyze Keynesian and classical theory in a unified theoretical framework, influenced by Clower, Leijonhufvud, and Patinkin, contending that monopolistic competition was crucial:

> We shall argue that monopolistic competition must be a central feature of the Keynesian model. As a matter of fact, in the neoclassical tradition, consistency of the model does not require a more explicit mechanism for price setting. Once the fixed-price method is used, the mere logical consistency of the model requires that one specifies how prices move from one period to the next. It is then surely logically consistent to specify an adjustment process as a function of excess demands observed in very period, as in Grossman, B. Hansen. *We certainly did not want to stick with such a specification, for it amounts to a reintroduction of some kind of auctioneering.* It is undoubtedly better to assume at the start that prices are quoted by agents belonging to the system and revised in every period in the light of the information received from the past. (Grandmont and Laroque 1976:53–54)

Similarly, they were led, by the logic of their model, to imperfect competition.[24] However, not everyone accepted the link between disequilibrium and imperfect competition. Drèze, for example, continued to work on models of decentralized price setting by firms that dispensed with any auctioneer but without monopolistic exploitation in equilibrium, extending the theory to increasing returns as well as to downwardly rigid prices.[25]

The economists discussed up to this point turned to imperfect competition not because of the existence of unions, large firms, barriers to entry and other such institutional reasons, but because they saw it as a logical consequence of the fact that prices had to be set by agents in the model. There was, however, no inconsistency between this approach and modeling imperfect competition as the result of institutional factors. The latter approach is illustrated in "A Model of Imperfect Competition with Keynesian Features" by Oliver Hart (1982), who was until 1981 a colleague of Hahn's at Churchill College Cambridge.[26] Instead of assuming that agents were rationed, with the implication that prices were not set optimally, Hart assumed that firms set prices so as to maximize profits, given the production plans of other

---

[23] E-mail from Grandmont to the authors, December 13, 2011.

[24] They did not cite articles by Arrow, Hahn, or Negishi on this point, Arrow and Hahn (1971).

[25] See Dehez and Dreze (1988) and Dreze (1991, 1999).

[26] He acknowledges Hahn's assistance in writing the paper.

firms. Not only did he assume that wages were set by unions that had monopolistic power,[27] but he also assumed that firms had monopoly power in product markets. The key element of Hart's modeling strategy was ensuring that unions and firms were all small relative to the economy as a whole, though of significant size relative to their own markets, for without this there would arise a situation of bilateral monopoly that would have very peculiar properties. He concluded that if competition were imperfect in this way, there could be equilibrium with a low level of unemployment and output. Furthermore, increasing demand for current consumption would have a multiplier effect on output and a balanced-budget fiscal expansion could stimulate the economy. These were the most obvious "Keynesian features" of his model.

But was he justified in describing this as Keynesian, given that Keynes did not rely on monopoly power to generate unemployment? Hart pointed out that

Under imperfect competition, as under fixed prices, an agent's actions will depend not only on prices but also on realized transactions, i.e. quantities. As Clower [1965] has emphasized, this seems to be a crucial feature of any Keynesian model.... [In] an imperfectly competitive equilibrium an agent will generally want to buy or sell more at the going price. (Hart 1982:134)

To this extent, his model was Keynesian, even though markets cleared and there was no rationing. But Hart was cautious in claiming his model to be Keynesian, for he recognized that insofar as unemployment arose from imperfect competition rather than from the failure of the market system to provide appropriate signals (the key characteristic of Keynesian economics according to Leijonhufvud), it was "closer to the ideas of such 'pre-Keynesians' as Pigou" (Hart 1982:135). On the other hand, he continued, in that each agent was small relative to the economy as a whole, albeit significant in its own market, "the model may not be so far removed from the atomistic world that Keynes had in mind" (Hart 1982:135).

CONCLUSION

What united this group of economists was their commitment to general equilibrium theory: for all of them, rigorous theorizing meant starting from the framework of general equilibrium theory and developing it to deal with macroeconomic issues. With the notable exception of Drèze, who

---

[27]   A similar approach was taken by, for example, McDonald and Solow (1981).

developed his ideas independently,[28] in the 1970s, these general equilibrium theorists developed general equilibrium models that explained Keynesian phenomena – that provided microfoundations for Keynesian macroeconomics. However, this was not their only aim. They were economists who started from the assumption that the Arrow-Debreu general equilibrium model had flaws that needed attention, something that was evident even before it received its canonical formulation in Debreu's *The Theory of Value* (1959). Not only did markets not work in the manner specified by the Arrow-Debreu model, *they could not do so*. Markets were obviously incomplete: in particular, it was clear that there were many eventualities against which it was impossible to get complete insurance, as the Arrow-Debreu model assumed. Just as fundamentally, equilibrium was achieved in the Arrow-Debreu model only through a deus ex machina, the fictitious auctioneer who was not part of the model (Debreu was silent on the question of stability) and, crucially, *could not* be part of it, for to model the auctioneer as part of the economy would be to imply that operating markets had a real resource cost, violating of the assumption that there were no transactions costs. In the story told here, it is the followers of Arrow and Debreu who sought to act on this, but theory was being taken in these directions with their active support.

To a substantial extent, therefore, it can be argued that this literature arose out of the internal problems within general equilibrium analysis. The Walrasian model, as interpreted by Arrow and Debreu, was fundamentally flawed as a general account of the economy. The proponents of disequilibrium theory recognized this and were seeking to find a more general way of portraying the operation of markets. Negishi and Hahn focused on the inevitability of monopoly if agents were to change prices themselves in a decentralized economy. Drèze focused on missing markets. Bénassy explored imperfect competition as a way to explain how prices were set. All of them assumed that agents made rational decisions based on the constraints that they perceived themselves to face and that the challenge facing macroeconomics was to explain how those perceived constraints were determined when some or all markets were out of equilibrium. Of course, they were taking up the challenge posed by Leijonhufvud (1968), namely, that of developing a theory of "economics without the auctioneer" that could explain Keynesian phenomena. However, in that the literature can

---

[28] The bibliography in Drèze (1975) is notable for its brevity. Aside from Debreu (1959) the only references are two discussion papers by Bénassy. Given that these were dated 1973–74 and that Drèze's paper had first been circulated as a discussion paper in 1972, there is no reason to think that he was anything other than generous in his citation practice.

clearly be traced back to the work of Hahn and Negishi in the early 1960s, it is clear that there were independent sources of this desire to develop the theory of general competitive equilibrium.

One of the reasons why these economists may have wanted to develop theory in this way was that, perhaps to a greater extent than many of their Anglo-Saxon counterparts working on general equilibrium theory, Drèze, and many of his French counterparts at CEPREMAP were heavily involved in applied economics and in government. Drèze's interest in this field arose out of his involvement in public economics (incidentally, a survey of work in *France*). Malinvaud was involved in a heavily statistical project (with Moses Abramovitz) on French economic growth and in the early 1970s spent three years working on planning for the French government. Laroque spent part of his career developing French national income statistics. Perhaps this made them take more seriously the need for a general equilibrium theory that could relate more closely to real-world phenomena.

The economists discussed in this chapter had an asymmetric relationship with macroeconomists. Their work drew on the macroeconomic literature: Clower, Leijonhufvud, and Barro and Grossman had a strong influence on almost everyone involved in non-Walrasian general equilibrium modeling. However, there was much less influence in the other direction because, though some were aware of the general equilibrium literature, most macroeconomists took little notice of it. There were many reasons for this. In part, it was clearly because these models did not address the pressing problems of inflation and unemployment that needed to be solved. In other cases, it was because they could not understand the mathematics. For example, Patinkin, in a letter to Solow on July 2, 1989,[29] admitted that he did not attend to the details of the work of Drèze or Bénassy, and even, in a letter to Grandmont on June 12, 1987,[30] that he was not mathematically competent to judge it. However, before considering the effects of this literature and that discussed in earlier chapters, it is useful to turn to the question of how the problem of microfoundations was conceived and some of the surveys that introduced this literature to a wider audience.

---

[29] Don Patinkin Papers, Box 62. David M. Rubenstein Rare Book and Manuscript Library, Duke University.
[30] Don Patinkin Papers, Box 55. David M. Rubenstein Rare Book and Manuscript Library, Duke University.

EIGHT

Macroeconomics and Microeconomics

THE CONCEPT OF MICROFOUNDATIONS

The language of "microeconomic foundations of macroeconomics" or "microfoundations of macroeconomics" dates from around 1970, the most significant usage being by Edmund Phelps (1969), whose subsequent book *The Microeconomic Foundations of Employment and Inflation Theory* (Phelps et al. 1970), discussed earlier in Chapter 7, popularized the idea. The idea that theories of the economy as a whole should be based on theories about individual behavior is probably older than the discipline, but the term "microeconomic foundations," or "micro-foundations," with its clear implication of a hierarchy, was generally absent from the literature until the late 1950s, when it was used by Sidney Weintraub, a Keynesian economist offering unorthodox ideas on inflation and employment (S. Weintraub 1956, 1957, 1958). He, however, only went part of the way toward what became the established terminology, for he did not use the term "macroeconomics," which came into widespread use only in the 1960s.[1] The change that took place in the 1970s is illustrated in Figure 8.1, which shows the number of times the combination "microfoundations" and "macroeconomics" was used in journals classified under economics in JSTOR.[2] Note that there are two aspects to this: talking of macroeconomics and talking about macroeconomics as needing microeconomic foundations.[3]

---

[1] This is why Sidney Weintraub (1957, 1958) is not picked up, for he did not use the term macroeconomics.

[2] This could be refined by adding a list of synonymous terms, for many variants have been used. However, this indicates the trend, which is all that matters for the argument being made.

[3] The reason for plotting the number of papers that use both terms is to avoid counting articles that are on the microfoundations of other fields. Clearly, articles can, and did, discuss macroeconomics without ever using the term but these statistics serve to indicate broad trends.

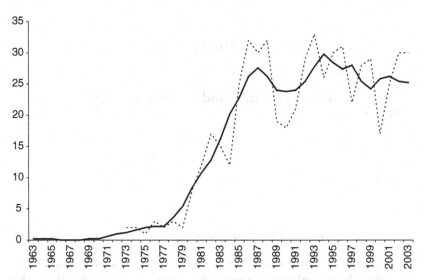

Figure 8.1. Microfoundations and macroeconomics in JSTOR economics articles
Source: Number of articles in JSTOR economics journals containing the words "micro-foundations" and "macroeconomics." Raw data and five-year moving average.

Given that the ideas had been in circulation for much longer, the emergence of this new terminology is, in itself, not of great importance. Hoover (2012), for example, writes about "microfoundational programs" going back to the *General Theory* (Keynes 1973[1936]). However, it can be argued that the emergence of this terminology, of microeconomics and macroeconomics, with the latter being grounded in the former, went along with a stabilization or standardization in the way economists viewed their discipline. At the beginning of the 1970s, the problem of microfoundations was seen to involve many things, whereas by the end of the decade it was coming to mean the grounding of macroeconomic models on models of individual optimizing behavior, with macroeconomic phenomena being, for the most part, a reflection of relationships that could be found at the level of the individual agent and in which the dominant framework was the theory of general competitive equilibrium.

A glimpse into the way the microeconomic foundations of macroeconomics were conceived in the early 1970s is given by Stanley Fischer's (1975) short survey of developments in monetary theory that had taken place since Harry Johnson's (1962) survey. His first topic was what he called "the new micro foundations of money." The objective of this literature was to go beyond the conventional approach of grounding a demand for money function on no more than "an informal and usually picturesque" account of why money is used (Fischer 1975:157). This immediately ran up against the problem that there was no room for money in general equilibrium theory as conventionally formulated. In response to this, theorists, had tried various approaches to modeling the use of money, all involving the use of "transactions costs and/or informational considerations" (p. 158). He then turned to "disequilibrium theory", defined as theorizing about models where trade takes place at false prices. This literature had, he claimed, succeeded in making more precise what he called "the basic Leijonhufvud position" (p. 159), but he remained agnostic about where it would lead:

> While disequilibrium analysis has succeeded in presenting models in which many Keynesian notions – particularly that of effective demand – are clarified, it remains to be seen whether the same analytical structure will prove useful when applied to situations in which price determination is endogenous. (Fischer 1975:161)

Simultaneous price and quantity adjustment was, he contended, the outstanding problem in this literature. In this, he reflected a position taken by Milton Friedman, who argued that this was the crucial component of his own monetary framework, differentiating it from both naïve Keynesianism, which took prices as given, and a naïve quantity theory of money, that took the level of output as given (see R.A. Gordon 1974).

One feature of Fischer's survey is that these two aspects of the problem of microeconomic foundations were considered separately. He also provided, separated from the discussion of disequilibrium analysis by a section on money and growth, a survey of work on rational expectations and the Phillips curve. Fischer thus offered three distinct approaches to the microeconomic foundations of monetary economics, though the term "micro foundations" was used only in relation to one of them; the common theme that ran through them was the lack of any satisfactory theory of "the short run dynamics and costs of inflation and unemployment" (Fischer 1975:165). The one place where he linked different approaches was where, in expounding disequilibrium theory, he noted that the theory developed by Phelps (cited in the context of rational expectations) could be used to justify Leijonhufvud's assumption that quantity adjustments were more rapid than price adjustments, conjecturing that this reflected the influence of Armen Alchian on both Leijonhufvud and Phelps.

DISEQUILIBRIUM THEORY IN THE MID-1970S

A much fuller picture of the variety of approaches to the microfoundations of macroeconomics in the early 1970s is provided in the proceedings of two conferences that took place in the mid-1970s. The first was held at the Institute for Advanced Studies in Vienna, on July 3–5, 1974, on the topic "Equilibrium and Disequilibrium in Economic Theory." Its aim was to bridge the gap between, on one hand, general equilibrium theory in what the editor described as the Walrasian and Edgeworthian tradition and, on the other hand, "the theoretical and policy problems raised in the framework of Keynesian and post-Keynesian macroeconomics". (Schwödiauer 1974:ix). Although the editor wrote about spanning the range from abstract general equilibrium theory to applied macroeconomics, the papers were almost uniformly technical and theoretical. The second was held in Spain in 1975 under the auspices of the International Economic Association and was titled "The Microeconomic Foundations of Macroeconomics" (Harcourt 1977). Both conferences attracted a wide range of distinguished contributors.

The main focus of the volume edited by Gerhard Schwödiauer, *Equilibrium and Disequilibrium in Economic Theory* (1978), was abstract general equilibrium modeling, the tone being set by the Introduction, subtitled "Economic Equilibrium and Disequilibrium from a Dynamic Point of View." The section of the book on disequilibrium and macroeconomics was preceded by papers that dealt with fundamental problems relating to general equilibrium theory, critiques of general equilibrium theory, short- and long-run dynamics, and the extension of general equilibrium theory to encompass problems as diverse as marketing costs, imperfect competition, uncertain product quality, and the stock market. However, despite the fact that the majority of chapters were on other topics, the volume was sufficiently large (thirty-six chapters spread across nearly eight hundred pages) that the twelve chapters on disequilibrium and macroeconomics provided a broad coverage of the field.

The included chapters were by several of the economists discussed in this book. Negishi tackled the problem of the existence of equilibrium without full employment. Bénassy's chapter contained the macro model, described previously in Chapter 5, and a substantial discussion of the theory of imperfect competition, outlined previously in Chapter 7. Barro and Grossman explored Clower's arguments about consumption, money, and liquidity in a world in which consumers were making inter-temporal choices subject to lifetime budget constraints. Beyond these contributions, the other chapters illustrate the depth of interest in the field, only three years after Barro and Grossman's first article. There were discussions of non-tâtonnement, false trading, and the multiplier, and ideas of disequilibrium were applied to a flow-of-funds model and international trade and

finance. There was also an attempt to think about disequilibrium in a stochastic context.[4]

Although the contributors may not necessarily have been in complete
agreement, the case for general equilibrium theory lying at the heart
of macroeconomics was generally taken as given. In his Introduction,
Schwödiauer's (1978:3) opening words were "The theory of general economic equilibrium, or, rather, a collection of general equilibrium models ...
can nowadays rightly be considered the theoretical basis and core of economic science." He went on to observe that modern general equilibrium
theory was based on "methodological individualism," recognizing that "at
the bottom of every collective social phenomena are the actions of individual human decision makers and ... for this reason, the modeling of
individual decision making plays an indispensible role in the analysis and
explanation of economic macro-phenomena."

The International Economic Association volume was very different, being
less technical, not focused in the same way on general equilibrium theory, and
being more directed toward asking questions about the relationship between
microeconomics and macroeconomics that Schwödiauer tended to take for
granted. Although it was edited by Geoffrey Harcourt, then at Cambridge
and probably best known for his survey of the capital controversy (Harcourt
1972), the vision behind the conference was that of John Hicks, from whose
Value and Capital (1939) much of the modern literature relating macroeconomics to general competitive equilibrium microeconomics stems. *Value
and Capital* had provided a modern, preference-based, exposition of the theory of general equilibrium before using this as a framework within which to
explore questions of capital, dynamics, and expectations. The IS-LM model,
the workhorse of macroeconomics from the 1940s to the 1960s, was a miniature general equilibrium model, written while he was working toward this
book. However, Hicks was less content with this model than were most macroeconomists (Hicks 1974), and in 1973, he wrote a paper that was used as
the basis for this conference, being used to select topics and participants and
being circulated to participants to set the agenda.[5]

The striking feature of the discussions recorded in this volume is their
variety. In his background paper, Hicks had, according to Harcourt
(1977:2), forecast that the conference would be concerned with three
main problems: (a) the concepts of capital and income, for these relate

---

[4]   The complete list of authors has not been provided because to do so would make the par-
      agraph read even more like a catalogue.
[5]   Hicks's paper was circulated amongst those participating in the conference, but was not
      published; we have not been able to obtain a copy.

the present and the future; (b) how far macroeconomic relations could be considered "projections of accepted principles in micro-economics" (examples being the consumption and investment functions); and (c) problems that had come down from Keynes, including equilibrium and money. Thus, although the volume contained reflections on general equilibrium theory, the problem of microfoundations was seen to involve *much* more than this.

General equilibrium theory was approached from three angles, several of the contributors (Hahn, Grandmont, Laroque, Malinvaud, and Younès) having been involved in the developments discussed previously in Chapter 7.[6] Hahn, for example, argued for imperfect competition. He discussed general equilibrium with fixed prices, but he contended that even if they took account of spillover effects and quantity constraints pioneered by Clower, such models did little more than provide theoretical foundations for what macroeconomists had been doing for years. The problem was that such an approach necessarily left out many of the problems with which Keynes, who had denied that unemployment was connected to wage rigidity, had been concerned. In contrast, Grandmont and Laroque discussed "temporary Keynesian equilibrium" (in which prices could not adjust flexibly) while Malinvaud and Younès explicitly referred to "new concepts" of equilibrium in which they did not assume that all transactions took place at the same price: that was something that should be proved, not assumed. It was recognized that these papers did not cover the full range of approaches being followed in macroeconomics, several contributors noting the absence of the information-theoretic approach to microfoundations taken by Edmund Phelps, who was unable to be at the conference.

There were also discussions that did not focus on general equilibrium theory. More radically, though less formally and moving beyond the confines of general equilibrium theory, Erich Streissler challenged the idea that it was necessary to assume optimizing agents, an assumption that, he contended, played an essential role in macroeconomic analysis. Results could instead be derived by considering the entry and exit of individuals into and out of the market. Even the law of demand could be derived without assuming individual optimization. There was discussion of aggregation of production relations and, more generally, of which aggregates macroeconomics should be concerned with. There were also discussions of the role of money in the economy, the consequences of inflation (by Leijonhufvud) and the behavior of firms and investment.

---

[6] Hahn was unable to be present but provided a paper, included in the volume.

According to Harcourt,[7] Hicks "dominated the topics and questions to be tackled but ended in despair, feeling that we had not gone anywhere!" Harcourt also recalled that Hicks "told me he thought we could never pull the disparate themes of the conference together into some sort of unified structure but that [in editing the volume] I had succeeded in doing so". Thus, in the final session Hicks opined that

[We have] not done what we were setting out to do. We had met to discuss a rather central issue in economics; but it had been shown that economists were not in a good state to discuss central issues. Economics was an expanding universe: we were each shooting off on our own paths ... We had been supposed to be discussing the microeconomic foundations of macroeconomics, but we had come to realise that there were several kinds of macroeconomics, each probably requiring its own foundations, and though they overlapped, they were not wholly the same. (Harcourt 1977:373)

Hicks's growing distance from the central currents in economics as it had evolved after the Second World War (see Hahn 1990) may have been one reason for the choice of contributors to the conference and the volume, but there is a sense in which the volume, especially if taken together with the very different, but more narrowly technical Schwödiauer (1978) volume, nonetheless captures the diversity of approaches to microfoundations in the early 1970s. The microeconomic foundations of macroeconomics could mean many things, and there was no agreement on how the problem should be tackled, as shown by the discussions reported by Don Moggridge and Susan Howson, regarded by Roy Weintraub (1978)[8] as the best part of the book. In contrast, by the end of the decade, though there were dissenters, macroeconomics was moving toward a fairly broad agreement on how the problem of the relationship between microeconomics and macroeconomics was to be approached.

GENERAL SYSTEMS ANALYSIS

On January 5, 1975, Roy Weintraub, a young general equilibrium theorist, wrote to Mark Perlman, editor of the *Journal of Economic Literature*, inquiring about whether he would be interested in a survey of recent developments in general equilibrium theory in relation to the problems in monetary theory that inspired them, under the title "Microfoundations of Macrotheory."

---

[7] E-mail from Harcourt, August 30, 2010.
[8] Unless otherwise mentioned, all references and in-text mentions of "Weintraub" refer to Roy.

He claimed that a taxonomy based on the distinctions between Walrasian and Edgworthian approaches and between equilibrium and disequilibrium would cover a range of recent developments. Perlman responded that he would like it to be called "The Microfoundations of Macroeconomics: A Survey" and that though several people had approached him about writing such an article, none of them had delivered anything. It was to be aimed at economists who were not specialists in general equilibrium theory. The article that resulted (Weintraub 1977) was the first (of those now listed in JSTOR) to use the terms "microfoundations" and "macroeconomics" together. In it, he proposed to bring together discussion of the temporary equilibrium approach found in Arrow and Hahn (1971), non-tâtonnement processes, and re-contracting.

Weintraub had started his academic career in mathematics, and in the University of Pennsylvania's applied mathematics department he had written a Ph.D. thesis, supervised by Lawrence Klein, on *The Stability of Stochastic General Equilibrium Systems* (Weintraub 1969), the main results of which were presented at the American Economic Association meetings at the end of the year (see Weintraub 1970). Although a thesis in mathematics, concerned with ideas that would appear far from those discussed in this book, Weintraub (1969:105) motivated his consideration of stochastic models as a way to account for market imperfections as random disturbances.[9] During a year's leave spent at the University of Bristol, in 1970–71, he followed this with a book manuscript, *An Approach to General Equilibrium Dynamics* (1972). Here, he presented his work as motivated by what he called "the rebirth of the Keynes-Classics debate" brought about by Clower and Leijonhufvud, which had stimulated a revival of interest in general equilibrium theory (Weintraub 1972:1). His contention, clearly stated in the Preface, was that the fate of macroeconomics had become entwined with that of general equilibrium theory. The key figure was Patinkin, who had provided macroeconomics with "a microeconomic foundation for theorizing," implying that "if general equilibrium theory was a settled area, then macroeconomic theory was essentially settled also" (ibid.). Yet, many Keynesian economists rebelled against Patinkin's conclusion that the Keynesian system was a special case of the classical. The significance of Clower (1965) was that, though it was not the first attempt to criticize general equilibrium theory, he was the first "to score a 'verified hit' on the Walrasian theory" (Weintraub 1972:2). After noting how Leijonhufvud had filled out Clower's argument, Weintraub noted that these issues had

---

[9] He cited Negishi (1961).

been taken up in two books on general equilibrium theory, Bent Hansen's *A Survey of General Equilibrium Systems* (1970) and Kenneth Arrow and Frank Hahn's *General Competitive Analysis* (1971). His own book would, he concluded, use the dynamic features of the standard model to show that general equilibrium models could not support the type of macroeconomics that many economists felt was valid (Weintraub 1972:2–3).

This manuscript was never published, but became the basis for two short books, *General Equilibrium Theory* (Weintraub 1974) and *Conflict and Co-operation in Economics* (Weintraub 1975). This was the point at which Weintraub contacted Perlman. The resulting article (Weintraub 1977) appeared under the title Perlman had suggested. Not only did publication in the *Journal of Economic Literature* give this article a prominence that such an article might not otherwise have achieved; it was then expanded into *The Microfoundations of Macroeconomics* (Weintraub 1979), a book in the newly established series of textbooks based on *Journal of Economic Literature* surveys, published by Cambridge University Press.[10]

The dominant theme in Weintraub's series of writings was that general equilibrium theory could be foundational for economics. His concern was not whether general equilibrium theory was the appropriate foundation for macroeconomics, but with "the most appropriate type of general equilibrium theory" (Weintraub 1972:4). General equilibrium theory served as "the bridge between microeconomics (partial equilibrium) and macroeconomics (aggregative analysis)," standing apart from both (Weintraub 1972:7). It could, he hoped, be used to end what he called the "grand schism" in economic theory:

Currently, economic theory is rent by this grand schism, between (depending on whom one reads), Keynesians and neo-Keynesians, Keynes and the Classics, neo-classicists and Keynesians, conservatives and liberals, good and evil. ...[11] This controversy has been difficult to follow because the combatants' weapons have been models, mathematics, polemic, jargon, and self-righteousness, weapons which serve as a smokescreen around "real" intentions. Consequently, though many economists

---

[10] Weintraub went on to develop what he described as the doctrine historical element in his survey in two further books. *General Equilibrium Analysis: Studies in Appraisal* (1985) explored more rigorously the notion that this episode could be viewed as a research program in the sense of Imre Lakatos. *Stabilizing Dynamics* (1991) abandoned this methodological framework in favor of one that owed more to the sociology of science, focusing on the stabilization of knowledge. Although we have been influenced by this last book's approach to writing intellectual history, this turn away from engagement as an economist to writing about economics goes beyond the issues that are the concern of this chapter and will not be discussed further.

[11] At this point, he cited Hines (1971) as providing the only guide to this literature.

are just now making their peace with the capital measurement protagonists, new heroes and villains are coming on the scene asking, for general equilibrium theory, "whose side are you on?" (Weintraub 1972:3–4)

General equilibrium theory is an outsider whose position in a field clouded by obfuscation and ideological dispute is not clear. Yet, this outsider can sort out the confusion that reigns.

The key to using general equilibrium theory to resolve disputes in economics, Weintraub claimed, was to see it as concerned with systems. General equilibrium theory could be separated from the microeconomics on which it rested, which might or might not be the standard model of perfect competition,[12] and was best seen as a branch of general systems theory, an idea that had been pursued by Kenneth Boulding, whose book, *Beyond Economics* (1968) was cited in the opening sentence of Weintraub's manuscript as the source of the tripartite division discussed in the previous paragraph. The manuscript, therefore, began not with the general equilibrium model, but with two chapters on the mathematics of systems.

General Equilibrium Theory (Weintraub 1975) took up this theme, presenting general systems theory, associated with Bartalanffy (1968) and represented in economics by Janos Kornai's *Anti-Equilibrium* (1971) as a newly available common language with the potential to unify different disciplines through finding structures that were common to them all. Economists had been "speaking 'systems' for many years without realising the fact" (Weintraub 1974:9). The case for using general equilibrium theory was not that it was correct, but that it was the most complete available model: if it were, as critics claimed, too simple, then the appropriate response was not to abandon it but to modify it. This accounts for why his book paid much attention to problems often associated with macroeconomics, such as expectations and money.

The potential of general equilibrium theory was, paradoxically, demonstrated by debates over Keynesian economics. It might be true that Keynesian critics, such as George Shackle, Sidney Weintraub, and Paul Davidson had worked out why neoclassical theory, represented by Patinkin, tamed and distorted Keynes's vision of how the economy worked. However, progress had risen not from their work but from the work of those who embraced general equilibrium theory: "It has been a minor triumph of general equilibrium theory, however abstract and rarefied as it may seem, that it has reconstituted the Keynesian revolution and breathed new life

---

[12] He cited Telser (1972) but without mentioning issues of strategy and game theory (which occur later in the text).

into those issue of pure theory with which Keynes grappled but which the neoclassicals ignored" (Weintraub 1974:54).[13] Clower and Leijonhufvud were presented, along with Frank Hahn (1965), as the general equilibrium theorists who had shown the context in which the problems identified by Keynes needed to be placed. Weintraub's second book dealt with game theory rather than the microfoundations of macroeconomics, yet it is worth noting that he presented game theory as helping to solve the problem of uncertainty posed by Keynes (Weintraub 1975:12–13).

SURVEYING MICROFOUNDATIONS: ROY WEINTRAUB

This background explains the article that Weintraub proposed to write for the *Journal of Economic Literature*. He wanted to "link up ... recent advances in general equilibrium theory with the problems in monetary theory that inspired them."[14] Three months after Perlman responded positively to his suggestion about writing it, Weintraub had drafted a paper and circulated it to friends for comment (with a copy to Perlman). Following those comments, he submitted a revised draft to Perlman in June 1975, who sent it to referees.

One of those friends was Hyman Minsky, the exchange with whom shows clearly the stance that Weintraub was taking. Minsky, in a letter to Weintraub, 14 April 1975, argued that shortfalls in revenue might require a modification of the equilibrium sufficiently great to call into question the validity of speaking in terms of equilibrium. Weintraub replied by arguing that equilibrium had no necessary connection with theories of equilibrium as they currently existed:

> For myself, I'm not so convinced that the sort of analysis you prefer, "identifying the disequilibrating factors at work within any 'temporary' equilibrium," is logically distinct from general systems analysis, of which Walrasian G. E. theory is a special case. Thus if you tell me what defines a "state", a configuration of prices, outputs, institutions, expectations etc., my task is to specify with some clarity the forces at work to transform that state over time. Equilibrium is a terminal state in that sense.[15]

However, at the same time as he was arguing that Minsky was engaging in general equilibrium analysis, he emphasized that new forms of that theory,

---

[13] Weintraub (1985) reaffirmed this in his criticism, at the American Economic Association meetings, of what he perceived as Joan Robinson's inability to grasp the concept of equilibrium in the neo-Walrasian program.

[14] Weintraub to Perlman, January 6, 1975. Unless otherwise stated, all Weintraub correspondence refers to papers in the possession of E. R. Weintraub.

[15] Weintraub to Minsky, April 29, 1975.

not assuming smoothly adjusting prices, market clearing, and the absence of any surprises, were needed. General equilibrium theory did not have to be "barter nonsense in a timeless world".

However, despite the enthusiastic reaction of Weintraub's friends, who included many that one would have expected to be critical, the first referee, whose views Perlman reported on September 1, 1975, recommended rejection. His reason, which echoes the view of the subject presented in the first section of this chapter, was that it was not a survey of microfoundations, but of general equilibrium. Microfoundations was a much broader topic. Rejection was recommended on the grounds that the paper was more suitable for *Econometrica* than for the *Journal of Economic Literature*. Despite this, and despite a second report recommending rejection on the grounds the paper would not make sense to a non-specialist, Perlman encouraged Weintraub to persist, telling him, on October 8, that the problem with the paper was that it was too concise and needed expanding. Weintraub responded to this, on November 10, by proposing to include a discussion of how economists had understood the problem of microfoundations and to expand his draft to explain the theories more fully. That draft was sent to Perlman on February 4, 1976, who then obtained five referee reports.

This time, the reaction was more positive, with reports that shed light on the way the topic was viewed. One, by Michio Morishima, at LSE, saw the popularity of the topic as a possible reason for publication, despite reservations about the paper that would cause him to reject it. However, he criticized the work that Weintraub was surveying on the grounds that it did not produce refutable results – he did not expect important result to be obtained and thought that there were many better articles than those that appeared in Weintraub's bibliography. An anonymous referee echoed the narrowness of the literature surveyed and questioned where the literature was leading:

Weintraub does not really broach the question "What will serious macroeconomists learn from all this?" Several leading macroeconomists have been aware of most of this work which Weintraub surveys and have been publicly (and, in the case of Harry Johnson, even more privately) skeptical of its ultimate worth.[16]

This was substantiated with two long quotations from Fischer (1975), and the observation that even Arrow and Hahn (1971) had shown that it was impossible "to tell a satisfactory tale about adjustment to equilibrium"

[16] Referee report dated March 18, 1976, page 1.

(ibid.:3). This referee and Morishima caused Weintraub to enter a further round of revisions, drawing on exchanges he had been having in the meantime with Jan Kregel and Don Patinkin, though this time in the belief that he would be producing the final draft. That was delivered on 30 August 1976. By this time, he was already in touch with an editor at Cambridge University Press about the expanded version of the article that was to be published under the title, *Microfoundations: The Compatibility of Microeconomics and Macroeconomics* (1979).

"The Microfoundations of Macroeconomics: A Critical Survey" argued boldly that general equilibrium theory offered a framework that was sufficiently broad to encompass both macroeconomics and microeconomics: "So viewed, general equilibrium theory is coextensive with the theory of the microfoundations of macroeconomics" (Weintraub 1977:1–2). However, this time, the theories that it could integrate were framed differently, as (1) the allocation of given outputs, (2) the determination of the level of output through aggregate supply and demand analysis,[17] and (3) the theory of distribution. The link was that, whichever problem was being tackled, it was necessary to confront questions of multi-market equilibrium. Weintraub explicitly rejected narrow conceptions of general equilibrium theory, such as the theory of perfectly competitive equilibrium. For him, "*a general equilibrium model is simply some specification of states of the world and a set of rules that structure the manner in which those states change over time*" (Weintraub 1977:2, emphasis in original). It thus made complete sense to use general equilibrium theory to analyze the microfoundations of macroeconomics, even though such an association might, he recognized, "induce cognitive dissonance in some economists" (ibid.).

After framing his objective in this way, instead of starting with the discussion of systems, Weintraub this time started with a long section (five-and-a-half pages) on the history of the microfoundations of Keynesian economics, in which Patinkin played the key role as laying down the standard view that Keynesian economics was the economics of disequilibrium and his analysis of disequilibrium in the labor market being taken up and developed by Clower. In an interesting juxtaposition, Weintraub then argued that Sidney Weintraub (1957, 1958), Leijonhufvud (1968), and Edmund Phelps (1970) all questioned, in different ways, whether Keynesian economics as the term had come to be understood, was indeed consistent with Keynes's economics. After showing, through a series of examples, that the Arrow-Debreu model *could* be developed to incorporate expectations and uncertainty, he turned

---

[17] This was one of Sidney Weintraub's ideas.

to an argument made by Jan Kregel, with whom he had been engaged in correspondence while revising his paper, that models of individual choice were incapable of explaining macroeconomic phenomena. Some "post Keynesians" (a term he attributed to Kregel [1973]) used a notion of explanation that could be traced to the adoption of a Marshallian approach.[18] The details of this argument are of less significance than is Weintraub's response (1977:8), which was to defend general equilibrium theory. The Marshallian approach could explain neither inter-relations between markets nor why certain institutional structures were likely to emerge; in contrast, general equilibrium theory had achievements to its credit (though these were left somewhat vague).

The result was that a paper that Morishima, in his referee report, had criticized for failing to express its author's point of view now offered a clear thesis: that general equilibrium theory was the way forward in microeconomics, but that it needed to be "sufficiently rich and flexible to phrase, and suggest answers to, questions that can also be posed using a Marshallian logic" (Weintraub 1977:8). The problem of the microfoundations of macroeconomics had been reformulated as the problem of how to design a suitable general equilibrium model. The stage was thus set for the survey of recent developments in general equilibrium theory that showed how richer and more flexible models were being developed, classified in a way that echoed work going back to his thesis, as Walrasian equilibrium and disequilibrium, and as Edgeworthian equilibrium and disequilibrium, a distinction also used by Schwödiauer (1978).

RECONSIDERING THE THEORY OF UNEMPLOYMENT

Of the all the surveys of the literature on the microfoundations of macroeconomics, the one that was most widely cited was a slim volume by Edmond Malinvaud, *The Theory of Unemployment Reconsidered* (1977b) based on the Yrjö Jahnsson Lectures delivered January 1976. Malinvaud was a senior figure at several of the institutions in Paris where research on macroeconomics was undertaken.[19] When a student in Paris, at the École Polytechnique and the École Nationale de la Statistique et de l'Administration Économique (ENSAE), Malinvaud had been part of an informal group (that also included Debreu) centered on Maurice Allais. He was a guest of the Cowles Commission in 1950–51, where he met Debreu, then a research assistant

---

[18] Recall that at this time, Clower and Leijonhufvud were arguing for a Marshallian approach to macroeconomics (see Chapter 6 of this book).

[19] Most biographical information is taken from Krueger (2003).

there, with whom he subsequently kept in touch. He then made his career at the Institut national de la statistique et des études économiques (INSEE) and the École nationale de la statistique et de l'administration, with visiting positions at Berkeley in 1961 and 1967. Particularly important was his role in running, with René Roy, the seminar that brought together economists from different parts of Paris.

Malinvaud has since recalled that, while at the Cowles Commission, and possibly for some time after, he had disagreements with Debreu over the relations between microeconomics and macroeconomics. Debreu's position was that general equilibrium would provide the general model, which could be aggregated as necessary for specific problems. Against this, Malinvaud "thought that he was seriously underestimating the distance from the general equilibrium theory of Arrow and Debreu to the actual macroeconomic problems" (Krueger 2003: 190).

Before the mid-1970s, Malinvaud was well known for his contributions to capital accumulation and resource allocation, econometrics, and for a highly successful graduate microeconomics textbook (Malinvaud 1953, 1966, 1972). Nevertheless, as recalled in an interview given to Alan Krueger (2003:189–90), starting in 1957, he taught macroeconomics at INSEE, where he covered Keynes's theory of temporary equilibrium. He remembers that he found the theory incomplete, mainly for failing to give adequate account of the role of business profitability (Krueger 2003:191). In 1962, he took part in the International Economic Association (IEA) conference during which Clower's (1965) paper was first presented and, like many others, including Patinkin, did not appreciate the implications of Clower's approach at the time (see Brechling's [1965:305] record of the debates). The disequilibrium theories developed by others in the early 1970s provided the theory for which he was looking and on which he drew in his Jahnsson lectures:

When I saw the work that was done on fixed price general equilibrium by people like Barro, Bénassy, Grandmont, Grossman, Laroque and Younes, I realized that it provided precisely what I was up to, namely a model to explain the respective roles of wage push shocks and aggregate demand shocks on changes in employment. This is what I tried to explain in my 1977 monograph.

He was actively involved in discussions of the theories being developed by Grandmont, Laroque, and Younès in the mid-1970s, through the Roy-Malinvaud seminar. As mentioned earlier, Younès (1975) went so far as to claim Malinvaud should be considered a co-author of a paper that appeared under his own name. In fact, Malinvaud's later recollection (1987:229) was that his decision to contribute to this literature was heavily influenced by Younès.

Faced with the macroeconomic problems that emerged after 1973, Malinvaud decided that the work of his colleagues (he cited Bénassy, Grandmont, Laroque, and Younès), together with that of Barro and Grossman provided "a model to explain the respective roles of wage push shocks and aggregate demand shocks on changes in employment" (Krueger 2003:191).

Although Malinvaud proceeded to analyze a general equilibrium with rationing, he chose not to describe it as a disequilibrium model:

> The objection [to general equilibrium analysis of involuntary unemployment] comes from a misunderstanding of what general equilibrium analysis really is. Economists have been brought up to think that the very notion of equilibrium implies that, for each commodity, supply must equal demand, which of course cannot be the case for labour if some involuntary unemployment remains. But a general equilibrium is an abstract construct that has no logical obligation to assume equality between supply and demand. (Malinvaud 1977b:5)

He argued against using the term "disequilibrium analysis," saying that it was "plain equilibrium analysis, but operating with a specific concept of equilibrium" (Malinvaud 1977b: 5–6). The alternative was a dynamic model, which would be very difficult to formulate and to handle: it would raise at least as many questions as would equilibrium analysis. General equilibrium provided a shortcut.

Malinvaud then proceeded to justify the modeling strategy of taking prices as given. He pointed to empirical evidence that, for many commodities, quantities adjusted first (order books, waiting lines, inventories, delivery dates, and so on) but then he also followed Drèze in pointing to theoretical reasons why prices might respond slowly. Given later developments in macroeconomics, it is significant that he cited Phelps et al. (1970). He then proceeded to offer a model, simplified by setting coefficients equal to unity wherever possible, similar to those used by Barro and Grossman and Bénassy discussed previously in Chapter 5.

Like Barro, Grossman, and Bénassy, Malinvaud analyzed macroeconomic disequilibrium in terms of three regimes, introducing the terminology of "Keynesian unemployment" (excess supply in both commodity and labor markets), "classical unemployment" (excess supply of labor and excess demand for commodities) and "inflation" (excess demand in both markets).

The lecture ended with the classification of equilibria into Keynesian, classical and repressed inflation, previously offered by Barro and Grossman.

Using diagrams, such as Figure 8.2,[20] Malinvaud explored the effects of changes in exogenous variables, and showed why classical unemployment

---

[20] See Malinvaud (1977) p. 96. This can be compared with Figure 5.3 in Chapter 5.

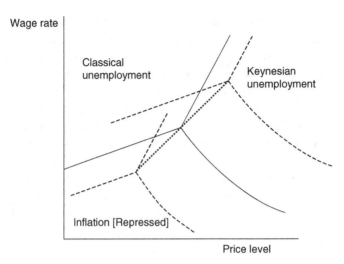

Figure 8.2. Malinvaud's explanation of Keynesian unemployment

was observed less frequently than the other two regimes: fluctuations in aggregate demand (in his view the most common source of disturbance) would shift the Walrasian equilibrium, along with the other curves, up and down, approximately along a ray from the origin. If prices and wages were sticky, and the real wage remained close to its long-run values, the economy would move between Keynesian unemployment and inflation, as shown in Figure 8.2.[21] He then explored the consequences of the real wage being too low, of wages and prices responding more quickly in response to excess demand than to excess supply, and why unemployment in 1976–77 was classical (essentially that there had been a large, negative productivity shock). Of particular significance, by analyzing the effects of productivity shocks and changes in oil prices, Malinvaud was able to argue that the model was able to account for the stagflation episode of the 1970s. His ideas about medium-term dynamics, involving changes in prices and wages, were developed further in his Marshall Lectures, delivered in Cambridge in 1978, and published as *Profitability and Unemployment* (1980). During the 1980s, concepts of Keynesian and classical unemployment were used to analyze the problem of unemployment, prominent examples of such work including Bruno and Sachs (1985) and Coen and Hickman (1987).

---

[21] All that is necessary for this result is that fluctuations are on a line that is less steep than the two positively sloped boundaries in Figure 8.2.

In focusing on what he called "fixed-price general-equilibrium analysis", Malinvaud turned away from both dynamic adjustments to equilibrium. This took him away from Clower's and Leijonhufvud's notion that non-clearing markets states have self-reinforcing tendencies ("deviation-amplifying"). As pointed out by Alan Coddington (1983:33), Clower (1965) had discussed the consequences of being in disequilibrium and the difficulties of getting out of that state, not how an economy gets into disequilibrium in the first place. This contrasts with Malinvaud (1977), where other arrangements (rationing of goods) fulfill the function that relative prices would otherwise carry out and take the pressure off relative prices (Coddington 1983:33). It also took Malinvaud away from imperfect competition, used by Bénassy to provide an account of how prices were set.

SURVEYING TEMPORARY GENERAL EQUILIBRIUM THEORY: GRANDMONT

In the same year, Jean-Michel Grandmont (1977) provided another survey of the field, offering a slightly different perspective, perhaps not surprisingly, given that it was published in *Econometrica*. His starting point was clear – the Arrow-Debreu model of general competitive equilibrium. This model, he argued, was useful as a benchmark but it failed to account for important features of the real world, including money, active stock markets, and the fact that some adjustments were made by quantity rationing. Expectations of an imperfectly known future were important and were being handled by theorists in ways that were developments of the temporary equilibrium approach adopted by Hicks (1939) and Patinkin (1965). However, though much work had been done, Grandmont (1977:537) concluded that "the subject has not yet reached a degree of maturation which permits the statement of the theory in a general and concise way." Instead, he chose to focus on a number of specific issues.

Where Grandmont departed from other surveys was that, in examining the logic of temporary equilibrium, he placed more emphasis on dynamics – on sequences of temporary equilibria. This provided, he argued, a suitable framework within which to explain why money was used, and to think rigorously about the quantity theory of money, as formulated by Patinkin. Though he did not discuss the macroeconomic literature associated with Lucas, he incorporated rational expectations through modeling sequences of temporary equilibria as stochastic processes.

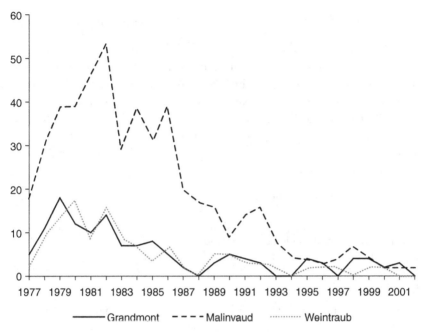

Figure 8.3. Citations of Grandmont (1977), Malinvaud (1977), and Weintraub (1977, 1979)
Source: Social Science Citation Index.

Grandmont's was a survey of the technical issues associated with temporary general equilibrium theory, engaging with much work that lies outside the concern of this book.[22] However, its significance lies in the fact that he was presenting a framework that could, he argued, incorporate quantity rationing and "disequilibrium" alongside rigorous treatments of money, financial assets, and rational expectations. They were all part of a coherent strategy for going beyond the Arrow-Debreu model. So, despite its title, the focus of Grandmont's survey was disequilibria, as it looked at temporary equilibria with predetermined prices and wages, with ensuing quantity rationing (see Grandmont 1977, sec. 4, on "Temporary Equilibria with Quantity Rationing").

These three surveys were all widely cited, as shown in Figure 8.3. Neither Weintraub's nor Grandmont's, however, was as widely cited as Malinvaud's survey, cited 499 times during the period.

---

[22] This includes Hahn's work on money and general equilibrium and that of Roy Radner on sequence economies.

DEBATING MICROFOUNDATIONS: RESPONDING TO
WEINTRAUB AND MALINVAUD

The range of attitudes to disequilibrium theory can be seen by considering the responses to the books by Weintraub and Malinvaud.[23] The clear-
est response came from those Keynesians who were beginning to use the
term "Post Keynesian" to describe their own work. As the son of Sidney
Weintraub, knowing many of his correspondents as family friends,
Weintraub was in the thick of it. He expressed this forcefully in a April 2,
1976, letter to Perlman:

> For your personal information, this has been the most difficult thing I've ever
> attempted because of my naive belief that intellectual vested interests were strong
> only in my family. Left, right, center all have sent me encouragement about how
> much better a piece it would be if I only took the trouble to really understand their
> implicit message. In this vein I have been literally disinherited and disowned for
> this survey, "an obscene act of public parricide." As Voneggut says, however, "and
> so it goes."

A day earlier, on April 1, 1976, he had made a similar remark to Patinkin:

> My "Microfoundations . . ." survey paper seems to be causing more of a reaction than
> I had expected. The Post-Keynesian group (Kregel, Davidson, S. Weintraub, etc.)
> have written me and then written me off, the monetarists who refereed the piece at
> first pass at the JEL saw grievous error everywhere, and now, with your comments, I
> see that as written the survey can't hold the Keynesian center either. I am beginning
> to suspect that what I am trying to do cannot be done in 30–40 pages.

Kregel is included in this list, for he was certainly a skeptic about general
equilibrium theory,[24] but in an April 20, 1976, letter to Weintraub, he nonetheless saw value in Weintraub's survey and sympathized with his position:

> I can quite understand how you can get upset by people rabbiting on about Walras,
> etc. when there is a really rather GE or systems theory that you'd rather they were
> talking about (It's sort of like the people who attribute all sorts of things to Keynes
> that he never said or thought and which I get upset about). But there still are people
> who have not yet gotten the message (Harry G. [Johnson] is one that I can think
> of right off hand) and given this fact I think I would consider your survey justified,
> perhaps more than that.

---

[23] Because both surveys were published as books that were widely reviewed, it is possible to
document reactions to Malinvaud's and Weintraub's surveys in a way that is not possible
with ones that were only published in journals.

[24] As an undergraduate in Bristol, in the year when Weintraub was writing his unpublished
book manuscript, Backhouse remembers being told by Kregel that Weintraub was writing
a book on general equilibrium theory, even though general equilibrium theory was hope-
lessly out of date.

In the same letter, Kregel explained that his objection was to the fact that in this entire literature, "disequilibrium transactions, information, decentralised institutions etc are discussed outside the context of money and production." He added that he could not forget an occasion when Clower lectured for a week on "monetary" problems without mentioning money or production and then confessed he was not sure how to include them.

Not surprisingly, Hahn, a general equilibrium theorist who had contributed to the literature being surveyed, was much more favorable, and when the expanded version of the survey (Weintraub 1979) appeared, he praised it, noting that it sought a bridge between general equilibrium theory and Keynesian economics. While he praised the book's treatment of short-period equilibria, Drèze equilibria, and Patinkin, however, he criticized it for serious omissions, notably implicit contracts and other theories of labor market disequilibrium, and rational expectations.

John Hicks (1979) responded to Weintraub's expanded survey in typically Hicksian fashion, by reflecting on his own work, and introducing new terminology. He suggested that the real issue cut across the micro-macro divide and concerned the type of microeconomics that was needed to support Keynesian ideas: what was missing was micro-Keynesianism (Hicks 1979:1452). He claimed that Weintraub had begun to catch sight of this in two places. One was his discussion of what Hicks though to be Keynes's "rather wicked" chapter 12 on the irreducibility of uncertainty to mathematics, but the more important place was where, at the end of the book, he turned to "Edgeworthian disequilibrium." The analysis surveyed by Weintraub, though highly abstract, led to the conclusion that in a world in which it is not possible for everyone to know everything about everyone else with whom he or she might be engaging in trade, there is a need for both intermediaries and a unit of account (money). He then suggested, echoing the remarks that Kregel had made privately to Weintraub, that there was a need to consider credit, capital markets and the issue of trust between individuals.

There was a similar range of responses to Malinvaud's lectures, though there was much stronger criticism, presumably because, through presenting highly specific, simplified model, Malinvaud was offering a much clearer target. Although aimed at the specific model, much of this criticism was addressed to the literature as a whole. One of the more enthusiastic reviewers, writing in the *Economic Journal*, was James Mirrlees (1978), later to win the a Nobel Memorial Prize for work on principal-agent theory. He was, however, critical of Malinvaud's conclusions. Citing Hahn's work (presumably on conjectural equilibria), he pointed out that it was not difficult to change the assumptions to produce models in which several equilibria are possible. Christopher Green (1978), reviewing the book in the *Canadian Journal of Economics*, argued that Malinvaud should have questioned the concept of involuntary unemployment, the 1930s meaning of which had, be claimed, become empty. Alan Coddington (1978), in a very long review discussed at greater length later in this chapter, despite clearly considering the book to address fundamental problems, questioned whether it was appropriate to analyze the consequence of sticky prices independently of their causes. This was a fundamental feature of the disequilibrium macroeconomic literature.

Richard Kahn (1977), a prominent member of the original "Cambridge Circus" in the early 1930s, attacked the association between sticky prices and unemployment. In particular, according to Kahn, Malinvaud's "classical unemployment" derived from the assumed coexistence of diminished returns with sticky mark-up pricing through the business cycle. Kahn claimed that sticky prices are typical of firms that operate with increasing returns. In the end, Malinvaud's classical unemployment disappears and the only determinant of unemployment is effective demand.

The strongest criticism of Malinvaud came from Melvin Reder, a Chicago economist, in the *Journal of Political Economy*:

What is missing are variables reflecting the anticipation of future wages, prices and (future) quantity constraints (on the sale of labor and the purchase of goods) as well as the relation of actual initial stocks of goods and money to desired levels of these stocks. The states of these omitted variables influence the short-run behavior of the endogenous variables as much or more than the variables explicitly considered. Moreover, movements in actual and anticipated values of wages, prices, and perceived quantity constraints will never be mutually independent.[25] Therefore, Malinvaud's careful derivation of individual supply and demand functions ... is simply an algebraic exercise. The effect of anticipations of future wage rates, product prices, and quantity constraints are built into the (static) supply and demand functions, whose shapes and positions will vary with these anticipations. Also, variations in the current values of these variables will impact upon their anticipated values so that short-run equilibria depend upon variables not included in the model. (Reder 1979:664–65)

This passage is quoted at length because it sums up, very concisely, the objections to Keynesian theorizing, of which Malinvaud's is representative, that were being made by Robert Lucas and the new classical macroeconomics.

---

[25] A paragraph break has been omitted at this point.

After his 1977 book, Malinvaud continued for a few years to contribute to fixed-price general equilibrium analysis, especially in connection with the notion of "classical unemployment" and the modeling of the effects of supply shocks (Malinvaud 1980, 1982). It was at that time that Malinvaud published in French a macroeconomic textbook, revised and translated in three volumes from 1998 through 2000. Volume two included a chapter on "unemployment and price rigidity" (Malinvaud 1998:879–910), which reproduced the basic ideas of the 1977 book. Hence, although Malinvaud continued to explain unemployment along the lines of his fixed-price model, he did not develop it beyond the ideas introduced in the mid-1970s. Malinvaud (1998:957–66) discussed some of the literature on the connection between imperfect competition and macroeconomic disequilibrium (see Bénassy 1993), reaching the conclusion that it renders the model too complicated to generate clear policy conclusions and is to a great extent not compatible with notion of disequilibrium unemployment. That is why he believed purely fixed-price models provided a better starting point, as clarified in the 2003 interview:

It's very difficult to have something which would be closer to the actual operation of competition in the economy than assuming exogenous prices ... Difficult for formulation the model in a persuasive way, for studying comparative statics properties that would be relevant ... that would be appropriate to the study of the short-term or medium-term macroeconomic phenomena. (Malinvaud interview in Krueger 2003:192)

Malinvaud recognized that the disequilibrium approach had limitations but had nonetheless been useful. Going beyond the disequilibrium approach involved tackling problems in which the difficulty went beyond those involved in endogenizing prices or incorporating imperfect competition:

It is true that the research line explored by Barro and Grossman, my two monographs and a number of European colleagues 20 years ago, proved to be little rewarding for these colleagues. ... My own conclusion is that the research in question enlightened our understanding of macroeconomic disequilibria. ... But further progress at the same overall level is very, very difficult to achieve. That's what I tried to say about imperfect competition, but it is more general. (Malinvaud interview in Krueger 2003:192–93)

Mirrlees adopted a similar position. He was critical of Malinvaud's model, claiming that the results Malinvaud obtained were less general than readers might assume, but concluded that the book "shows what the new macroeconomics is all about, and should set further work off in the right directions" (Mirrlees 1978:159).

Malinvaud has subsequently made it clear that he considered a sales constraint to be an integral part of Keynesian economics and advanced the criticism that economists often put forward models of imperfect competition that did not involve one.[26] He did not see the distinction between new Keynesian and disequilibrium macroeconomics as crucially important, since the rationalization of price and wage stickiness should be understood as a complement to, not as a substitute for, non-market clearing analysis. In particular, the widespread notion that inflation in the 1970s and 1980s made the sticky prices hypothesis incredible was not warranted, Malinvaud believed, in view of the then current ideas about cost-push inflation and price expectations once an inflationary spiral is in place.

As someone who had written an influential appraisal of Keynesian economics, containing the conclusion that "for a generation brought up on Keynesian ideas ... a sense of intellectual liberation" was "far more likely" to come from the approach associated with Clower and Leijonhufvud than from "fundamentalist" Keynesianism (Coddington 1976:1272), Coddington might be thought likely to have endorsed Malinvaud's book wholeheartedly. Yet, he was critical, raising objections that are worth discussing at length because they reflect reactions that, if less clearly articulated, were increasingly being levied against disequilibrium macroeconomics:

The basic presupposition of the approach to which Malinvaud's three lectures provide an introduction is that it is both possible and useful to analyze the consequences of sticky prices independently of their causes. That is: it is a worthwhile analytical tactic to work with prices that are given in the short-run, without attempting to provide any explanation of what determines them, or why they are not responding more rapidly to market conditions. The problems of price adjustment are then acknowledged but side-stepped by appealing to the longer-run model in which price changes have eliminated all excess demands: the familiar model of Walrasian equilibrium. Like any analytical tactic that promises to yield tractable problems, it is worth trying provided we are fully aware of its limitations. (Coddington 1978:1017)

Here, he clearly states the analytical strategy being followed, of breaking down complex adjustment processes into two stages, the first involving considering the consequences of sticky prices apart from their causes, leaving the explanation of price changes to later. He then went on to note that this strategy necessarily introduced an element of dysfunction into the economic system, which was not necessarily justified. "Friction" or "inertia" might be a rational response to the ambiguity of market signals and the

---

[26] Correspondence with the authors, April 27, 2005,

difficulty in discriminating sustained changes in economic conditions from ones that were transient. He also noted that whereas Malinvaud's approach presumed that there was too little price adjustment, it was possible that misreading of transient changes might lead to excessive price adjustment. The problem was that like the IS-LM model it was intended to displace, Malinvaud's model was static:

any construction based on single-period decision models for households and firms cannot accommodate a distinction between transient and sustained changes. The Malinvaud approach shares this limitation with other methods that attempt to analyze a process of adjustment by conceiving of the process as being in a state of suspended animation. In particular, it shares the limitation with that indispensable method of analyzing cyclical movements by ignoring the fact that there is a cycle: the IS-LM model. (Coddington 1978:1017–18)

Although phrased rather differently, and not citing other work, Coddington was offering a critique of disequilibrium macroeconomics that reflected very closely the concerns that motivated those involved in the Phelps volume (Phelps et al. 1970) and the new classical macroeconomists (discussed earlier in Chapter 6). He can be read as arguing not just that disequilibrium models are problematic, but that the theoretical strategy on which they are based is necessarily limiting.

Across the Atlantic, criticisms were more forthright. Green, though finding interest in Malinvaud's discussion (in his third lecture) of why, though unemployment had been Keynesian in 1975 (there being excess supply in labor and product markets), classical unemployment (excess supply of labor accompanied by excess demand for products) might emerge once demand picked up. However, despite this, he concluded that the book was limited in that it "reconsidered" unemployment "only within the narrow framework of the old Keynesian-classical debate." He listed several factors that Malinvaud ignored, from the political business cycle to job-search theories, before noting that "at no point is the concept of involuntary unemployment questioned, although the 1930s meaning is almost empty today" (Green 1978:777).

Reder, though he used many of the same arguments as Coddington and Green, drew much more critical conclusions. Rather than simply observing that Malinvaud's model was too static, he argued that the omitted variables (expected values of future wages, prices and quantity constraints, and relations between actual and desired stocks) were as important, and possibly more important, than the variables Malinvaud considered. Moreover, movements in actual and anticipated values would "*never* be mutually independent" as Malinvaud's method assumed (Reder 1979:664, italics added). Short-period equilibrium had to be derived from "an ongoing dynamic process." Like Coddington, he noted that prices might overreact to market signals:

Moreover, as recent microtheory has been at much pains to show, sticky wages and prices may arise from individual optimization under long-term contracts, either implicit or explicit, as well as from government fiat. Contractually induced price rigidity may be more or less responsive (to market forces) than (say) governmentally decreed prices, and attempts by private parties to set prices and wages in a manner inconsistent with arbitrarily assigned levels could generate behavior well outside anything considered in Malinvaud's model. (Reder 1979:667)

It is worth noting that, like Barro (see Chapter 6 of this book), Reder is here stressing long-term contracts (as well as government regulation) as the cause of rigidities; the idea that disequilibrium has to be modeled because, as Arrow, Hahn, and others had argued, the model of perfect competition was logically incomplete, was lost from view. He concludes by contending that Malinvaud's short-run model was either "the taxonomic framework for a familiar kind of macroeconomic policy characterized by Abba Lerner's parable of the 'Economic Steering Wheel'" or "simply a formal exercise, albeit an elegant one" (Reder 1979, p. 669). Either way, it was of little interest from his perspective.

SURVEYING MACROECONOMIC DISEQUILIBRIUM THEORY: DRAZEN

In 1980, *Econometrica* published a second survey of the field, focusing more narrowly on disequilibrium theory. The origin of this article goes back to Stanley Fischer. Fischer obtained his Ph.D. from MIT in 1969, the year after Solow and Stiglitz (who was in the previous year's class) published their paper in the *Quarterly Journal of Economics*. When Patinkin visited MIT, Fischer was his assistant, and the two kept in contact. Fischer had the idea that there should be a survey of the literature on disequilibrium macroeconomics presented at the 1978 summer meeting of the Econometric Society, and he invited Allan Drazen, who had obtained his Ph.D. from MIT in 1976, to write one. Although claiming not to know anything about the subject at that point, Drazen jumped at the opportunity to present a paper at what was a small and exclusive conference.[27] The paper was favorably received, and Robert Gordon, his discussant, who was in the editorial board

---

[27] The source is an e-mail from Drazen, September 3, 2010. He says that Fischer approached him six months before the meetings, which were held in June.

of *Econometrica,* suggested that he submit the paper there, which Drazen did in August, only two months after the June meeting.

Drazen opened his survey by pointing out that what he called "the pioneering work in macroeconomic disequilibrium theory" by Patinkin, Clower, Barro and Grossman, and others had "been succeeded by an outburst of theoretical work by Hahn, Bénassy, Grandmont, and others" (Drazen 1980:283). His view was that skepticism about such work arose from ignorance: many economists outside the field of general equilibrium theory either did not know about this work or did not understand it. Thus, where economists such as Coddington or Reder saw the disequilibrium literature as oversimplified, missing what might be crucial phenomena, Drazen believed that the general equilibrium theorists were in the process of developing answers to many of the questions that the pioneering work had left unanswered. His role was to make this more complex theory accessible to a wider audience (though presumably not that wide an audience, given that the paper was published in *Econometrica*).[28]

Drazen started by surveying the early work. Agreeing with many of the critics of disequilibrium macroeconomics he argued that the crucial question was not what happens when prices were fixed, but why prices do not move. Because of their failure to address this, he concluded, like Coddington and Green, that the Barro and Grossman model was "similar to earlier interpretations of Keynes which used wage rigidity to prove the existence of an unemployment equilibrium" (Drazen 1980:286). In contrast, Leijonhufvud offered interesting and suggestive ideas, without providing rigorous analysis or operationalizing his concepts. "What looks promising often fails to be convincing on slightly closer examination, and we are left, once again, with exogenous price inflexibility" (ibid.). Thus, he was able to conclude that, "in spite of Clower's brilliant contribution" much of the pioneering work "ends up sounding like early interpretations of Keynes," leaving unanswered the fundamental question of whether unemployment equilibrium is simply the result of wage rigidity.

From here, Drazen went into the general equilibrium literature (much of which was discussed earlier in Chapter 7). He began with distinction between Drèze-equilibrium, in which constrained demands depend on constraints in *all* markets, including the market in question, and

---

[28] It is not surprising that Drazen does not cite these critics of disequilibrium macroeconomics, most of whose views were expressed in reviews of Malinvaud's book. What is more surprising is his failure to cite Weintraub (1977). Drazen explains this by saying that he probably did not know about the article but that if he did, the explanation is probably that he saw his own paper as technical, and so cited the more technical literature.

Bénassy-equilibrium, in which constrained demands depend only on constraints in *other* markets. This immediately presented agents as responding to market signals rather than constrained by arbitrary rules. Discussion of rationing schemes leads on to the question of the conditions under which agents' desire to "break" the constraints they face will be consistent with equilibrium.[29] Given this focus on individual choices, the survey proceeded naturally to models where prices are endogenous. Observing that much of this literature cited the remarks of Arrow (1959) that were discussed in Chapter 7, this took Drazen into various models of imperfect competition, including, inter alia, Negishi, Bénassy, Hahn, Grandmont, and Laroque.

Based on such work, Drazen drew several conclusions. Perhaps his fundamental conclusion was that the idea of a conjectural equilibrium, in which agents have no incentive to change their prices given their conjectures about the market conditions they face, *did* provide an alternative to sticky wages as an explanation of unemployment. Drawing extensively on Hahn (1977, 1978), he explored the question of what it meant for conjectures to be rational, and whether rational conjectures could support a non-Walrasian equilibrium (with unemployment). He left open the question, perhaps crucial to the literature, of whether the "disappointing" nature of the results that had been obtained reflected "an underlying problem with rational conjectural equilibrium" or "the fact that work is just beginning in an extraordinarily difficult area" (Drazen 1980:296).

Drazen also explored the possibility that models of imperfect competition with perceived demand curves might solve long-standing problems in monetary economics. He quickly dismissed the idea, taken up by Clower (1967), that money acts as a constraint on transactions, arguing that it is "the nonsynchronous nature of trading" that leads to the use of money. This is linked to the literature under review because, he pointed out, it is also what leads to quantity-constrained equilibria. Drazen claimed that the literature was under-developed because, although none of the existing models of price dynamics was satisfactory, and although monopolistic competition was the most promising route, "As far as I know, there has been almost no work on convergence and dynamics in non-Walrasian models with monopolistic price setting" (Drazen 1980:303).[30] His conclusion was that the dynamics of non-Walrasian models was an open area meriting further work.

---

[29] Equilibrium in the sense of a fixed point of the system, not in the sense of a point where supply and demand are equal.

[30] The sole exception he cited was Fisher (1976).

Drazen's conclusion about disequilibrium theory was that though it had "advanced our understanding", much work remained to be done, for some of the results had been disappointing. One can only conclude that it was the hope that further work would solve the outstanding problems that led to an optimistic appraisal of the literature.

Reformulating equilibrium theory à la Clower and Hahn (to whose work on conjectural equilibrium this paper owes a large debt) indicates that Keynesian theory may be the more general theory after all, and it may, after all these years, give a sound basis to macroeconomics. (Drazen 1980:304)

Perhaps that conclusion reflected the enthusiasm of a young economist surveying a field created by his elders, and on which he had not previously worked, because he did not publish further papers on macroeconomic disequilibrium theory: after trying to work further in the field, he concluded that the approach was less promising than he had thought.

CONCLUSION

After the publication of the Barro-Grossman (1971) model, there was an explosion of literature on disequilibrium theory, illustrated by Figure 8.4. Citations of Lucas (1972) are shown as a benchmark, along with a count of the number of papers in JSTOR that use the words "microfoundations" and "macroeconomics."[31] The first point to note is that from 1973 to 1978, Barro and Grossman were more frequently cited than Lucas, and from 1978 to 1988, citations of Malinvaud closely matched those of Lucas. Also noticeable is the rise in the use of the label "microfoundations," following Roy Weintraub's survey. Although microfoundations could be interpreted in different ways, as was evident from the International Economic Association conference reported in Harcourt (1977), it came to be interpreted, as it had been at the Vienna conference, as relating to the relationship between macroeconomics and general equilibrium theory.

The most widely cited exposition of disequilibrium theory at the end of the 1970s was Malinvaud (1977).[32] Why was this? Clearly, the exposition was very elegant, rendering the discussion of rationing schemes, and the relationship between micro and macro, more accessible than in previous accounts: it was addressed to the general economist in a way that

---

[31] This could be improved by adding more linguistic variations, but this is sufficient to indicate the trend. This series has been smoothed by taking a three-year moving average. Citation counts are not smoothed.

[32] See Figure 8.2 earlier in the chapter.

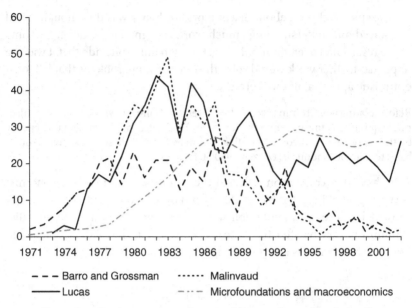

Figure 8.4. Citations counts and usage of the term "microfoundations"

Grandmont (1977), Drazen (1980), and even Weintraub (1977) were not. He also introduced the widely used terminology of Keynesian and classical unemployment (reflecting the fact that it was part of a fixed-price model, the third regime came to be called "repressed inflation"). It will also, no doubt, have been important that he presented the theory offering an explanation of what had happened during the 1970s, something that other authors, writing before stagflation had set in, could not do.

Although Drazen (1980) devoted a section of his survey to "Models with Endogenous Price Setting," and Weintraub (1977) discussed Edgeworthian models, the main focus of surveys was on models with fixed prices. No doubt this was because the distinctive feature of these models was taken to be the way quantity constraints could generate equilibria with unsatisfactory properties. One result of this was to make it easier to see these models as dealing with the consequences of institutionally determined price and wage rigidities rather than as steps toward a more general theory of price adjustment. This reduced interest in the theory because, although Malinvaud claimed that models of equilibrium with rationing were needed to make sense of stagflation, a much more common response was to take the view that markets appeared to be fairly competitive and that the assumption of price-rigidity did not make sense in a world where one of the major macroeconomic problems was rapid inflation. Although for Clower, Leijonhufvud, Hahn, Negishi, Bénassy, Grandmont, and Laroque, amongst others, the search for non-Walrasian microfoundations had been motivated by a concern to find a more general, logically consistent and more realistic theory of market processes than was offered by Walrasian theory, and though they had developed models of price setting (which inevitably involved an element of imperfect competition), these were sidelined. The result was that non-Walrasian, or "disequilibrium" theory lost out to the new classical macroeconomics of Lucas and those who followed him in using market-clearing models.

NINE

After the 1970s

A common perception is that disequilibrium macroeconomics was very rapidly displaced by equilibrium, market-clearing models inspired by Phelps and Lucas. This is symbolized by the fact that, as documented previously in Chapter 6, Barro and Grossman, the two economists most closely associated with it, abandoned the approach. The change in Barro's reputation from being one of the leading exponents of macroeconomic disequilibrium modeling to being one of the leading new classical macroeconomists was particularly dramatic. However, as Figure 8.2 suggests, interest in disequilibrium theory continued through the 1980s and into the 1990s. This chapter outlines the form that interest took. It starts with an account of how the ideas of the pioneers, Patinkin, Clower, Leijonhufvud, Solow, and Stiglitz developed after the 1970s.

DEFENDING DISEQUILIBRIUM THEORY

Solow and Patinkin never abandoned disequilibrium macroeconomics. Solow has recently claimed that

After the Barro-Grossman book, and even more so after Edmond Malinvaud's little book [1977], I was one of the very few Americans who took that disequilibrium-macro line of thought seriously. (Barro and Grossman were not among them!) I used to teach it regularly in our basic graduate macro course; I never came across anyone else who did.[1]

Solow (1979:345) presented the disequilibrium macroeconomics as a way forward, augmenting it with a long explanation of why prices and wages might be sticky. He claimed that "the difference between the equilibrium

---

[1] Letter from Solow to the authors, July 12, 2004.

view and the disequilibrium view is not that in one theory agents are assumed to optimize and in the other they are not. The difference is in the constraints they are assumed to take into account."

So, by 2000, Solow stood out among U.S. economists in defending disequilibrium macroeconomics: "I hold the minority view that the fixed-price models of Malinvaud (1977) and Bénassy (1986) and others were never given a fair trial by American economists" (Solow 2000:152). (As explained earlier, European economists were generally more receptive to the idea that markets were typically not in equilibrium.) He suggested that the absence of an adequate account of how prices eventually move, plus related ambiguities about the concept of effective demand, were behind the negative verdict. In contrast, his own view (1979:346) was that stickiness of prices and wages remained a basic fact that should be part of macroeconomic models, regardless of the macroeconomists' inability to explain why they are sticky.

However, with the exception of the disequilibrium model he adapted from Solow and Stiglitz (1968) and Malinvaud (1977) to investigate the consequences of supply shocks (see Solow 1980), he did not try to develop the analysis of non-clearing markets. Indeed, in a book that reflected many years of collaboration with Frank Hahn, he pursued a different approach to developing an alternative to the new classical economics.[2] In response to the question of why he and Stiglitz did not do this, Solow responded that it was probably not an answerable question. It was almost tautological to say that they were both doing things that seemed more interesting and more exciting, though he concluded, "Of course if the 1968 paper had got other economists excited, I'm sure that we would have kept working at those disequilibrium-type problems. As I've said, I still think it's a real unsolved problem."[3] The nature of this "unsolved problem" was mentioned in Solow's reaction to Patinkin's new 1989 preface:

I always rather liked that stuff [Bénassy et al] and taught it when it was being ignored in American universities. Solow-Stiglitz (1968) lives on only in acknowledgments from Benassy and Grandmont, probably because we were concerned only with macro and not at all with micro-foundations... What version of "excess supply" creates effective pressure on wages and prices? The Benassy version is not very satisfactory, but nothing better has come along. It's a genuine problem for disequilibrium macroeconomics.[4]

---

[2] Hahn and Solow (1995) is discussed later in this chapter.
[3] Letter from Solow to the authors, July 12, 2004.
[4] Letter from Solow to Patinkin, June 14, 1989. Don Patinkin Papers, Box 62. Rubenstein Rare Book and Manuscript Library, Duke University.

Like Solow,[5] Patinkin ceased to be actively involved in research into disequilibrium macroeconomics. His work on applied economics relevant to Israel took much of his time, and he moved more and more into the history of Keynesian economics and the Chicago school (see Mehrling 2002; Backhouse 2002). However his commitment to keeping *Money, Interest and Prices* in print, a task that took considerable effort, and available to be used as a graduate textbook, and his clear statements about the importance of chapter 13, suggest that he remained sympathetic toward disequilibrium macroeconomics. In correspondence with Leijonhufvud of February 12, 1974, Patinkin informed him that "one of the things I want to get around to shortly... is to examine the recent developments in the theory of unemployment (namely, the work of Clower and yourself, and the literature to which that has given rise) in order to see if it provides an answer to the difficulties noted in the aforementioned footnote in my book." As mentioned in Chapter 3 above, Patinkin (1965:323n9) had been unable to explain why firms unable to sell all they want cannot find buyers by reducing their relative prices rather than accepting as given an absolute sales constraint, a problem he identified as the main stumbling block in the field of disequilibrium macro (see also Howitt 1990:10–11n12). A couple of years later, Patinkin drafted a "research proposal" titled "A Reexamination of Keynesian Economics,"[6] which listed the "theory of unemployment" as one of the items in the agenda:

One of the basic problems in the theory of unemployment is to explain the relationship between such unemployment and the profit-maximizing behavior of firms. Some years ago I expounded my own interpretation of this theory – but also indicated some unsolved problems that arose in connection with this interpretation (1965, chap. 13). In the past few years, this question has been treated from different viewpoints by Clower (1965, 1967), Davidson (1967), Grossman (1969), Barro and Grossman (1971, 1976), and others. I am not too satisfied with the solution that these economists have offered, and so am planning to return to the question with the hopes of being able to advance the analysis further. One of the basic questions that arise here is the analysis of an economy in disequilibrium – under which conditions one must reinterpret the role of *tâtonnement* and of Walras' Law. There are some serious analytical questions here which, to my mind, have not been solved.

However, with the exception of his entry on "Walras' Law" in *The New Palgrave – A Dictionary of Economics* (Patinkin 1987), Patinkin did not

---

[5] See also Solow's interview in Klamer (1983), where he argued that, despite its problems, the disequilibrium approach was the only alternative to Walrasian equilibrium.

[6] July 1976, pp. 3–4. Don Patinkin Papers, Box 43. Rubenstein Rare Book and Manuscript Library, Duke University.

succeed in his endeavors (Leijonhufvud is not listed in the last quotation because Patinkin intended to deal separately with the 1968 book, which "does not correctly represent Keynes' analysis"). The development of the fixed-price literature (Dreze, Bénassy, Malinvaud) did not help things either, as pointed out by Patinkin at the proceedings of a conference on "The Notion of Equilibrium in Keynesian Theory" organized by Mario Sebastiani in Perugia in 1987: "I looked at the development of the literature, what is called fixed-price and quantity restraints, as an attempt to deal with those problems, although frankly I still feel that some of the basic problems still remain."[7] The core of the problem was economic, not mathematical: "You can develop a whole complicated mathematical theory of quantity restraints, but in most of the literature I don't see the person going back to ask why the quantity restraint exist. Which was what bothered me and continues to bother me." In his introduction to the third edition of *Money, Interest and Prices* (1989:xx), Patinkin argued that the new classical economists had rejected disequilibrium macroeconomics because it seemingly violates the assumption of rational economic behavior, but that this situation had changed with the arrival of new Keynesian economics in the 1980s, which "on the basis of various assumptions, has rationalized the seemingly irrational." Patinkin had in mind the assumption of imperfect competition plus efficiency-wage theory, and referred to the survey by Stanley Fischer (1988), with whom he still kept in touch.[8]

In the 1989 introduction Patinkin also mentioned his argument, against Clower (1965) that a proper formulation (that is, one that takes into account quantity constraints) of Walras' Law holds in all situations, not just in equilibrium (see Patinkin 1987). That entry was Patinkin's first printed incursion into disequilibrium macroeconomics since *Money, Interest and Prices*. As Patinkin explained in correspondence of October 4, 1987, with Fischer, the entry "makes the record straight" in establishing his priority in the disequilibrium approach, something Clower and Leijonhufvud did not acknowledge.

Perhaps the reason for this was that, as explained earlier in Chapter 4, Clower and Leijonhufvud never accepted that their message was captured

---

[7] Notes on Perugia Conference, Robert W. Clower Papers, Box 4. David M. Rubenstein Rare Book and Manuscript Library, Duke University. See also Sebastiani (1992).

[8] In correspondence with James Tobin of January 1 1992, Patinkin wrote, "I am still happy to claim paternity" for the disequilibrium approach. "You seem to think that it assumes price rigidity, and that is particularly true of the French literature on disequilibrium macroeconomics. But in accordance with my consistent emphasis on the fact that the analysis of the General Theory does not depend on price rigidity, that is not the way I developed this idea in chapters 13–14 of my book." Don Patinkin Papers, Box 62. Rubenstein Rare Book and Manuscript Library, Duke University.

by the Barro and Grossman model, Furthermore, by the middle of the 1970s, they had both moved away from the macroeconomic mainstream. Clower (1984:263) moved into what he chose to call general process analysis. This involved ceasing to think of markets in terms of impersonal forces of supply and demand and, instead, analyzing them in terms of interactions between trading institutions. Leijonhufvud's concern with the organization of markets was evident as early as 1973. It was also central to the criticism of the early disequilibrium-macro literature by an economist who worked closely with both Clower and Leijonhufvud, Peter Howitt in the *American Economic Review (AER)* symposium, where he referred to his joint work with Clower (Howitt 1979; Clower and Howitt 1978) on that topic. In Leijonhufvud's case, the interest in trading institutions led him to computational economics, which he later pursued in both UCLA and Trento. While Leijonhufvud's research program led him to develop further the inter-temporal coordination theme of the "Wicksell Connection" (see Leijonhufvud 1981), Clower's (1988) search for a "Marshall Connection" led him to charge Keynes (1972[1936], ch. 3) with "fraud" in the formulation of the theory of effective demand. According to Clower (1994), Keynes's Marshallian model cannot account for sales constraints because it assumes (perfectly competitive) "thick" markets, as opposed to (imperfectly competitive) "thin" markets (see also Marcuzzo 1999). Hence, Clower (1994) agreed with Barro (1994b) that non-clearance of the output market remained the sine qua non of Keynesian macroeconomics.

AGAINST THE TREND

Hahn and Solow were significant not only because of their own work, some of which was discussed earlier in Chapters 5 and 7, but also because, through their positions at Cambridge and MIT, they were closely involved with many of their younger colleagues who were trying to develop alternatives to the new classical macroeconomics. Many of the most influential macroeconomic theorists in the 1980s and 1990s were their students. For many years, they discussed macroeconomics, and their shared aversion to the new classical economics, eventually publishing *A Critical Essay on Modern Macroeconomic Theory* (1995).[9]

Hahn and Solow (1995:1) described the motivation for their book as negative, to offer "respectable theoretical resistance" to the main trend in

---

[9] We leave aside the uninteresting semantic question of whether they count as "new Keynesians."

macroeconomics in the early 1980s.[10] They accepted the desirability for macroeconomic models to be the exact aggregation of micro models, but questioned the assumption "that the actual economy can be read as if it is acting out or approximating the infinite-time discounted utility maximizing program of a single, immortal 'representative agent'" constrained only by resources and the production technology (Hahn and Solow 1995:2). Such an approach, they contended, led to a Panglossian view, in which the status quo was the best of all possible worlds. Its main flaw was that no one had ever shown how a decentralized economy could behave in this way. Decentralized economies, Hahn and Solow contended, characterized by pathologies that could not even be mentioned within the framework within which macroeconomics was coming to be discussed.

Their approach was thus to start with the new classical model, gradually modifying it, to show that the new classical vision rapidly became untenable. The first step was to replace the immortal, all-seeing representative agent with an overlapping-generation model of households. Even this was enough to undermine the stability of the system. They proceeded to introduce wage stickiness and monopoly power derived from increasing returns to scale in production. Their point here was that very different policy conclusions could be reached, even if one accepted many new classical assumptions: they were, they argued, "boring from within (Hahn and Solow 1995:9).

The definition of "equilibrium" with which they worked is that equilibrium is a situation in which "no agent finds it in his interest to deviate from the status quo if such a deviation is possible," a definition they describe as "uncontroversial" (Hahn and Solow 1995:86). Thus they did not criticize the market-clearing approach of the new classical economics for being an equilibrium theory. Rather, they criticized it because "it contains no credible arguments about feasible choices out of equilibrium and is thus incomplete" (ibid.). They then proceeded to provide an explanation of how involuntary unemployment, a concept to which some new classical economics found theoretically incoherent, could arise: it was, they argued, a meaningful concept the defense of which did not require delving into philosophical ideas about free will. Hahn and Solow even argued, using a theory based on ideas of fairness, that involuntary unemployment might persist in long-run equilibrium.

---

[10] Note the number of economists in the Dramatis Personae who obtained their Ph.D. at MIT. Many of these spent some time at Cambridge. An indication of those working with Hahn is given by the contributors to Hahn (1989).

The point here is that Hahn and Solow were neither rejecting nor accepting the notion of disequilibrium, as it was understood in the disequilibrium macroeconomics literature. They were simply arguing in a different way, starting from the assumption that economic agents are rational, optimizing subject to constraints. When realistic features are introduced into the constraints facing agents, features such as involuntary unemployment could emerge. That might involve situations that could be described as disequilibrium, but there was no necessity for this.

Methodologically, one of their most important departures from the new classical model is taken in their final chapter, titled simply "Macroeconomics". Although they concede that exact aggregation (having a model in which one can show rigorously how the microeconomic relationships imply macroeconomic ones) is desirable, they explore models in which the two are more loosely related.[11] Given that it goes against the dominant view, their justification for this is worth stating:

> The models we propose pay attention to micro foundations in the sense that they are suggested by or analogous to or loosely abstracted from the micro models analyzed in chapters 4 and 5. But we do not insist that they arise literally by exact aggregation. This strikes us as a perfectly reasonable way to go about macroeconomics. We hope to gain in flexibility and plausibility far more than we lose in abstract purity. (Hahn and Solow 1995:105)

In other words, they offered a pragmatic justification for the model: "it is not one we would defend unto death", but it contains "interesting and plausible" microfoundations (Hahn and Solow 1995:6). Reflecting the new possibilities opened up by developments in information technology, they used computer simulations to explore the model's disequilibrium behavior.

STRUCTURAL SLUMPS AND RATIONAL EXPECTATIONS

Lucas repeatedly presents his work as continuing the program set out by Phelps. He refers, as has become customary, to the Friedman-Phelps natural rate hypothesis and the Friedman-Phelps approach. The difference between Friedman and Phelps was simply that Phelps laid out the general equilibrium framework underlying that hypothesis more fully than did Friedman.

---

[11] This arguably represents a modification of the view expressed in Hahn (1983:223) which had argued, referring to Lucas, that the project of "providing microeconomic foundations for macroeconomics" was "absurd" on the grounds that macroeconomics could be separate from microeconomics. When the relationship is loose, macro and micro theories can be different.

Hence, given his own emphasis on rigorous mathematical models, he can present himself as being closer to Phelps than to Friedman. Thus, in his key paper, he wrote, "Phelps foresees a new inflation and employment theory in which Phillips curves are obtained within a framework which is neoclassical except for 'the removal of the postulate that all transactions are made under complete information.' This is precisely what is attempted here" (Lucas 1972:104). What this overlooks is that Phelps did not reach the same conclusions as Lucas, as is made clear by his reference to dynamic monopsony, which might be seen as echoing Arrow's concern, discussed earlier in Chapter 7, that there could not be perfect competition out of equilibrium, or his emphasis on the existence of involuntary unemployment, a concept that Lucas found problematic, in his model of the natural rate.

Indeed, in his Arne Ryde Memorial Lecture delivered at Lund University in 1988, Phelps (1990) offered a history of macroeconomic thought based on seven schools, of which he identified himself with the "New Keynesian School" (discussed further in the next section) and especially the "Structuralist School" started by Phelps himself in the 1980s and fully developed in his 1994 book on *Structural Slumps*. As pointed out by Leijonhufvud (2004:814), Phelps shared with the New Keynesians the view that labor markets tend to converge to equilibria with jobs rationed at equilibrium wage rates. This means that the natural rate of unemployment is not an efficient state but one that can be improved by economic policy. Phelps's study of staggered wages and prices – started in his 1968 and 1970 papers and continued in a set of influential papers produced by Phelps and his Columbia colleagues (Guillermo Calvo, John Taylor) in the late 1970s and early 1980s (see, e.g., Phelps 1978) – may be regarded as his main contribution to New Keynesian macroeconomics. The term "Calvo pricing" (Calvo 1983) came to denote models in which firms could change prices only certain randomly determined times, an assumption that was widely used in the late 1980s and 1990s. The Western European experience with persistently high rates of unemployment since the 1980s led Phelps to investigate the determinants of the size of the natural rate. Phelps (1994b) put forward a model of the natural rate path as endogenous, determined by non-monetary forces, called "a non-monetary equilibrium theory of unemployment movements." It should not be confused with real business cycle theory (see Woodford 1994).

The first macroeconomic school discussed in Phelps's 1990 lecture was, following a chronological order, the "Macroeconomics of Keynes." The main theoretical feature of the *General Theory* pointed out by Phelps (1990:2) was the role of uncertainty as an obstacle blocking expectations from the successful coordination of economic activity and thereby entailing a "fundamentally anti-equilibrium" stance (in the expectational sense). That was precisely the theme of Leijonhufvud's 1968 reinterpretation of the economics of Keynes, as Phelps himself noticed (1990:17). Phelps (1990:5) saw Keynes's outlook as parallel to the intellectual revolution that took place in the first half of the 20th century in art and philosophy. He argued that Keynes played a role in economics similar to roles played by Picasso and Braque in painting, Schoenberg and Berg in music, Eliot and Pound in poetry, and Nietzsche and Sartre in philosophy. From that perspective, Keynes "brought to economics the outlook generally called modernism: the consciousness of the distance between self and others, the multiplicity of perspectives, the end of objective truth, the vertiginous sense of disorder" (1990:5). Phelps further suggested that this parallel applied also to the later part of the twentieth century, when in economics and other fields a "post-modern" tendency to go back to "classical values" revealed itself. During the 1980s, macroeconomics, according to Phelps, was the field for a seesaw battle between the "modernists" – defined as the "asymmetric information camp and the expectational disequilibrium crowd" – and the "post-modernists" formed by "the classicals in modern dress who march in such banners as New Classical and neo-classical". Phelps's motivation to write his historical survey was to assess what he perceived as the "Methodenstreit" that was taking place in economics at the time.

Significantly, Phelps (1990:12) saw his "island parable" as pertaining to the "Macroeconomics of Keynes," in the sense that it led to a reinterpretation of Keynes's vision about the labor market as one in which the worker does not have enough information about wage rates in another sector of the economy. The next school examined by Phelps, the monetarist tradition led by Milton Friedman, was seen as "intellectually a direct descendent from Keynes" but differing in giving more importance to disturbances in money supply and less so to disturbances in the prices of capital assets in relation their production costs (Phelps 1990:28). The introduction of rational expectations by the New Classical School into the flexible wage and price microfoundations models of the late 1960s – which, in Phelps's (1990:52) view, had been devised as providing support for some Keynesian propositions – led to an anti-Keynesian reformulation of macroeconomic theory and policy. According to Phelps's historical account, the New Keynesian School largely accepted the rational-expectations hypothesis, but represented a "second army" (after the early microfoundations literature of the late 1960s) in the effort to establish microfoundations for the Keynesian claims of persistence of slumps (from permanent shifts in aggregate demand) and the effectiveness of stabilization policy. The New Keynesian counterattack came in two waves, represented by the staggering model put forward at Columbia and MIT and the menu-costs approach developed by George Akerlof, Greg Mankiw, and others. Supply-side macroeconomics was another school of thought that had some influence in the United States in the 1970s and 1980s, but it was seen by Phelps as focused mainly on policy instead of providing new theoretical insights.

The last two schools discussed by Phelps deal with the effect of real forces in the generation of macroeconomic oscillations. Real business cycle theory is not just another manifestation of new classical macroeconomics, since it dispenses with the information problem of inferring the data in unknown parts of the economy by adopting the single (or representative) agent. Phelps's historical survey ends with an exposition of his own "Structuralist School," which may be regarded as his main contribution to macroeconomics after his seminal papers of the late 1960s (see Dimand 2008). Since the oil-price increase of 1973–74 and the persistently high rates of unemployment in the 1980s, it became clear, in Phelps's view, that his former model of the natural rate of unemployment should be changed to take into account the effects of real shocks and real wage rigidity on the equilibrium path of the natural rate. Bruno and Sachs's (1985) well-known book on stagflation was considered by Phelps the pioneer in the use of structuralist models to explain the pattern of employment series between the mid-1970s and mid-1980s. Phelps mentioned also Malinvaud (1980), reflecting Bruno and Sachs's extensive reference to Malinvaud's (1977b, 1980) treatment of that issue.

Phelps (1990, ch. 1) referred to the criticism of rational expectations contained in the volume he co-edited with Roman Frydman, *Individual Forecasting and Aggregate Outcomes: "Rational Expectations" Examined* (1983), a book that they described as "the logical sequel to" Phelps et al. (1970). Interestingly, the conference on which the volume was based, held in December 1981, was called "Expectations Formation and Economic Disequilibrium". Frydman and Phelps started with the observation that after the Second World War, Keynesian economics had largely been framed in terms of the Walrasian approach, modeling individuals as maximizing utility or profit based on full information. The Phelps et al. (1970) volume had laid the foundation for an alternative theory through postulating that agents faced incomplete information and taking into account that acquiring and transmitting information was a costly activity. However, that volume, while it looked at how individuals behaved, paid little attention to the expectations, necessarily about how other people would behave, on which that behavior was based – to "the agent's model of the other agents' model" (Frydman and Phelps 1983:3).

Of course, Lucas had solved this problem by turning to rational expectations, but there were problems with this approach. For rational expectations to be operational, agents would have to be able to agree on the relevant economic theory and to be able to learn the parameters that they needed to know in order to generate their forecasts. The contributors to Frydman and Phelps (1983), therefore, focused on issues of learning, the consistency of different individuals' expectations, and the implications of people holding mistaken beliefs. Although the title of the conference had used the word "disequilibrium," that term was rarely used and where it was used, it was, with one exception, used to describe a situation where learning was not complete, or errors had not been corrected: it was not a notion around which discussion was organized.

The one exception to this use of the term disequilibrium was in the chapter by Leijonhufvud, where he posed the question, "Equilibrium or disequilibrium theory?" He presented "monetarists", from Friedman to Lucas and real business cycle theorists, as favoring an equilibrium approach, analyzing economies as passing through a series of equilibria. In contrast, the Keynes-Wicksell approach involved disequilibrium. However, whereas Leijonhufvud argued that the question of equilibrium versus disequilibrium analysis "ought not to be evaded altogether" – he admitted that he had no firm answer (Leijonhufvud 1983:218) – his discussant, Hahn, was very critical of this position. The problem with the new classical macroeconomics was not that it was equilibrium theory, but that it was *Walrasian* equilibrium theory: Walrasian theory was an important benchmark, but there was no reason to believe that it applied to any real-world economy (Hahn 1983:224). It was, Hahn contended, wrong to follow Leijonhufvud in describing all non-Walrasian economics as "disequilibrium economics":

> In its own way, this nomenclature is as mendaciously partisan as, say, is Marxian "exploitation." It has the implication not only that this kind of theory is not "quite proper" but also that such a state of the economy will not persist. In any event, it is sloppy. An equilibrium state is one where all agents take the actions that in that state they prefer to take, and these actions are mutually compatible. At least that is what the term traditionally means. It does not *define* equilibrium as a Pareto-efficient state, nor does the term apply only to Walrasian economies. Fixed price models are neither equilibrium nor disequilibrium models until a theory of price is proposed. If an agent finds it optimal to set a price independent of the state of demand for his product, or if a group of agents (union and employer) find this optimal, then this has as much claim to the title of equilibrium price as does the Walrasian "market

clearing" price. Names matter, and the muddle that Leijonhufvud discerns is often grounded in simple illiteracy. (Hahn 1983:228)

Hahn was using the same definition of equilibrium as Frydman and Phelps used in their introduction to the volume, and views such as these may explain why, despite the word appearing in the title of the conference, the term "disequilibrium" was rarely used in the volume. The significance of Hahn's making these remarks is that even though he could claim that Lucas's conclusions were "absurd," he found things to praise in Lucas's recognition that macroeconomics and microeconomics needed to be integrated (Hahn 1983:223). The problem was not equilibrium theorizing for there was a sense in which all theorizing had to argue in terms of equilibrium and disequilibrium, but the type of equilibrium theorizing that Lucas and the new classical economists used.

THE CONSOLIDATION OF THE "NEW KEYNESIAN" ECONOMICS

Stiglitz's main contribution to disequilibrium macroeconomics after the Solow-Stiglitz 1968 paper was arguably the special issue of the *Quarterly Journal of Economics* on "Implicit Contracts and Fixed Price Equilibria" (Azariadis and Stiglitz 1983), that he edited together with Costas Azariadis, and which featured a fixed-price model with rational expectations (Neary and Stiglitz 1983). While Grossman (1979) had seen implicit contracts as an alternative to the disequilibrium approach, Azariadis and Stiglitz (1983:1) hoped that the microfoundations of the fixed-price method would be strengthened by bringing together contributions from both fields.

Stiglitz's own contribution to the symposium, co-authored with Peter Neary, had first been presented, to the Econometric Society, in 1979. That made the rationing approach more dynamic by pursuing the argument that decisions would be influenced not simply by quantity constraints faced in the current period, but also on expectations concerning such constraints in the future:

we show that if individuals expect there to be unemployment next period, it is more likely ... that there will be unemployment this period; whereas if individuals expect there to be excess demand for goods next period, then it is more likely that there will be excess demand for goods this period. As a result, for any particular set of current wages and prices, there may exist multiple expectational equilibria that exhibit "bootstraps" properties; e.g. households expect that they will be unable to sell all their labor both this period and next, then it will turn out that they will be unable to sell all their labor; but had they expected there to be inflationary pressures this period and next, then that would have turned out to be the case instead. (Neary and Stiglitz 1983:200)

They went on to analyze equilibria in which individuals held rational expectations about future constraints, showing that the introduction of rational expectations, contrary to what was widely claimed, was not sufficient to undermine Keynesian results: the key assumption in undermining Keynesian results was the assumption that prices adjusted instantaneously to clear markets. They used these results, which they claimed captured Keynesian insights better than did the static model, to argue that the key innovation in the new classical macroeconomics was not rational expectations:

These results suggest that the critique of the effectiveness of government policy presented by "new classical macroeconomists" ... rests primarily on their assumption that prices and wages adjust instantaneously to clear markets, and *not* on their use of the rational expectations hypothesis. (Neary and Stiglitz 1983: 225)

Neary and Stiglitz concluded by arguing that achieving equilibrium through price adjustments might be slow and difficult. Shifts in expectations might cause significant changes in the prices needed to achieve market-clearing equilibrium and disequilibria might arise in markets other than the ones in which prices were sticky. They therefore conjectured what they called a "dynamic second-best theorem," according to which "with limited flexibility of some prices, increasing the flexibility of other prices may reduce rather than increase the ability of the system to return to Walrasian equilibrium" (Neary and Stigltiz 1983:225).[12]

In this paper, Neary and Stiglitz were clearly still developing disequilibrium macroeconomics into what could, potentially, be a general theory, for a major component of their thesis was that the assumption of rational expectations did not, as was widely believed, lead to "new classical" conclusions. Another economist who argued such a case was John Flemming (1987), who was one of the very few to take up Keynes's claim that, far from being the cause of unemployment, wage stickiness could stabilize an economy. To make this point, he used a model that was as close as possible to the Walrasian model, with rational expectations and a goods market in which prices adjusted instantaneously, modifying it by assuming that wages were sticky, adjusting slowly toward equilibrium – the minimum needed to generate Keynesian unemployment. The model was stable and greater

---

[12] It is interesting to note that, though this was not the basis for their argument, their stress on the importance of dynamic complications as the cause of unemployment echoes Keynes (see Backhouse and Laidler 2004).

wage flexibility would cause full employment to be reached more quickly. However, and this was the key point, greater wage flexibility would make wages less predictable and so prices would be less responsive to wages. The result was that greater wage flexibility increased the sensitivity of real wages and employment to disturbances. Adjustment to full employment might be faster, but fluctuations in employment would be greater. There could, there-fore, be no presumption that an economy with more flexible wages would necessarily exhibit lower employment, on average, than one in which wages were sticky. Whether the benefits of wage stickiness (reducing the sensitiv-ity of the economy to shocks) were greater than the benefits (faster adjust-ment to full employment) depended on the monetary policy being pursued, for this would influence errors that people made. This result, Flemming pointed out, was a standard second-best result:

A policy designed to increase wage flexibility, which one might expect to be "a good thing", can only be relied upon to raise welfare if other policies notably monetary policy – are also optimised. If wages are less than perfectly flexible, the optimization of money supply policy is by no means trivial. (Flemming 1987:173–74)

Azariadis and Stiglitz (1983:2) could still describe the notion of quantity-constrained equilibrium as a "very interesting concept," but the New Keynesian manifesto written a few years later by Greenwald and Stiglitz (1987:121), expressed the view that the fixed-price assumption "fails to square with evidence" and "cries out for theoretical justification." Perhaps this is why, when Gregory Mankiw and David Romer published a two-volume selection of readings on the *New Keynesian Economics* (1991), their introduction did not mention the search for disequilibrium micro-foundations. Starting with the Keynesian consensus of the 1960s, based on the IS-LM model and the Phillips curve, they argued that the new classi-cal macroeconomists, who shattered this consensus, "argued persuasively, that Keynesian economics should be replaced with macroeconomic theo-ries based on the assumptions that markets always clear and that economic actors always optimize" (Mankiw and Romer 1991, vol. I:1). They went on to claim that "because wage and price rigidities are often viewed as central to Keynesian economics, much effort was aimed at showing how these rigidi-ties arose from the microeconomics of wage and price setting" (ibid.).

Summarizing what was distinctive about the new Keynesian economics, Mankiw and Romer (1991, vol. I:2) claimed that it was the only approach that rejected the so-called classical dichotomy (the theory that supply and demand for goods determines relative prices and that the quantity of money determines the overall price level) and believed that "real market imperfections" were "crucial for understanding economic fluctuations." The reason was that wages and prices were sticky: "The classical dichotomy fails because prices are sticky. Real imperfections are crucial because imperfect competition and rigidity in relative prices are central to understanding why prices are sticky" (ibid.). Thus, their "whirlwind tour" of the new Keynesian economics covered the costs of changing prices, the staggering of wages and prices, imperfect competition, and factors specific to labor, credit, and goods markets that included asymmetric information. They did have a section on coordination failures, centered on Cooper and John (1988),[13] who had established, contra both the new classical monetary explanations of the cycle and real business cycle theory, that fluctuations in confidence or animal spirits might drive economic fluctuations. However, they went on to explain how coordination failures could arise from specific externalities, citing thick-market externalities (that it is easier to find people to trade with if markets are thick than if there are few potential buyers or sellers).

A crucial element in this new Keynesian literature was a model of imperfect competition produced a few years earlier by Dixit and Stiglitz (1977). This was important because it provided a tractable general equilibrium model of monopolistic competition with differentiated products, enabling it to become one of the main tools of New Keynesian macroeconomic modeling. Dixit and Stiglitz assumed a consumer with a taste for variety and a utility function featuring additive separability. The rise in the use of this model in macroeconomics was part of a much broader resurgence of interest in monopolistic competition that extended to international trade and growth theories, to such an extent that it came to be seen as representing a second revolution in the field of monopolistic competition after Chamberlin and Robinson in the 1930s (see Brakman and Heijdra 2004; Warsh 2006) – though it was considered a more successful one because of the range of its applications.[14]

During the 1970s and 1980s, the New Keynesian Economics came to be seen as the main alternative to the new classical macroeconomics and real business cycle theory. It was an elastic term. Mankiw and Romer, as we have just seen, could present it as providing explanations of why prices and wages were sticky, making it possible to present it as a natural, more

---

[13] This was the first article reprinted in Volume II of their collection.

[14] Not all work on international trade adopted an imperfect competition framework. Arida and Bacha (1987) argued that a disequilibrium framework based on the assumption that the wage rate and the exchange rate changed slowly provided a model that was useful for the analysis of semi-industrialized countries and hence policy problems faced by Latin American countries.

rigorous, extension of disequilibrium macroeconomics. At the same time, Phelps, whose concerns with information and structural problems ran much deeper than this, could claim to be a new Keynesian. However, though the label new Keynesian was sufficiently elastic to cover much of the ferment of new macroeconomic thinking that erupted in response to the new classical macroeconomics and real business cycle theory, it came to be strongly associated with institutionally caused wage stickiness (notably unions, long-term contracts, menu costs, and asymmetric information). Reviewing the collection edited by Mankiw and Romer, Huw Dixon (1992:1273) criticized the narrowness of their view of new Keynesian macroeconomics:

It is far too narrow geographically, in that it takes a narrowly American (Bostonian) view of macroeconomics. It is far too narrow historically, in that it fails to recognise work done before 1980. Of course, these two narrownesses are linked: in the 1970s most of the serious work on imperfect competition and macroeconomics was being done in Europe and Japan. I find it incredible that there is not even a reference to Jean-Pascal Bénassy's or Takashi Negishi's papers from the late 1970s.[15] Sadly, very few of the many European contributions from the 1980s are cited, and certainly none included in this parochial collection. However, the most important narrowness of their vision is their failure to realise that the significance of imperfect competition goes far beyond a 'Keynesian' short-run. When you replace the auctioneer with wage- and price-setting agents the whole nature and significance of equilibrium changes. Not only will the equilibrium tend to be inefficient, but there is the possibility of multiple equilibria that can be ranked in welfare terms. Imperfect competition opens up the possibility and desirability of effective macroeconomic intervention.

The collection did contain four papers on imperfect competition, but he clearly felt that they were not the ones that offered the most radical critiques of the Walrasian approach.

Insofar as the new Keynesians took this position, they placed themselves in succession to the fixed-price approach of Barro and Grossman, later reinforced by Malinvaud's stress on fixed prices, rather than to the more radical critiques of general equilibrium modeling that involved imperfect competition. In doing this, they were ignoring precisely those approaches to disequilibrium theory that provided an explanation of how prices were set. The four papers included saw imperfect competition not as a solution to the problem of how prices are set, but as the result of institutional and technological barriers to competition.

---

[15] Mankiw and Romer (1991) contains Hart (1982), which cites Bénassy (1976a, 1978). Although Hart was by then at MIT, his paper was conceived when working with Hahn in Cambridge.

MODELING TRANSACTIONS AND PRICE SETTING

Not everyone avoided language of disequilibrium. MIT industrial economist and econometrician Franklin Fisher, in a book, *Disequilibrium
Foundations of Equilibrium Economics* (1983), that drew on over a decade
of work on the subject, was still prepared to argue, on purely theoretical
grounds, that "disequilibrium questions cannot be avoided. If 'equilibrium'
is to have any substantive meaning, one must be willing to countenance the
possibility of encountering disequilibrium states" (Fisher 1983:7). Accepting
that led him to conclude that it was essential to consider non-tâtonnement
processes such as those first developed by Negishi and Hahn in the early
1960s. Fisher's main contribution to Walrasian disequilibrium theory was
what Roy Weintraub (1979:118–21) described – drawing analogy with the
better-known "Hahn process" – as the "Fisher process," advanced in Fisher
(1976). The problem tackled by Fisher was to investigate how economic
agents change prices in the absence not just of the tâtonnement but also of
any auctioneer. Fisher suggested that commodities should be distinguished
in such a way that firms and households are associated with the good they
specialize in. Despite the conceptual problems involved in the "Fisher process," such as the nature of the demand curves facing sellers in their particular markets, Fisher (1983) kept stressing the need to study disequilibrium
states. According to Francesca Busetto (1995), Fisher's analytical difficulties
illustrated a general problem that beset the microeconomic non-tâtonement
literature, which included general monopolistic equilibrium of the type
pursued by Hahn and Negishi as well as fixed-price equilibria with quantity
rationing such as developed by Drèze and Bénassy: its inability, to provide
a proper analysis of the observed non-intentional behavior of economic
agents out of equilibrium.

Another challenge to the dominance of perfect competition modeling
can be found in the work of Peter Diamond, who obtained his Ph.D. from
MIT in 1963 and returned as a faculty member in 1966. In the late 1970s
and 1980s, he wrote a series of papers on search models, the key ideas of
which were explained in two lectures, given in Stockholm in 1982, and
published as *A Search-Equilibrium Approach to the Micro Foundations of
Macroeconomics* (1984). Although his starting point was the Phelps volume (Phelps et al. 1970), he started his lectures by emphasizing the difference between his own work and the earlier literature. Unlike many new
Keynesians, he was not simply modeling imperfections that happened to
exist, but, in a manner reminiscent of Leijonhufvud's use of Alchian's work

(see Chapter 4), he was challenging the general equilibrium framework that was coming to dominate macroeconomics.

Most writers apply search theory to the labor market, while implicitly or explicitly closing the model in the familiar general-equilibrium way; that is, a Walrasian auctioneer clears all markets. Of course, the auctioneer is a fiction. My starting point has been to build a model that avoids any such mechanism, a model that does not assume a frictionless, costless, perfect resource allocation device.... My alternative assumptions are that all trades in the economy take place between two individuals, rather than between an individual and "the market," and that it is time-consuming to locate a trading partner. (Diamond 1984:1–2)

Using this approach, in which agents would make individual bargains with other traders (the same product would not always sell at the same price) and in which the costs of having to find new trading partners would make it sensible to cultivate long-term relationships and for some people to set up as dealers (shopkeepers), Diamond developed a theory in which, though agents were rational, markets would not clear in that demand and supply would not be equal.[16] He claimed that it was an alternative to the simple Keynesian model in which prices are fixed and rationing emerges in the short run, but, unlike the new classical model, it was compatible with it.

Diamond analyzed the problem of disequilibrium through modeling the technology through which trade took place, showing that, even if people were rational, market disequilibrium might emerge. A step even further in this direction was taken in the literature on what came to be described as "agent-based" modeling. One strand in this approach is represented by Peter Howitt, who obtained his Ph.D. from Northwestern in 1973, and who worked with both Clower and Leijonhufvud. Explicitly citing a remark by Leijonhufvud that "the real problem of macroeconomics was to understand how order can arise from the interactions of people following simple rules to cope with a complex environment," and citing Leijonhufvud's (1993, 2006) work on computational economics (Howitt 2008:161), he argued that, when faced with uncertainty, people generally follow rules of thumb because, even if they could work out optimal decisions, it would be far too costly to do so. This is a view of how people behave when they know that they do not fully understand the situation the face that is well supported by psychological research. The crucial feature of this approach, which justifies the term "agent-based," is that each agent

---

[16] In models of search equilibrium, in which matching buyers and sellers is costly, terminology such as market clearing has to be treated cautiously.

makes decisions that can in principle be different from the decisions made by other agents, in a way that is not possible in models with either market clearing or rational expectations. Without making such an assumption, Howitt argued, it is impossible to understand how the actions of heterogeneous agents are co-ordinated.

This approach differs from Diamond's in that it starts from the assumption that people follow rules of thumb that will not be optimal though, like Diamond's, it involves focusing not on homogenous markets but on interactions between individual agents. Given the complexity of the systems and the need to assess behavior by seeing how it works out in practice, the only practical way to analyze them is through computer simulation. Thus, simulating a model in which behavior is determined by a series of such rules, Howitt was able to show that on average real GDP may be higher in a world where wages are sticky (though not completely rigid) than if they were completely flexible. Such methods, of course, only became feasible as a result of developments in information technology and simulation techniques: in the 1970s and early 1980s, they would have been impossible.

Howitt's paper has been discussed because of its close connection, through Leijonhufvud, with the earlier literature on disequilibrium macroeconomics. It is, however, one of a variety of behavioral "agent-based" approaches to macroeconomics, that have attracted adherents as experimental and behavioral economics has taken off since the 1990s. Drawing on the way they are based on a shared discontent with the dynamic stochastic general equilibrium model that forms the basis for the new neoclassical synthesis, David Colander (1996, 2006) tried to bring some of these together under the heading "post-Walrasian economics."

IMPERFECT COMPETITION AS A THEORY OF PRICE SETTING

During the 1980s, the dominant approach to macroeconomic theory came to be what was eventually called dynamic stochastic general equilibrium (DSGE) model. This had its origins in the work of Lucas and the new classical macroeconomics, discussed earlier in Chapter 6. Toward the end of the 1970s, it had become clear that the monetary shocks approach explanation of the cycle did not work: extensive econometric testing was showing that it did not explain the time path of key variables. Ironically, a solution to the problem was, according to Snowdon and Vane (2005:295), first pointed out by the Keynesian economist James Tobin (1980:789) when, asking whether the classical models were plausible enough to guide policy (he concluded that they were not), he observed that

Of course the real equilibrium of a full-information model could move around, driven by fluctuations of natural endowments (like weather), technologies (and thus factor marginal productivities), and tastes (e.g., leisure versus work). If these fluctuations are serially persistent random processes, the observations they generate may look like business cycles in certain variables.

This was the approach adopted by Fynn Kydland and Edward Prescott (1982) in their highly influential article "Time to Build and Aggregate Fluctuations" (1982) and was labeled "real business cycle theory" by John Long and Charles Plosser (1983). As was mentioned in Chapter 6, this adopted many features of new classical methodology: modeling inter-temporal choice in a stochastic framework involving competitive markets – using what was later called a DSGE model. All that was necessary was to postulate real shocks instead of demand shocks as the driver of the cycle.

However, the effects of real business cycle theory had a far deeper effect on macroeconomic theory than this. There were two main reasons for this. The first was that Kydland and Prescott proposed a new technique for estimating macroeconomic models that they called "calibration." Because the models being used were representative agent models, in which the behavior of macroeconomic variables was essentially the same as that of individual agents, it was possible to find values for the key parameters by looking at microeconomic evidence. Once the key parameters were found, the model could be simulated and the results compared with the macroeconomic data that needed to be explained. Given that the models were stochastic, testing them involved comparing the statistical properties of the outputs generated by the model with those of macroeconomic data. Such comparisons could also be used to establish values of parameters that could not be estimated directly from microeconomic data (this was the calibration element).

This approach was strongly criticized, so it would be an exaggeration to say that it became the dominant approach to econometric modeling. However, it added one more element at a time when econometrics was in flux, with the possibilities being opened up by developments in information technology making it possible to generate new techniques that only a decade previously econometricians could only dream about. Around the same time, for example, Christopher Sims (1980) was challenging the belief that so-called structural models – econometric models in which the equations were believed to represent behavioral relations present in the real economy – were in fact properly identified, arguing instead for techniques such as vector autoregressive (VAR) modeling that sought merely to describe the time series properties of the data. Sims did not endorse the calibration methods employed by real business cycle theorists (see Sims

1996:112–15), but his work arguably helped create a climate in which there was more receptiveness to such methods than would otherwise have been the case.

On the economic theory side, real business cycle theory had the effect of integrating growth theory with the analysis of short-run fluctuations in economic activity. The variable used to measure technology shocks was the Solow residual – that component of output growth that could not be explained by the growth of capital and labor, or other inputs. More important, the theoretical model used was a stochastic growth model, this providing a unified theoretical framework.

However, as Tobin had noted in 1980, the use of such a model had problems:

Theories of this genre, as Gottfried Haberler observed decades ago, explain cycles not as economic mechanism but as the reflection, in an intrinsically stable structure, of exogenous shocks. Their serial correlation, moreover, is assumed rather than justified by argument or evidence. More important, such theories do not explain nominal variables. In particular, they do not explain the short-run positive associations of employment and output on the one hand, and prices on the other. That is the function of the third ingredient, asymmetrical incompleteness of information. (Tobin 1980:798)

He was skeptical about whether any economic mechanism was being provided to explain the cycle, for all that was necessary was that shocks be applied to a system that would otherwise be stable. Perhaps, at a time when, after the Lucas (1976) critique, there was skepticism about whether Keynesian models actually explained anything, and there was skepticism about structural econometric modeling, this was seen as less of an issue than it might have been a decade earlier. The most important of Tobin's criticisms, however, was that it was necessary to explain the relationship between real and nominal magnitudes, the problem that had arguably been central to macroeconomics for many decades. Tobin clearly thought that using workers' misperceptions of prices, the mechanism first explored by Phelps in his search for microfoundations in the late 1960s, was inadequate. His remark was prescient in that during the 1980s, economists sought to modify the underlying model in ways that took it away from real business cycle theory. This search for better models was driven both by skepticism about the theory and by the empirical failings of real business cycle models.[17]

---

[17] As our focus is on macroeconomic theory, the details of this will not be pursued here. Some of the issues involved can be found in the exchanges, in particular between Sims, David Hendry, Adrian Pagan, and Martin Eichenbaum, in Backhouse and Salanti (2000).

During the 1980s, the DSGE models pioneered by the new classical and real business cycle theorists progressively lost their perfectly competitive microfoundations as an increasing number of economists turned to imperfect competition. As in the 1970s, in some cases this was because economists believed that large firms possessing market power were important in reality. However, in other cases, it was that imperfect competition was needed to provide a theory of price adjustment, or else that it was needed to explain what was going on in the world.

This process started early. In the same year that Kydland and Prescott (1982) published their "Time to Build" article, Julio Rotemberg published an article, drawn from his 1981 Princeton University Ph.D. thesis, in which he worked out a rational expectations equilibrium for a model in which firms believe that changing prices is costly (Rotemberg 1982). He described his work as related both to Lucas's models and, crucially, to the disequilibrium model of Barro and Grossman: "This model is therefore a relative of the Barro-Grossman (1976) model in that it is the slow response of prices which is placed at the centre of the explanation of business cycles" (Rotemberg 1982:517). The difference was that, whereas Barro and Grossman simply postulated price stickiness, his model assumed that firms set prices optimally, taking account of the fact that it was costly to change them, possibly because consumers react unfavorably to price changes. Despite working with a general equilibrium model and assuming rational expectations, the model exhibited the serial correlation of output that was characteristic of Keynesian models. Imperfect competition was crucial to this result.

A later paper that illustrates the way DSGE modeling moved away from its origins is Lars Svensson's "Sticky goods prices, flexible asset prices, monopolistic competition and monetary policy" (1986). He started from the assumption that conventional models exaggerated the flexibility of the price level, one of the reasons being that money was an asset, alongside other assets, and as an asset, its price would adjust instantaneously whenever there was new information. However, in practice, the prices of goods fluctuated much less than did, say, share prices or exchange rates. Informational lags could not explain this. His solution was to postulate that product prices were set by imperfectly competitive firms seeking to maximize their stock market values. Thus, although he adopted the approach, by then standard, of a DSGE model, the result was "stationary stochastic rational-expectations equilibria where nominal goods prices do not respond to the current state of the economy" (Svensson 1986: 386). Prices were set by profit-maximizing firms before the current state of the economy was observed, meaning that they reflected past information. The result was a model in which "there is excess demand for goods in some states, and excess supply in other states," concluding that "the paper, with its equilibria with endogenous price-setting and underutilization of resources, might be considered as a contribution to the literature on non-Walrasian equilibria, as surveyed for instance by Drazen (1980)" (Svensson 1986:386). The crucial feature of the model was that firms set their own prices, which required imperfect competition.

A year later, Olivier Blanchard and Nobuhiro Kiyotaki (1987) reached a similar conclusion about the importance of competition. Their conclusion, using a model they compared with Hart (1982) (discussed in Chapter 7) was that monopolistic competition could not, on its own, explain why fluctuations in aggregate demand affected output, the key feature of Keynesian economics. However, they went on to argue that if imperfect competition were combined with other imperfections, such as costs of changing prices, it could do so, and hence explain how economies would respond to demand shocks.

The models discussed so far assumed monopolistic competition, but this was not the only way imperfect competition was handled. Rotemberg went on to tackle, with several co-authors, the implications of oligopoly. For example, in an article with Woodford (Rotemberg and Woodford 1992), he assumed that industry was characterized by collusion, in which deviations from the agreed price would be punished by other firms reducing prices in the following period. This provided a mechanism through which demand shocks could affect prices and hence output: if there is a positive demand shock in one period, this raises the benefits of trying to undercut competitors relative to the losses that will result from being punished in the future. The result is that high demand will be associated with lower profit margins and higher output.

One of the many economists to explore the macroeconomic implications of imperfect competition in this way was Bénassy, whose Ph.D. thesis had been one of the first attempts, after the very early work of Hahn and Negishi, to tackle the problem. Although he produced several books during the intervening years (Benassy 1982, 1986), his approach can be summed up by looking at *The Macroeconomics of Imperfect Competition and Nonclearing Markets: A Dynamic General Equilibrium Approach* (2002), in which he sought to synthesize what he described as "four central paradigms in economic theory":

1.   General equilibrium theory;
2.   Keynesian theory, represented by Hicks, Patinkin, Clower and Leijonhufvud;

3. Imperfect competition, of which the general equilibrium formulation was due to Negishi;
4. Rational expectations and "their integration into dynamic general equilibrium macroeconomic models by Lucas (1972) or Kydland and Prescott (1982)" (Benassy 2002:xi).

Like much macroeconomic theory since the 1970s, his theory was based on a dynamic, and sometimes stochastic, general equilibrium approach.

He started his book by reviewing early contributions to the literature on fixed-price equilibria and quantity rationing, including not only his own but those of Drèze and Barro and Grossman. However, though they served to place what he was doing in a historical perspective, these chapters were the prelude to the book's main argument, in which he offered a synthesis comprising models with imperfect competition and nominal rigidities in inter-temporal deterministic and stochastic settings. He thus drew on work such as that of Rotemberg and Woodford (1992, 1995) on DSGE models with imperfect competition and he adopted the widely used device of so-called Calvo pricing (see Calvo 1983), as a way to model the effects of staggered wage and price contracts. The modeling of contracts though Calvo pricing was central to the mechanism whereby the effects of monetary shocks were propagated through the economy, and to the strong persistence of such shocks, a feature that distinguished both of their models from most real business cycle models with money. Thus, Bénassy's strategy was to start from market-clearing models and to generalize them to non-Walrasian settings in order to obtain a more general and arguably relevant class of models with non-clearing markets and imperfect competition. This objective echoed his early work, in which imperfect competition provided the theoretical basis on which disequilibrium theory could be constructed, though the techniques employed – including inter-temporal modeling and rational expectations – were those pioneered by Phelps and Lucas.

THE NEW NEOCLASSICAL SYNTHESIS

In 1997, at a conference organized by the National Bureau of Economic Research, Marvin Goodfriend and Robert King argued that there had emerged a "new neoclassical synthesis." As one might expect of two economists affiliated to the Federal Reserve Bank of Richmond, Virginia, this synthesis related to the operation of monetary policy, extending to both theory and practice. They claimed that there had emerged a consensus both on how monetary policy should be conducted and, more important for our purposes, that there was a consensus on how policy should be analyzed. There is a parallel here with the neoclassical synthesis proposed by Samuelson over four decades earlier, discussed in Chapter 2, in which a synthesis of views on policy was underwritten by an integration of theoretical frameworks previously thought to be incompatible.

As we explained in Chapter 2, the work often taken to sum up this synthesis was Michael Woodford's *Interest and Prices* (2003). Woodford, after taking his first degree at the University of Chicago, obtained a Ph.D. from MIT in 1983. Influenced by his thesis advisor, Solow, he was encouraged to work on integrating sticky prices into the inter-temporal general equilibrium model that was becoming fashionable with the rise of new classical and real business cycle models. In the early 1990s, he wrote a series of papers (including work discussed earlier in this chapter) with Rotemberg, who had obtained his Ph.D. from MIT a year ahead of him. In his book, he drew on the results of this collaboration and work with other collaborators during the 1990s. In it, he sought both to tackle the problem of integrating microeconomics and macroeconomics into a framework that could explain observed fluctuations in economic activity and to bridge the gap between the perspectives of monetary theorists and central bankers. Whereas monetary theory had traditionally analyzed monetary policy in terms of its effect on monetary aggregates (the money supply was, for example, central to the work of Friedman and Patinkin and had been central to debates over "monetarism" in the 1970s), central bankers had long focused on interest rates (this focus on interest rates provided the link with Wicksell discussed in Chapter 2): the rate of interest was the regulator of commodity prices.

When summing up this synthesis, Woodford (2009:269–74) picked out five elements: (1) inter-temporal general equilibrium foundations, which may involve either perfect or imperfect competition; (2) the use of structural econometric models; (3) endogenous expectations that take account of the policy regime; (4) disturbances arising from real shocks; and (5) the conclusion that monetary policy can be effective in controlling inflation.

Woodford placed this work as a direct descendent of new classical and real business cycle models. "The methodological stance of the New Classical school and the real business cycle theorists has become the mainstream," he wrote (2007:269) for macroeconomic models needed microfoundations and theories of the business cycle should be integrated with theories of economic growth. DSGE modeling was thus central to macroeconomics, a stochastic growth model providing the underlying theoretical framework.

However, and this was a crucial point differentiating his work from real business cycle theory, this did not mean models of perfect competition:

The dynamic stochastic general equilibrium (DSGE) models now used to analyze the short-run effects of alternative policies often involve imperfect competition in both labor markets and product markets, wages and prices that remain fixed for intervals of time rather than being instantaneously adjusted to reflect current market conditions, and an allowance for unutilized resources as a result of search and matching frictions. The insistence of monetarists, New Classicals, and early real business cycle theorists on the empirical relevance of models of perfect competitive equilibrium, a source of much controversy in past decades, is not what is now generally accepted. Instead, what is important is having general-equilibrium models, in the broad sense of requiring that all equations of the model be derived from mutually consistent foundations, and that the specified behavior of each economic unit make sense given the environment created by the behavior of the others. At one time, Walrasian competitive equilibrium models were the only kind of models with these features that were well understood, but this is no longer the case. (Woodford 2009:269–70)

Although Woodford was, perhaps in the interests of maintaining the appearance of consensus, cautious in claiming no more than that DSGE models "often" incorporate imperfect competition, he might perhaps have argued that imperfect competition was essential, for without some sort of imperfect competition, it would have been difficult to solve two key problems. Imperfect competition was needed to develop a theory of price setting, without which it would be hard to provide rigorous microeconomic foundations, and it was needed to explain cyclical fluctuations in output and employment.

After the 2008 crisis, Woodford's optimism about the monetary policy regime that he advocated appeared unjustified – doubts were raised about whether monetary policy could control inflation and there appeared to be a need for more interventionist, discretionary, policy than he had envisaged; success in stabilizing inflation and growth in the 1990s and 2000s appeared to have been bought at the cost of building structural imbalances that, in retrospect, appeared unsustainable, and as a result, the practice of DSGE modeling was called into question. Clearly, the main failing of the framework summarized in *Interest and Prices*, linked to Woodford's optimism that the problem of how to conduct monetary policy had, effectively, been solved, was the lack of attention paid to developments in financial markets, and which Woodford (2010) later sought to remedy. However, it is also possible that had greater emphasis been placed on the crucial turn to imperfect competition, and less on the new classical legacy, some of this criticism might have been mitigated.

CONCLUSION

The common perception that disequilibrium macroeconomics died at the end of the 1970s, killed by its failure to explain macroeconomic events is incorrect. Although battles between a small number of clearly defined schools of thought may make for good drama and even for textbook accounts that are simple for students to memorize, what happened in macroeconomics was far more complex. Chapter 5 drew attention to the work of economists, such as Portes and Quandt, who developed econometric methods relevant to such models and who applied them to planned economies; it also noted that Clower and Leijonhufvud, rejecting the Barro-Grossman interpretation of their work, had moved in directions that took them away from the main currents in macroeconomics. As this chapter shows, economists continued to develop models with inflexible prices in which rationing and spillover effects gave rise to Keynesian problems. Others accepted much of the Lucasian framework – rational agents operating in competitive markets – but found specific reasons why wages would not adjust to clear the labor market. Others identified much more widespread problems with the perfect competition model, developing theories of how transactions costs, informational problems, and, above all, imperfect competition could produce results that were, at least in some respects, closer to those of disequilibrium theory than those of the new classical macroeconomics.

Although such work could be seen as providing more rigorous microeconomic foundations for disequilibrium theory, they rendered the term "disequilibrium" even more problematic: if there is monopolistic competition, supply will not equal demand, but there can still be equilibrium in the sense that firms are maximizing profits. It thus became increasingly common to favor the term non-Walrasian macroeconomics, this term being used to encompass all models that departed from the perfect competition assumed by Lucas, the new classical macroeconomists, and the real business cycle theorists. Another term that gained currency in the 1980s was "new Keynesian macroeconomics." This was a very loosely defined term, covering models that used a wide variety of assumptions, including asymmetric information, menu costs, implicit contracts, monopolistic competition, and multiple equilibria, to generate Keynesian results. Thus, in 1992, a "survey of research strategies" in macroeconomics naturally included a chapter on methodological issues in new Keynesian economics (Stiglitz 1992) and another on the "non-Walrasian" approach to macroeconomics (Silvestre 1992). The latter drew not only on the author's own extensive work on the subject, but also on analyses of monopolistic price adjustment, of the econometrics of disequilibrium and of the economics of centrally planned economies. This literature overlapped with the new Keynesian literature surveyed by Stiglitz, but was not co-extensive with it. However, though most economists were abandoning the term disequilibrium in favor of "new Keynesian" or "non-Walrasian," there remained economists who still used the term. Thus, at the end of our period, Bénassy (2002) published a book with a title that included the phrase "imperfect competition and nonclearing markets." Disequilibrium theory had given rise to a variety of new developments.

TEN

Conclusion

KEYNESIAN ECONOMICS AND GENERAL
EQUILIBRIUM THEORY

The search for non-Walrasian or disequilibrium microfoundations was central to the transformation of macroeconomics that took place in the 1970s. Its roots lie in the late 1930s and 1940s, when economists from Hicks to Lange and Modigliani sought to make sense of Keynesian economics in terms of general equilibrium models inspired by Walras. Out of this came what was, at that time, the most rigorous attempt to integrate money into general equilibrium theory, Patinkin's *Money, Interest and Prices*. Patinkin's conception of equilibrium was essentially Walrasian in that he thought in terms of perfect competition and markets that would eventually clear. However, though it took a long time for economists to realize this, his analysis of the labor market contained ideas that later formed the basis for disequilibrium, non-Walrasian theories in which there could be no assurance that markets would ever achieve equilibrium.

The search for disequilibrium microfoundations thus had two sources. One was the continuing concern, even in the 1960s, to find a better theoretical basis for Keynesian macroeconomics. Here, Clower was the crucial figure, his dual-decision hypothesis not only justifying the Keynesian consumption function – central to Keynesian economics – but also showing, much more clearly than had Patinkin, how trading out of equilibrium could cause supply and demand functions to be very different from the way they were generally modeled. Walras's law, that excess demands sum to zero, might not hold and there would be spillover effects – disequilibrium in one market alters supplies and demands in other markets. The other source of the literature on disequilibrium theory was general equilibrium theory itself. It had been known, since the 1950s when the modern theory of general competitive equilibrium, associated above all with Arrow and Debreu, was being developed, that there were significant logical and empirical problems with the theory. The mechanism of the tâtonnement, involving "re-contracting" or a fictitious auctioneer who changed prices – a deus ex machina – was clearly unrealistic but non-tâtonnement processes, in which trade took place at disequilibrium prices, were difficult to analyze, even if the theorist was willing to make arbitrary assumptions about what determined the trades that took place out of equilibrium. There was also recognition of the need to replace the assumption of perfect competition with imperfect competition, resulting in early models of Hahn and Negishi around 1960.

The subsequent story of the search for microfoundations involves the interaction between these two lines of theorizing, both legitimately described as non-Walrasian or disequilibrium theory, and the Walrasian or equilibrium theorizing to which Lucas and others turned in the 1970s. Disequilibrium theory became entwined not only with theories of imperfect competition, without which it was hard to have a theory of price-adjustment, but also with arguments about information. Ironically, Alchian, who had seen the importance of information early in the 1960s, influenced both Leijonhufvud, whose book *On Keynesian Economics and the Economics of Keynes* inspired many to look for disequilibrium foundations for macroeconomics, and Phelps, whose work on the labor market enabled his successors to construct equilibrium theories of the business cycle in which markets were perfectly competitive. There were also different approaches to the problem of equilibrium within the general equilibrium literature. Drèze, seeing price rigidity as a form of income insurance, started from the general equilibrium theory of Debreu to develop a theory of equilibrium with rationing in competitive markets. Bénassy, in contrast, in his Ph.D. thesis, *Disequlibrium Theory*, drew on Clower's dual-decision hypothesis and used models with fixed prices only as the first step to developing models in which competition was imperfect and price formation was endogenous.

General equilibrium models involving imperfect competition and non-tâtonnement were complicated and so were ignored by many economists. Leijonhufvud offered a vision of economic activity in disequilibrium that, though it inspired many macroeconomists, was not instantiated in any formal, mathematical model. When models were constructed, they were generally models with fixed prices such as that of Barro and Grossman (1971). Because economists continued, for the most part, to assume perfect competition, if prices changes were modeled, it was through some adjustment mechanism linking price changes to excess demands. Even if "effective" excess demands were used, this involved the use of what Lucas was later to criticize as "free parameters." Thus, when economists saw themselves as being faced with a choice between, on one hand, Keynesian models that took prices as given or as responding only slowly to market signals or, on the other hand, new classical models in which prices were endogenous, determined by optimizing agents buying and selling in competitive markets, Keynesian models seemed incomplete. Even though disequilibrium models, as they were still called, were developed to encompass inter-temporal choice and even rational expectations, they were widely seen as models of what happened when prices were rigid rather than as steps towards a more general theory of how market economies worked.

During the 1970s, economists did develop models of imperfect competition that could explain how prices were set, from the early model of Bénassy to the later models of Hahn and Hart at the end of the decade, and imperfect competition was one of the ideas used by the new Keynesians to undermine new classical policy recommendations. However, this did not stop people claiming that there was no theory of how prices were set out of equilibrium. One reason was the widespread belief, that can be traced back to Keynes, that macroeconomics should assume perfect competition. Imperfect competition was associated with institutional barriers to competition. Monopoly power in the labor market, for example, was linked to trade unions, which had a very high profile in the 1970s, especially in Europe, when many days were lost to strike action; but from the 1980s, their power was significantly reduced in many countries. Clearly, there were barriers to entry in some product markets, but monopoly power did not seem, to many economists, to be sufficiently pervasive to justify a universal assumption of imperfect competition. They thus lost sight of Arrow's point that imperfect competition was a necessary consequence of trade taking place out of equilibrium, and that disequilibrium trades must happen whenever it requires time for markets to get into equilibrium. There was also the fact that, as was the case even for Patinkin, much of the general equilibrium literature that modeled price setting was technically very difficult. The result was that equilibrium modeling – Walrasian models in which markets were perfectly competitive and generally cleared – became the dominant approach in macroeconomics. Disequilibrium theory, one of the hottest topics in macroeconomics in the first half of the 1970s, came to be seen as a detour, dealing with a special case, and not, as it had appeared at the time, as a more general approach to the problem of how markets worked.

However, despite the dominance of equilibrium theory, empirical evidence accumulated that showed the simple real business cycle model could not explain what was happening in the real world. In order to explain the data, real business cycle theorists had to introduce persistence – lags and rigidities that, even if they were not formally theorized as imperfect competition or other market imperfections, made their empirical models look more like those of their Keynesian critics. This opened the door to those who brought imperfect competition into DSGE models, creating what came to be called the new neoclassical synthesis.

Perhaps the most important lesson from this account of the search for non-Walrasian foundations for macroeconomics is that it was never homogeneous. The early contributors to this literature, notably Clower, Leijonhufvud, and Barro and Grossman (and sometimes Patinkin, Solow, Stiglitz, Bénassy, Drèze, Grandmont, and Laroque) were routinely bracketed together. However, as Chapters 3, 4, 5 and 7 show, these economists approached disequilibrium theory in ways that were very different, and as a result, even when they developed models that resembled each other, they viewed them in different ways. It is rarely recognized that Clower and Leijonhufvud never accepted that the model produced by Barro and Grossman captured the points they were trying to make. Thus, it is not surprising that, from the 1970s, those who had pioneered disequilibrium theory developed it in different directions, ranging from Barro's endorsement of new classical models, through Stiglitz's new Keynesianism, to Leijonhufvud's taking up computational and agent-based modeling. On top of that, those who were inspired by this literature responded by developing a variety of theories, many of which did not fit the oversimplified labels that were often used to sum up developments in the subject. Thus, Phelps, widely bracketed with Lucas, could also be described as a new Keynesian or as standing in a category of his own. Bracketing macroeconomists into well-defined "schools," though frequently done, is difficult. Also significant was the considerable divide between general equilibrium theory and macroeconomics: important communications did take place, but macroeconomists did not fully engage with the general equilibrium literature.

The search for non-Walrasian or disequilibrium microfoundations was a part of a broader search for microfoundations that took place after the Second World War when economists who were better trained in mathematics than their pre-war counterparts, and who had a different attitude towards what we now call economic modeling, engaged with Keynesian macroeconomics. This search was in turn only a part of macroeconomics, let alone economics as a whole. However, although it deals with only a part of what macroeconomists were doing, the story we tell in this book is central to the transformation of macroeconomics that took place during the 1970s. In the early 1970s, disequilibrium theory, stimulated by thinking that took place in the 1950s and 1960s, *before* the world economic crisis erupted in 1973–74, was exciting because it offered the possibility of a new paradigm – a new way of thinking about economics that some thought could explain phenomena that traditional Keynesian theories could not explain. It may have been pushed aside by the renaissance of equilibrium (market-clearing) theory into which it was technically easier to incorporate formal models of inter-temporal choice and inflation expectations but economists did not abandon the search: by the end of the 1990s, some of the ideas that arose out of the search for disequilibrium microfoundations formed the basis for a widespread consensus on how to construct macroeconomic models. However, this consensus was far from complete with many economists, including writers of introductory and intermediate textbooks, continuing to do macroeconomics in the "old Keynesian" way, and with a smaller number, including those who called themselves "Post-Keynesians," exploring more radical alternatives. The search for non-Walrasian microfoundations left a deep mark on macroeconomics.

A METHODOLOGICAL POSTSCRIPT

This story told in this book illustrates the view, often held by historians, that the history of ideas rarely yields a simple narrative of progress, even though participants (in our case economists) like to present it that way. The idea that, confronted with new evidence, economists developed new macroeconomic theories that were clearly more rigorous and therefore better than their predecessors is an oversimplification. The search for non-Walrasian microfoundations came before the turmoil of the 1970s and was not a response to it. Rather, it was a response to perceived theoretical – even logical – problems with Walrasian models. In contrast to the claims sometimes made, the advocates of disequilibrium theory *did* produce theories of why prices were inflexible. Some of these theories were instantiated in formal models involving imperfect competition, while others remained more informal, involving accounts of decision making in time and costs of making transactions. Ironically, given that disequilibrium theories were criticized for not explaining how individual agents set prices, those theories of price setting, and the arguments about the logical problems with the theory of competitive equilibrium, were brushed aside in favor of a model that did not solve the problem of how prices were set by assuming that markets could reach equilibrium instantaneously: for Lucas, it did not even make sense to talk of a market that was not in equilibrium.

New Keynesians took up the idea of imperfect competition, along with other ways of explaining why the labor market did not clear, but much of this literature, like the new classical economics, bypassed arguments that many advocates of disequilibrium macroeconomists thought important. New Keynesian models generally offered institutional explanations of why the labor market did not clear: the problem of disequilibrium was not seen, as it had been in many earlier writings, as a fundamental theoretical problem with the Walrasian competitive equilibrium approach. Imperfect competition was seen not as referring to the situation that must exist when markets were not in equilibrium – as a logically necessary feature of economies where economic activity takes place in time – but as a phenomenon that may or may not exist, depending on the characteristics of different markets.

One of the factors driving this history was the gap between the vision that drove the search for disequilibrium theory and the models in which that vision was instantiated. Clower and Leijonhufvud never accepted that wage rigidity was the cause of the problems they were analyzing, and disequilibrium theory was developed in large part to explain why Keynesian phenomena were *not* caused by sticky wages but were, as Keynes himself had claimed, the result of economic activity taking place in time. Clower and Leijonhufvud never tried to sum up their insights in a mathematical model. Barro and Grossman, in contrast, had a model that was simple, easy to manipulate, and teachable. Although Clower and Leijonhufvud, the two economists most consistently associated with the subject, rejected the notion; for most macroeconomists, disequilibrium economics meant equilibrium with fixed prices and, during the 1970s, it became common practice to explore the properties of fixed-price equilibria. Malinvaud's widely cited lectures, with his distinction between classical and Keynesian unemployment, certainly popularized non-Walrasian theory. However, through focusing on a fixed-price model, neglecting attempts that were being made to construct theories of how prices were determined, his book, paradoxically, made it easier for non-Walrasian theory to be rejected.

It is also worth nothing that, though it had started earlier, the heyday of disequilibrium theory was precisely the time when inflation was at its peak in many countries. Far from undermining it, stagflation was in part the motivation behind disequilibrium macroeconomics, for many economists saw the events of the 1970s as evidence that markets could not be in continuous Walrasian equilibrium. A new theory was needed, and it was far from obvious that the theory of general competitive equilibrium could provide the answer.

Thus, when Roy Weintraub, who was aware of the literature on imperfect competition, surveyed the field, he mounted a defense of general equilibrium theory not by defending theories based on perfect competition, but by arguing that general equilibrium was a much more general notion, that could encompass imperfections in the market process:

General equilibrium analysis has, for a number of years now, gone far beyond Walrasian typologies to a consideration of many issues, like transactions structures, information costs, speculation, imperfect adjustment, and search behaviour, which are nearer to traditional macroeconomic concerns.... Those who argue that the current theory is unrealistic fail to appreciate the attention being paid to real adjustment processes in real time. (E. R. Weintraub 1977:19)

However, the subject was "not susceptible to neat packages of integrated results," as a result of which he predicted that the short-term result would be eclecticism. On the narrower question of disequilibrium macroeconomics, he concluded that "Keynesian macroeconomics cannot be derived from any simple Walrasian microsystem.... the question of *appropriate* microfoundations for macroeconomic theory is still an open one" (E. R. Weintraub 1977:18). This remained true when the new neoclassical synthesis became established in the 1990s, for there remained significant numbers of economists who did not accept it. Macroeconomists remained divided over whether it was necessary to assume imperfect competition and on the importance of factors such as asymmetric information, some seeing them as offering new general theories, whilst others saw them as much more limited in their application. There were macroeconomists who rejected formal modeling altogether, or preferred more data-driven econometric modeling and others who sought microfoundations in new approaches, such as behavioral or "agent-based" modeling. After the 2008 financial crisis focused attention on features of the financial system that had up to then been ignored in most macroeconomic models, these disagreements became even wider.

Bibliography

Alchian, A. A. 1950 Uncertainty, Evolution and Economic Theory. *Journal of Political Economy* **58**:211–21.

　1963. Reliability of Progress Curves in Airframe Production. *Econometrica* **31**:679–93.

　1969. Information costs, pricing and resource unemployment. *Western Economic Journal* **7**:109–28.

　1970. Information Costs, Pricing and Resource Unemployment. In Phelps et al. *Microeconomic Foundations of Employment and Inflation Theory*. London: Macmillan, 27–52.

Amadae, S. 2003. *Rationalizing Capitalist Democracy: The Cold War Origins of Rational Choice Liberalism*. Chicago: University of Chicago Press.

Anonymous. 1988. Citation classics. *Current Contents* **13** (March):16.

Arena, R. 2010. From the "old" to the "new" Keynesian-neoclassical synthesis: an interpretatation." In B. W. Bateman, T. Hirai, and M. C. Marcuzzo (eds.) *The Return to Keynes*. Cambridge, MA: Harvard University Press, 77–93.

Arida, P., and Bacha, E. 1987. Balance of payments: a disequilibrium analysis for semi-industrialized economies. *Journal of Development Economics* 27:85-108.

Arrow, K. J. 1953. Le rôle des valeurs boursieres pour la repartition la meilleure des risques. *Econometrie*, 41–47. Paris: CNRS. Translated as Arrow 1964.

　1959. Towards a theory of price adjustment. In M. Abramovitz (ed.) *The Allocation of Economic Resources*. Stanford: University of California Press, 41–51.

　1964. The role of securities in the optimal allocation of risk-bearing. *Review of Economic Studies* **31**:91–96.

Arrow, K J., and Debreu, G. 1954. Existence of an equilibrium for a competitive economy. *Econometrica* **22**(3):265–90.

Arrow, K. J., Block, H. D., and Hurwicz, L. 1959. On the stability of the competitive equilibrium, II. *Econometrica* **27**:82–109.

Arrow, K. J., and Hahn, F. H. 1971. *General Competitive Analysis*. Edinburgh: Oliver and Boyd.

Atkinson, A. B., and Stiglitz, J. E. 1977. *Lectures in Public Economics*. New York: McGraw-Hill.

Azariadis, C. 1975. Implicit contracts and underemployment equilibria. *Journal of Political Economy* **83**(6):1183–1202.

189

Azariadis, C., and Stiglitz, J. E. 1983. Implicit contracts and fixed price equilibria. *Quarterly Journal of Economics* **98**:1–22.

Backhouse, R. E. 1980. Fix-price versus flex-price models of macroeconomic equilibrium with quantity rationing. *Oxford Economic Papers* **32**(2):210–33.

1981. Keynesian unemployment and the one-sector neoclassical growth model. *Economic Journal* **91**(361):174–87.

1982. Price flexibility and Keynesian unemployment in a macroeconomic model with quantity rationing. *Oxford Economic Papers* **34**(2):292–304.

1995. *Interpreting Macroeconomics: Explorations in the History of Macroeconomic Thought.* London: Routledge.

1998. The transformation of American economics, seen through a survey of journal articles. In M. S. Morgan and M. Rutherford (eds.) *From Interwar Pluralism to Postwar Neoclassicism.* Annual supplement to vol. 30 of *History of Political Economy.* Durham, NC: Duke University Press, 85–107.

2002. Don Patinkin: Interpreter of the Keynesian revolution. *European Journal of the History of Economic Thought* **9**(2):186–204.

2006. The Keynesian revolution. In R. E. Backhouse and B. W. Bateman (eds.) *The Cambridge Companion to Keynes.* Cambridge: Cambridge University Press, 19–38.

2008. Economics in the United States after 1945. In L. Blume and S. Durlauf (eds.) *The New Palgrave Dictionary of Economics*, 2nd ed. London: Palgrave, vol. 8, 522–533. Available at http://www.dictionaryofeconomics.com.

2010a. *The Puzzle of Modern Economics.* Cambridge: Cambridge University Press.

2010b. Economics. In R. E. Backhouse and P. Fontaine (eds.) *The History of the Social Sciences since 1945.* Cambridge: Cambridge University Press, 38–70.

Backhouse, R. E., and Bateman, B. W. 2011. *Capitalist Revolutionary: John Maynard Keynes.* Cambridge, MA: Harvard University Press.

Backhouse, R. E., and Fontaine, P. 2010a. *The History of the Social Sciences since 1945.* Cambridge: Cambridge University Press.

2010b. *The Unsocial Social Science? Economics and Neighboring Disciplines since 1945.* Durham, NC: Duke University Press.

Backhouse, R. E., and Giraud, Y. 2010. Circular Flow Diagrams. In M. Blaug and P. Lloyd (eds.) *Famous Figures and Diagrams in Economics.* Cheltenham: Edward Elgar, 221–29.

Backhouse, R. E., and Laidler, D. 2004. What was lost with IS-LM. In M. De Vroey and K. D. Hoover (eds.) *The IS-LM Model: Its Rise, Fall, and Strange Persistence.* Annual supplement to vol. 36 of *History of Political Economy.* Durham, NC, and London: Duke University Press, 25–56.

Backhouse, R. E., and Salanti, A. 2000. *Macroeconomics and the Real World, Volume I: Econometric Techniques and Macroeconomics.* Oxford: Oxford University Press.

Bailey, M. J. 1962. *National Income and the Price Level: A Study in Macroeconomic Theory.* New York: McGraw-Hill.

Baily, M. N. 1974. Wages and employment under uncertain demand. *Review of Economic Studies* **41**(1):37–50.

Barro, R. J. 1974a. Are government bonds net wealth? *Journal of Political Economy* **82**(6):1095–1117.

1974b. Suppressed inflation and the supply multiplier. *Review of Economic Studies* **39**:17–26. Reprinted in Barro 1981.

1976. Rational expectations and the role of monetary policy. *Journal of Monetary Economics* **2**(1):1–32. Reprinted in Barro 1981.

1977a. Consumption, income and liquidity. In G. Schwoediauer (ed.) *Equilibrium and Disequilibrium in Economic Theory*. Dordrecht: Reidel, 565–92.

1977b. Long-term contracting, sticky prices and monetary policy. *Journal of Monetary Economics* **3** (3):305–16. Reprinted in Barro 1981.

1979. Second thoughts on Keynesian economics. *American Economic Review* **69**:54–59.

1981. *Money, Expectations and Business Cycles: Essays in Macroeconomics*. New York: Academic Press.

1987. *Macroeconomics*. 2nd ed. New York: Wiley.

1994a. Interview in Snowdon, Vane, and Wynarczyk (1994).

1994b. The Aggregate-Supply/Aggregate-Demand Model. *Eastern Economic Journal* **20**:1–6.

Barro, R. J., and S. Fischer. 1976. Recent developments in monetary theory. *Journal of Monetary Economics* **2** (2):133–67. Reprinted in Barro 1981.

Barro, R. J., and Grossman, H. I. 1971. A general disequilibrium model of income and employment. *American Economic Review* **61**:82–93.

Barro, R. J., and Grossman, H. I. 1974. Suppressed Inflation and the Supply Multiplier. *Review of Economic Studies* **41**(1):87–104.

1976. *Money, Employment and Inflation*. Cambridge: Cambridge University Press.

Bartalanffy, L. 1968. *General System Theory: Foundations, Development, Applications*. New York: George Braziller.

Baumol, W. J. 1977. Say's (at least) eight laws, or what Say and James Mill may really have meant. *Economica* **44**:145–62.

1999. Say's law. *Journal of Economic Perspectives* **13**(1):195–204.

Becker, G. S., and Baumol, W. J. 1952. The classical economic theory: the outcome of the discussion. *Economica* **19**:355–76.

Bénassy, J.-P. 1973. *Disequilibrium Theory*. Ph.D. Dissertation, University of California, Berkeley.

1975. Neo-Keynesian disequilibrium theory in a monetary economy. *Review of Economic Studies* **41**:503–23.

1976a. The disequilibrium approach to monopolistic price setting and general monopolistic equilibrium. *Review of Economic Studies* **43**:69–81.

1976b. Théorie neokeynésienne du déséquilibre dans une économie monétaire. *Cahiers du séminaire d'économétrie* **17**:81–113.

1978. A neo-Keynesian model of price and quantity determination in disequilibrium. In G. Schwödiauer (ed.) *Equilibrium and Disequilibrium in Economic Theory*. Boston: Reidel, 511–44.

1982. *The Economics of Market Disequilibrium*. New York: Academic Press.

1986. *Macroeconomics: An Introduction to the Non-Walrasian Approach*. New York: Academic Press.

1987a. Disequilibrium analysis. In J. Eatwell, M. Milgate, and P. Newman (eds.) *The New Palgrave Dictionary of Economics*. London: Macmillan, vol. 1, 858–63.

1987b. Rationed equilibria. In J. Eatwell, M. Milgate, and P. Newman (eds.) *The New Palgrave Dictionary of Economics*. London: Macmillan, vol. 4, 88–92.

1993. Nonclearing markets: microeconomic concepts and macroeconomic applications. *Journal of Economic Literature* **31**:732–61.

Bénassy, J.-P. (ed.) 1995. *Macroeconomics and Imperfect Competition*. Aldershot: Edward Elgar.

2002. *The Macroeconomics of Imperfect Competition and Non-Clearing Markets*. Cambridge, MA: MIT Press.

(ed.) 2006. *Imperfect Competition, Non-Clearing Markets and Business Cycles*. Cheltenham: Edward Elgar.

2008a. Dynamic models with non-clearing markets. In S. Durlauf and L. Blume (eds.) *The New Palgrave Dictionary of Economics*, 2nd ed., vol. X. London: Palgrave, vol. 2, 568–75.

2008b. Non-clearing markets in general equilibrium. In S. Durlauf and L. Blume (eds.) *The New Palgrave Dictionary of Economics*, 2nd ed., vol. X. London: Palgrave, vol. 6, 62–69.

Blanchard, O. J. 2000. What do we know about macroeconomics that Fisher and Wicksell did not? *Quarterly Journal of Economics* **115**:1375–1409.

2003. *Macroeconomics*. 3rd ed. London: Pearson Education.

2008. Neoclassical synthesis. In S. N. Durlauf and L. E. Blume (eds.) *The New Palgrave Dictionary of Economics*. London: Palgrave, vol. 5, 896–99.

Blanchard, O. J., and Kiyotaki, N. 1987. Monopolistic competition and the effects of aggregate demand. *American Economic Review* **77**(4):647–66.

Blaug, M. 1992. *The Methodology of Economics*. 2nd ed. Cambridge: Cambridge University Press.

1997. *Economic Theory in Retrospect*. 5th ed. Cambridge: Cambridge University Press.

1999. *Who's Who in Economics*. 3rd ed. Cheltenham: Edward Elgar.

Bliss, C.J. 1975. The reappraisal of Keynes's economics: an appraisal. In M. Parkin and A. Nobay (eds.) *Current Economic Problems*. Cambridge: Cambridge University Press, 203–13.

Boianovsky, M. 2002a. Patinkin, the Cowles Commission, and the theory of unemployment and aggregate supply. *European Journal of the History of Economic Thought* **9**:226–59.

2002b. Simonsen and the early history of the cash-in-advance approach. *European Journal of the History of Economic Thought* **9**: 57–71.

2004. The IS-LM model and the liquidity trap concept: from Hicks to Krugman. In M. de Vroey and K. D. Hoover (eds.) *The IS-LM model: its rise, fall, and strange persistence*. Annual supplement to vol. 36 of *History of Political Economy*. Durham, NC, and London: Duke University Press, 92–125.

2005. Some Cambridge reactions to the *General Theory*: David Champernowne and Joan Robinson on full employment. *Cambridge Journal of Economics* **29**:73–98.

2006. The making of chapters 13 and 14 of Patinkin's *Money, Interest, and Prices*. *History of Political Economy* **38**:193–249.

2008. Patinkin, Don (1922–1995). In W. Darity (ed.) *International Encyclopedia of Social Sciences*, 2nd ed. London: Macmillan, vol. 10, 223–24.

2011. Was Patinkin a Keynesian economist? In A. Arnon, J. Weinblatt, and W. Young (eds.) *Perspectives on Keynesian Economics*. Berlin: Springer, 81–98.

Boianovsky, M., and Hoover, K. D. 2009. The neoclassical growth model and twentieth-century economics. In M. Boianovsky and K.D. Hoover (eds.) *Robert*

Solow and the Development of Growth Economics. Annual supplement to vol. 41 of *History of Political Economy.* Durham and London: Duke University Press, 1–23.

Boianovsky, M., and Presley, J. R. 2009. The Robertson connection between the natural rates of interest and unemployment. *Structural Change and Economic Dynamics.* **20**:136–50.

Boianovsky, M., and Trautwein, H.-M. 2006. Wicksell after Woodford. *Journal of the History of Economic Thought* **28**(2):171–85.

2010. Schumpeter on unemployment. *Journal of Evolutionary Economics.* **20**: 233–63.

Boschen, J., and Grossman, H. I. 1982. Tests of equilibrium macroeconomics using contemporaneous monetary data. *Journal of Monetary Economics* **10**(3):309–33.

Boulding, K. E. 1968. *Beyond Economics: Essays on Society, Religion and Ethics.* Ann Arbor: University of Michigan Press.

Brakman, S., and Heijdra, B. J. (eds.) 2004. *The Monopolistic Competition Revolution in Retrospect.* Cambridge: Cambridge University Press.

Branson, W. H. 1979. *Macroeconomic Theory and Policy.* 2nd ed. New York: Harper and Row.

Brechling, F. 1965. Summary record of the debate. In F. Hahn and F. Brechling (eds.) *The Theory of Interest Rates.* London: Macmillan, 283–360.

Bruno, M., and Sachs, J. D. 1985. *The Economics of Worldwide Stagflation.* Oxford: Basil Blackwell.

Burns, A., and Mitchell, W. C. 1946. *Measuring Business Cycles.* New York: NBER.

Burstein, M. L. 1986. *Modern Monetary Theory.* New York: St. Martin's Press.

Busetto, F. 1995. Why the non-tâtonnement line of research died out. *Economic Notes* **24**(1):89–114.

Bushaw, D., and Clower, R.W. 1960. On the Invariance of the Demand for Cash and Other Assets. *Review of Economic Studies* **28**(1):32–36.

Calvo, G. A. 1983. Staggered prices in a utility-maximizing framework. *Journal of Monetary Economics* **12**:383–98.

Champernowne, D. 1936. Unemployment, basic and monetary: The classical analysis and the Keynesian. *Review of Economic Studies* **3**:201–16.

Cherrier, B. 2011. The lucky consistency of Milton Friedman's science and politics, 1933–1963. In R. van Horn, P. Mirowski, and T. A. Stapleford (eds.) *Building Chicago Economics: New Perspectives on the History of America's Most Powerful Economics Program.* Cambridge: Cambridge University Press, 335–367.

Clower, R. W. 1952a. Mr Graaff's producer-consumer theory: A restatement and a correction. *Review of Economic Studies* **20**(1): 84–85.

1952b. Professor Duisenberry and traditional theory. *Review of Economic Studies* **19**(3):165–78.

1954. An investigation into the dynamics of investment. *American Economic Review* **44**(1):64–81.

1959. Some theory of an ignorant monopolist. *Economic Journal* **69**(276): 705–716.

1960. Keynes and the classics: a dynamical perspective. *Quarterly Journal of Economics* **74**(2):318–23. Reprinted in Walker (1984).

1965. The Keynesian counterrevolution: A theoretical appraisal. In F. H. Hahn and F. P. R. Brechling (eds.) *The Theory of Interest Rates.* London: Macmillan, 103–25.

1967. A reconsideration of the microfoundations for monetary theory. *Western Economic Journal* 6:1–8.

1975. Reflections on the Keynesian perplex. *Zeitschrift fuer Nationaloekonomie* 35:1–24.

1984. Afterword. In D. A. Walker (ed.) *Money and Markets: Essays by Robert W. Clower.* Cambridge: Cambridge University Press, 259–72.

1988. Keynes' *General Theory*: the Marshall Connection. In D. Walker (ed.). *Perspectives on the History of Economic Thought,* vol. II. Aldershot: Elgar, 133–47.

1994. The effective demand fraud. *Eastern Economic Journal* 20:377–85.

1999. Interview in Snowdon and Vane (1999).

Clower, R. W., and D. W. Bushaw. 1954. Price determination in a stock-flow economy. *Econometrica* 22:328–43.

Clower, R. W., and Howitt, P. 1978. The transactions theory of the demand for money: A reconsideration. *Journal of Political Economy* 86:449–66.

Coddington, A. 1976. Keynesian economics: The search for first principles. *Journal of Economic Literature* 14:1258–73.

1978. Review of Malinvaud 1977. *Journal of Economic Literature* 16(3):1012–1018.

1983. *Keynesian Economics: The Search for First Principles.* London: Allen & Unwin.

Coen, R. M., and Hickman, B. G. 1987. Keynesian and classical unemployment in four countries. *Brookings Papers on Economic Activity* 1987(1):123–406.

Colander, D. C. (ed.) 1996. *Beyond Microfoundations: Post Walrasian Macroeconomics.* Cambridge: Cambridge University Press.

(ed.) 2006. *Post Walrasian Economics: Beyond the Dynamic Stochastic General Equilibrium Model.* Cambridge: Cambridge University Press.

Committee on the Working of the Monetary System. 1959. *Report.* London: Her Majesty's Stationery Office.

Cooper, R., and A. John. 1988. Coordinating Coordination Failures in Keynesian Models. *Quarterly Journal of Economics* 103(August):441–63.

Costa, M.L. 2002.*General Equilibrium Analysis and the Theory of Markets.* Cheltenham: Edward Elgar.

de Antoni, E. 1999. R.W. Clower's intellectual voyage: The "Ariadne's thread" of continuity through changes. In P. Howitt, E. de Antoni, and A. Leijonhufvud (eds.) *Money, Markets and Method – Essays in Honour of Robert W. Clower.* Cheltenham: Elgar, 3–22.

2006. The auctioneerless economics of Axel Leijonhufvud: The "dark forces of time and ignorance" and the coordination of economic activity. *Cambridge Journal of Economics* 30:85–103.

De Vroey, M. 2004. *Involuntary Unemployment: The Elusive Quest for a Theory.* London: Routledge.

2006. Marshall versus Walras on equilibrium. In T. Raffaelli, G. Becattini, and M. Dardi *(eds.) The Elgar Companion to Alfred Marshall.* Cheltenham: Edward Elgar, 237–48.

Debreu, G. 1959. *The Theory of Value.* London: Wiley.

1974. Excess demand functions. *Journal of Mathematical Economics* 1:15–21.

Dehez, P. and Drèze, J. 1988. Competitive equilibria with quantity-taking producers and increasing returns to scale. *Journal of Mathematical Economics* 17:209–30.

Diamond, P. A. 1967. The role of a stock market in a general equilibrium model with technological uncertainty. *American Economic Review* 57:759–76.

  1984. *A Search-Equilibrium Approach to the Micro Foundations of Macroeconomics.* Cambridge, MA: MIT Press.

Dimand, R. 2008. Edmund Phelps and Modern Macroeconomics. *Review of Political Economy* 20(1):23–39.

Dixit, A. K. 1978. The balance of trade in a model with temporary equilibrium with rationing. *Review of Economic Studies* 45:393–404.

Dixit, A. K., and Stiglitz, J. E. 1977. Monopolistic competition and optimum product diversity. *American Economic Review* 67(3):297–308.

Dixon, H. 1992. Review of N. Gregory Mankiw and David Romer (eds) *New Keynesian Economics.* 2 volumes. Cambridge, MA: MIT Press. *Economic Journal* 102(414):1272–75.

  1997. The role of imperfect competition in Keynesian economics. In Snowdon, B., and Vane, H. (eds.), *Reflections on the Development of Modern Macroeconomics.* Cheltenham: Edward Elgar, pp. 158–203.

Drazen, A. 1980. Recent developments in macroeconomic disequilibrium theory. *Econometrica* 86:505–16.

Drèze, J. 1964. Some postwar contributions of French economists to theory and public policy. *American Economic Review* 54 (2):1–64.

Drèze, J. (ed.) 1974. *Allocation under Uncertainty: Equilibrium and Optimality.* London: Macmillan.

Drèze, J. 1975. Existence of an exchange equilibrium under price rigidities. *International Economic Review* 16:301–20. Reprinted in Dreze 1991a.

  1991. *Underemployment Equilibria: Essays in Theory, Econometrics and Policy.* Cambridge: Cambridge University Press.

  1999. On the dynamics of supply-constrained equilibria. In P. J.-J. Heerings, G. van der Laan, and A. J. J. Talman (eds.) *Theory of Markets.* Amsterdam: North Holland, 7–25.

Eichner, A. S. 1976. *The Megacorp and Oligopoly: Micro Foundations of Macro Dynamics.* New York: Cambridge University Press.

Eichner, A. S, and Kregel, J. A. 1975. An essay on post-Keynesian theory: a new paradigm in economics. *Journal of Economic Literature* 13(4):1293–1314.

Fair, Ray C., and Jaffee, D. M. 1972. Methods of estimation for markets in disequilibrium. *Econometrica* 40(3):497–514.

Fischer, S. 1975. Recent developments in monetary theory. *The American Economic Review* 65 (2, Papers and Proceedings):157–66.

  1977. Long-term contracts, rational expectations, and the optimal money supply rule. *Journal of Political Economy* 85:191–205.

  1988. Recent developments in macroeconomics. *Economic Journal* 98: 294–339.

  1996. Robert Lucas's Nobel memorial prize. *Scandinavian Journal of Economics.* 98: 11–31.

Fisher, F. M. 1976. A Non-Tatonnement Model with Production and Consumption. *Econometrica* 44(5):907–938.

1983. *Disequlibrium Foundations of Equilibrium Economics.* Cambridge: Cambridge University Press.

Flemming, J. S. 1973. The consumption function when capital markets are imperfect: The permanent income hypothesis reconsidered. *Oxford Economic Papers* 25:160–72.

1987. Wage flexibility and employment stability. *Oxford Economic Papers* 39(1):161–74.

Forder, J. 2010a. The historical place of the 'Friedman–Phelps' expectations critique. *European Journal of the History of Economic Thought* 17(3):493–511.

2010b. Friedman's Nobel lecture and the Phillips curve myth. *Journal of the History of Economic Thought* 32(3):329–48.

Friedman, M. (ed.) 1956. The quantity theory of money: a restatement. In M. Friedman (ed.) *Studies in the Quantity Theory Of Money.* Chicago: University of Chicago Press.

1957. *A Theory of the Consumption Function.* Princeton, NJ: Princeton University Press.

1968. The role of monetary policy. *American Economic Review* 58:1–19.

Friedman, M., and Schwartz, A. J. 1963. *A Monetary History of the United States, 1867–1960.* Princeton, NJ: Princeton University Press.

Frydman, R., and Phelps, E. S. 1983. *Individual Forecasting and Aggregate Outcomes: "Rational Expectations" Examined.* Cambridge: Cambridge University Press.

Gallegati, M., and Kirman, A. P. (eds.) 1999. *Beyond the Representative Agent.* Cheltenham: Edward Elgar.

Gans, J. S., and Shepherd, G. B. 1994. How Are The Mighty Fallen: Rejected Classic Articles by Leading Economists. *Journal of Economic Perspectives* 8(1):165–79.

Garretsen, H. 1992. *Keynes, Coordination and Beyond: The Development of Macroeconomic and Monetary Theory since 1945.* Aldershot: Edward Elgar.

Goldfeld, S. M., and Quandt, R. E. 1975. Estimation in a disequilibrium model and the value of information. *Journal of Econometrics* 3:325–48.

Goodfriend, M., and King, R. G. 1997. The new neoclassical synthesis and the role of monetary policy. *NBER Macroeconomics Annual* 12:231–83.

Gordon, D. F. 1974. A neoclassical theory of Keynesian unemployment. *Economic Inquiry* 11:431–59.

Gordon, R. A. (ed.) 1974. *Milton Friedman's Monetary Framework: A Debate with His Critics.* Chicago: University of Chicago Press.

Grandmont, J.-M. 1977. On temporary Keynesian equilibrium. In G. C. Harcourt (ed.) *The Microeconomic Foundations of Macroeconomics.* London: Macmillan, 41–61.

Grandmont, J.-M., and Laroque, G. 1976. On temporary Keynesian equilibria. *Review of Economic Studies* 43:53–67.

1977. On temporary Keynesian equilibria. In G. Harcourt (ed.) *Microeconomic Foundations of Macroeconomics.* London: Macmillian, XX–XX.

Grandmont, J.-M., Laroque, G., and Younès, Y. 1978. Equilibrium with quantity rationing and recontracting. *Journal of Economic Theory* 19(1):84–102.

Grandmont, J.-M., and Younès, Y. 1972. On the role of money and the existence of a monetary equilibrium. *Review of Economic Studies* 39:355–72.

Gray, J. A. 1976. Wage indexation: A macroeconomic approach. *Journal of Monetary Economics* **2**:221–35.

Green, C. 1978. *Canadian Journal of Economics* **11**(4):775–77.

Greenwald, B., and Stiglitz, J. E. 1987. Keynesian, new Keynesian and new classical economics. *Oxford Economic Papers* **39**:119–33.

Grossman, H. I. 1969. Theories of markets without recontracting. *Journal of Economic Theory* **1**:476–79.

1972a. Money, interest and prices in market disequilibrium. *Journal of Political Economy* **80**(2):223–55.

1972b. Was Keynes a "Keynesian"? A review article. *Journal of Economic Literature* **10**:26–30.

1974. Effective demand failures – a comment. *Swedish Journal of Economics* **76**:358–65.

1979. Why does aggregate employment fluctuate? *American Economic Review* **69** (Papers and Proceedings) 64–69.

1983. The natural-rate hypothesis, the rational expectation hypothesis, and the remarkable survival of non-market clearing assumptions. *Carnegie-Rochester Conference on Public Policy* **19**:225–46.

1987. Monetary disequilibrium and market clearing. In J. Eatwell et al. (eds.) *The New Palgrave – A Dictionary of Economics*. London: Macmillan, vol. 3, 504–506.

Gurley, J. G., and Shaw, E. S. 1960. *Money in a Theory of Finance*. Washington, DC: Brookings Institution.

Hahn, F. H. 1952. Expectations and equilibrium. *Economic Journal* **62**:802–19.

1955. Uncertainty and the cobweb. *Review of Economic Studies* **23**(1):65–75.

1965. Of some problems on proving the existence of equilibrium in a monetary economy. In F. H. Hahn and F. P. R. Brechling (eds.) *The Theory of Interest Rates*. London: Macmillan, 126–35.

1977. Exercises in conjectural equilibria. *Scandinavian Journal of Economics* **79**:210–26.

1978. On non-Walrasian equilibria. *Review of Economic Studies* **45**:1–17.

1983. Comment on Leijonhufvud. In R. Frydman and E. Phelps (eds.) *Individual Forecasting and Aggregate Outcomes: "Rational Expectations" Examined*. Cambridge: Cambridge University Press, 223–30.

Hahn, F. H. (ed.) 1989. *The Economics of Missing Markets, Information and Games*. Oxford: Clarendon Press.

Hahn, F. H. 1990. John Hicks the Theorist. *Economic Journal* **100**: 539–49.

Hahn, F. H., and Solow, R. M. 1995. *A Critical Essay on Modern Macroeconomic Theory*. Oxford: Blackwell.

Hansen, A. 1953. *A Guide to Keynes*. London: McGraw Hill.

Hansen, B. 1951. *A Study in the Theory of Inflation*. London: Allen and Unwin.

1970. *A Survey of General Equilibrium Systems*. New York: McGraw Hill.

Harcourt, G. C. 1972. *On Some Cambridge Controversies in the Theory of Capital*. Cambridge: Cambridge University Press.

(ed.) 1977. *The Microfoundations of Macroeconomics*. London: Macmillan.

Hart, O. D. 1982. A model of imperfect competition with Keynesian features. *Quarterly Journal of Economics* **97** (1):109–38.

Hartley, J. 1997. *The Representative Agent in Macroeconomics*. London: Routledge.

Hicks, J. R. 1937. Mr Keynes and the "classics": A suggested interpretation. *Econometrica* 5:147–59.

1939. *Value and Capital*. Oxford: Clarendon Press.

1957. A rehabilitation of "classical" economics. *Economic Journal* **67**:278–89.

1974. *The Crisis in Keynesian Economics*. Oxford: Basil Blackwell.

1979. Review of Weintraub 1979. *Journal of Economic Literature* **17** (4):1451–54.

Hines, A. G. 1971. *On the Reappraisal of Keynesian Economics*. London: Martin Robertson.

Hoover, K. D. 1988. *The New Classical Macroeconomics*. Oxford: Blackwell.

1991. Scientific research program or tribe? A joint appraisal of Lakatos and the new classical macroeconomics. In M. Blaug and N. De Marchi (eds.) *Appraising Economic Theories: The Methodology of Scientific Research Programmes*. Aldershot: Edward Elgar, 364–94.

(ed.) 1999. *The Legacy of Robert E. Lucas Jr.* 3 vol. Cheltenham: Edward Elgar.

2012. Microfoundational programs. In Duarte, Pedro Garcia & Lima, Gilberto Tadeu (Eds.). *Microfoundations reconsidered: The relationship of micro and macroeconomics in historical perspective*. Cheltenham: Edward Elgar, 19–61.

Howitt, P. 1979. Evaluating the non-market clearing approach. *American Economic Review* **69**:60–63.

1987. Macroeconomics: Relations with microeconomics. In J. Eatwell, M. Milgate, and P. Newman (eds.) *The New Palgrave – A Dictionary of Economics*. London: Macmillan, 273–76.

1990. *The Keynesian Recovery and Other Essays*. Oxford: Philip Allan.

2002. Leijonhufvud, Axel – On Keynesian economics and the economics of Keynes: a study in monetary theory. In X. Greffe, J. Lallemont, and M. De Vroey (eds.) *Dictionnaire des grandes oevres économiques*. Paris: Dalloz, 280–88.

2008. Macroeconomics with intelligent autonomous agents. In R. E. A. Farmer (ed.) *Macroeconomics in the Small and the Large: Essays on Microfoundations, Macroeconomic Applications and Economic History in Honor of Axel Leijonhufvud*. Cheltenham: Edward Elgar, 157–77.

Janssen, M. 1993. *Microfoundations – a critical inquiry*. London: Routledge.

2008. Microfoundations. In S. Durlauf and L. Blume (eds.) *The New Palgrave Dictionary of Economics*, 2nd ed. London: Palgrave Macmillan, 600–604.

Johnson, H. G. 1962. Monetary theory and policy. *American Economic Review* **52**(3):335–84.

1971. The Keynesian revolution and the monetarist counter-revolution. *The American Economic Review* **61**(2):1–14.

1976. Keynes's general theory: Revolution or war of independence? *Canadian Journal of Economics* **9**(4):580–94.

Kahn, R. F. 1977. Malinvaud on Keynes. *Cambridge Journal of Economics* **1**:375–88.

Keynes, J. M. 1937. The general theory of employment. *Quarterly Journal of Economics* 51(2):209–23.

1973[1936]. *The General Theory of Employment, Interest and Money*. The Collected Writings of John Maynard Keynes, VII. London: Macmillan.

King, J. E. 2009. *A History of Post Keynesian Economics*. Cheltenham: Edward Elgar.

Kirman, A. P. 1993. Whom or what does the representative agent represent? *Journal of Economic Perspectives* 6(2):117–36.

Klamer, A. 1984. *Conversations with Economists: New Classical Economists and Opponents Speak Out on the Current Controversy in Macroeconomics*. Totowa, NJ: Rowman and Littlefield.

Kornai, J. 1971. *Anti-Equilibrium: On Economic Systems Theory and the Tasks of Research*. Amsterdam: North Holland.

Kregel, J. A. 1973. *The Reconstruction of Political Economy: An Introduction to Post-Keynesian Economics*. London: Macmillan.

Krueger, A. B. 2003. An interview with Edmond Malinvaud. *Journal of Economic Perspectives* 17(1):181–98.

Krugman, P. 2009. How did economists get it so wrong? *The Times Magazine*, September 2.

Kydland, F. E., and E. C. Prescott. 1982. Time to Build and Aggregate Fluctuations. *Econometrica* 50 (6):1345–70.

Laidler, D. W. 1993. Hawtrey, Harvard, and the Origins of the Chicago Tradition. *Journal of Political Economy* 101 (6):1068–1103.

1999. *Fabricating the Keynesian Revolution: Studies of the Inter-War Literature on Money, the Cycle, and Unemployment*. Cambridge: Cambridge University Press.

Lange, O. 1938. The rate of interest and the optimum propensity to consume. *Economica* 5(17):12–32.

1942. Say's law: a restatement and criticism. In O. Lange et al. (eds.) *Studies in Mathematical Economics and Econometrics*. Chicago: University of Chicago Press, 49–68.

1944. *Price Flexibility and Employment*. Bloomington, IN: Principia Press.

Lee, F. S. 2000. On the genesis of Post Keynesian economics: Alfred Eichner, Joan Robinson and the founding of Post Keynesian economics. In A. Name (ed.) *Research in the History of Economic Thought and Methodology*: 18-C, *Twentieth Century Economics*. Greenwich, CT and Amsterdam: JAI/Elsevier, 3–258.

2010. *A History of Heterodox Economics*. London: Routledge.

Leijonhufvud, A. 1968. *On Keynesian Economics and the Economics of Keynes*. Oxford: Oxford University Press.

1969. *Keynes and the Classics: Two Lectures*. London: Institute of Economic Affairs.

1973a. Effective demand failures. *Swedish Journal of Economics* 75:27–48.

1973b. Life among the Econ. *Western Economic Journal* 11(3):327–37.

1974a. Maximization and Marshall. Marshall Lectures, unpublished.

1974b. Varieties of Price Theory: What Microfoundations for Macrotheory? UCLA Discussion Paper.

1974c. Keynes's Employment Function. *History of Political Economy* 6(2):164–70.

1981. *Information and Coordination: Essays in Macroeconomic Theory*. New York: Oxford University Press.

1983. Keynesianism, monetarism and rational expectations: some reflections and conjectures. In R. Frydman and E. Phelps (eds.) *Individual Forecasting and Aggregate Outcomes: "Rational Expectations" Examined*. Cambridge: Cambridge University Press, 203–23.

1998. Mr Keynes and the moderns. *European Journal of the History of Economic Thought* 5(1):169–88.

2000. *Macroeconomic Instability and Coordination: Selected Essays of Axel Leijonhufvud.* Cheltenham: Edward Elgar.

2004. Celebrating Ned. *Journal of Economic Literature* 42:811–21.

Levallois, C. 2009. One analogy can hide another: physics and biology in Alchian's 'economic natural selection'. *History of Political Economy* 41(1):163–81.

Levine, D. K. n.d. Armen A. Alchian. Available at http://levine.sscnet.ucla.edu/ General/ alchian.htm. Accessed on August 4, 2011.

Licandro, O., and Dehez, P. 2007. An interview with Jacques Drèze. In P. A. Samuelson and W. A. Barnett (eds.) *Inside the Economist's Mind: Conversations with Eminent Economists.* Malden, MA: Blackwell Publishing, 278–306.

Lipsey, R. G. 1960. The relation between unemployment and the rate of change of money wage rates in the United Kingdom, 1862–1957: A further analysis. *Economica* 27(105):1–31.

Long, J. B., and C. I. Plosser. 1983. Real Business Cycles. *Journal of Political Economy* 91(1):39–69.

Lucas, R. E. 1967a. Adjustment costs and the theory of supply. *Journal of Political Economy* 75(4):321–34.

1967b. Optimal investment policy and the flexible accelerator. *International Economic Review* 8(1):78–85.

1972. Expectations and the neutrality of money. *Journal of Economic Theory* 4(2):103–24.

1975. An equilibrium model of the business cycle. *Journal of Political Economy.* 83:1113–44.

1976. Econometric Policy Evaluation: A critique. *Carnegie-Rochester Conference Series on Public Policy* 5(1):7–29.

1980. Methods and Problems in Business Cycle Theory. *Journal of Money, Credit and Banking* 12(4):696–715.

1995. Autobiography. http://www.nobelprize.org/nobel_prizes/economics/ laureates/1995/lucas-autobio.html

2004. My Keynesian Education. In. M. De Vroey and K. D. Hoover (eds.) *The IS-LM Model: Its Rise, Fall, and Strange Persistence.* Annual supplement to vol. 36 of *History of Political Economy.* Durham, NC, and London: Duke University Press, 12–24.

Lucas, R. E., and Prescott, E. 1971. Investment Under Uncertainty. *Econometrica* 39(5):659–81.

Lucas, R. E., and Rapping, L. 1969. Real wages, employment, and inflation. *Journal of Political Economy* 77(5):721–754.

1970. Real wages, employment and inflation. In E. S. Phelps et al. (eds.) *Microeconomic Foundations of Employment and Inflation Theory.* New York: Norton, 257–305.

Lucas, R. E., and Sargent, T. J. 1978. After Keynesian Macroeconomics. In *After the Phillips Curve: Persistence of High Inflation and High Unemployment.* Conference Series No. 19. Boston, MA: Federal Reserve Bank of Boston.

(eds) 1981. *Rational Expectations and Econometric Practice.* London: George Allen and Unwin.

Lundberg, E. 1964. [1937]. *Studies in the Theory of Economic Expansion.* New York: A.M. Kelley.

Maddala, G. S., and Nelson, F. D. 1974. Maximum likelihood methods for models of markets in disequilibrium. *Econometrica* **42** (6):1013–30.

Malinvaud, E. 1953. Capital accumulation and the efficient allocation of resources. *Econometrica* **21**:233–68.

1966. *Statistical Methods of Econometrics*. New York: Elsevier.

1972. *Lectures on Microeconomic Theory*. Amsterdam: North Holland.

1977. *The Theory of Unemployment Reconsidered*. Oxford: Basil Blackwell.

1980. *Profitability and Unemployment*. Cambridge: Cambridge University Press.

1982. Wages and unemployment. *Economic Journal* **92**:1–12.

1987. The challenge of macroeconomic understanding. *Banca Nazionale del Lavoro Quarterly Review. #* **162**: 219–38.

1998–2000. *Macroeconomic Theory: A textbook on Macroeconomic Knowledge and Analysis*, 3 vols. New York: Elsevier.

Malinvaud, E., and Younès, Y. 1976. Une nouvelle formulation generale pour l'etude des fondements microeconomique de la macroeconomie. *Cahiers de seminaire d'econometrie* 18:63–109.

Mankiw, N. G. 1990. A quick refresher course in macroeconomics. *Journal of Economic Literature* **28**:1645–60.

Mankiw, N. G., and Romer, D. (eds) 1991. *New Keynesian Economics*. 2 vol. Cambridge, MA: MIT Press.

Mantel, R. 1972. On the characterization of aggregate excess demand functions. *Journal of Economic Theory* 7:348–53.

Marcuzzo, M. C. 1999. Thick markets and thin theories: R.W. Clower and the economics of J.M. Keynes. In P. Howitt, E. de Antoni, and A. Leijonhufvud (eds.) *Money, Markets and Method – Essays in Honour of Robert W. Clower*. Cheltenham: Elgar, 140–54.

McDonald, I. M., and Solow, R. M. 1981. Wage bargaining and employment. *American Economic Review* **71**(5):896–908.

McKenzie, L. 1954. On equilibrium in Graham's model of world trade and other competitive systems. *Econometrica* **22**:147–161.

Mehrling, P. G. 2002. Don Patinkin and the origins of postwar monetary orthodoxy. *European Journal of the History of Economic Thought* 9(2):161–85.

Minsky, H. P. 1975. *John Maynard Keynes*. New York: McGraw-Hill.

Mirrlees, J. A. 1978. Review of Malinvaud 1977. *Economic Journal* **88**:157–59.

Modigliani, F. 1944. Liquidity preference and the theory of interest and money. *Econometrica* **12**:45–88.

Mitchell, W.C. 1927. *Business Cycles: the Problem and its Setting*. New York: NBER.

Moggridge, D. E. 2008. *Harry Johnson: A Life in Economics*. Cambridge: Cambridge University Press.

Muellbauer, J., and Portes, R. 1978. Macroeconomic models with quantity rationing. *Economic Journal* **88**:788–821.

Muth, J. 1961. Rational expectations and the theory of price movements. *Econometrica* **29**: 315–35.

Neary, J. P., and Stiglitz, J. E. 1983. Toward a reconstruction of Keynesian economics: expectations and constrained equilibria. *Quarterly Journal of Economics* **98**(Suppl.):199–228.

Negishi, T. 1961. Monopolistic competition and general equilibrium. *Review of Economic Studies* **28**:196–201.

1976. Unemployment, inflation and the micro foundations of macroeconomics. In M. J. Artis and A. R. Nobay (eds.) *Essays in Economic Analysis*. Cambridge: Cambridge University Press, 33–49.

1994. *General Equilibrium Theory: The Collected Essays of Takashi Negishi*. Vol. 1. Aldershot: Edward Elgar.

Negishi, T., and Hahn, F. H. 1962. A theorem on non-tatonnement stability. *Econometrica* **30**:463–69.

Neumann, J. von. 1945. A model of general economic equilibrium. *Review of Economic Studies* **13**(1):1–9.

Patinkin, D. 1946. Market adjusting and inventory equations. Cowles Commission Staff Papers. Duke University, Don Patinkin Papers, box 4.

1947a. Multiple-plant firms, cartels and imperfect competition. *Quarterly Journal of Economics* **61**(2):173–205.

1947b. *On the Consistency of Economic Models: A Theory of Involuntary Unemployment*. Ph.D. diss., University of Chicago.

1948. Price flexibility and full employment. *American Economic Review* **38**:543–64.

1949a. Involuntary unemployment and the Keynesian supply function. *Economic Journal* **59**:360–83.

1949b. The indeterminacy of absolute prices in classical economic theory. *Econometrica* **17**:1–27.

1956. *Money, Interest and Prices*. Evanston, IL: Row, Peterson.

1959. Keynesian economics rehabilitated: A rejoinder to Professor Hicks. *Economic Journal* **69**:582–87.

1965. *Money, Interest and Prices*. 2nd ed. New York: Harper and Row.

1969. The Chicago tradition, the quantity theory, and Friedman. *Journal of Money, Credit and Banking* **1**(1):46–70.

1987. Walras' law. In J. Eatwell et al. (eds.) *The New Palgrave – A Dictionary of Economics*, vol. 4. London: Macmillan, vol. 4, 863–68.

1989. *Money, Interest and Prices*. 3rd ed. Cambridge, MA: MIT Press.

1990. On different interpretations of the General Theory. *Journal of Monetary Economics* **26**(2):205–43.

1995. The training of an economist. *Banca Nazionale del Lavoro Quarterly Review* **195**:359–95.

Pearce, K. A., and K. D. Hoover. 1995. After the revolution: Paul Samuelson and the textbook Keynesian model. *History of Political Economy* **27**(Suppl.):183–216.

Phelps, E. S. 1961. The Golden Rule of Accumulation: A Fable for Growthmen. *American Economic Review* **51**:638–43.

1967. Phillips curves, expectations of inflation and optimal unemployment over time. *Economica* **34**:254–81.

1968. Money Wage Dynamics and Labor Market Equilibrium *Journal of Political Economy* **76**:678–711.

1969. The new microeconomics in inflation and employment theory. *The American Economic Review* **59** (2, Papers and Proceedings):147–60.

1970a. Preface. In Phelps et al. *Microeconomic Foundations of Employment and Inflation Theory*. London: Macmillan, vii–viii.

1970b. Money wage dynamics and labor market equilibrium. In Phelps et al. *Microeconomic Foundations of Employment and Inflation Theory*. London: Macmillan, 124–66.

1970c. Introduction: The new microeconomics in employment and inflation theory. In E. S. Phelps et al. *Microeconomic Foundations of Employment and Inflation Theory*. New York: Norton, 1–23.

1978. Disinflation without recession: adaptive guideposts and monetary policy. *Weltwirtschaftsliches Archiv* 100; reprinted in E. S. Phelps *Studies in Macroeconomic Theory, Volume 1: Employment and Inflation*. New York: Academic Press.

1990. *Seven Schools of Macroeconomic Thought*. Oxford: Clarendon.

1995. The origins and further development of the natural rate of unemployment. In R. Cross (ed.) *The Natural Rate of Unemployment: Reflections on 25 Years of the Hypothesis*. Cambridge: Cambridge University Press, 15–31.

1994. *Structural Slumps*. Cambridge, MA.: Harvard University Press.

2006. Autobiography. http://www.nobelprize.org/nobel_prizes/economics/laureates/2006/phelps-autobio.html

Phelps, E. S., and Taylor, J. 1977. Stabilizing powers of monetary policy under rational expectations. *Journal of Political Economy* **85**:163–90.

Phelps, E. S. et al. 1970. *Microeconomic Foundations of Employment and Inflation Theory*. London: Macmillan.

Phillips, A. W. 1958. The relation between unemployment and the rate of change of money wage rates in the United Kingdom, 1861-1957. *Economica* 25:283–99.

Portes, R. 1969. The enterprise in central planning. *Review of Economic Studies*. **36**:197–212.

1970. Economic reform in Hungary. *American Economic Review* **60**(2):307–13.

1971. Decentralized planning procedures and centrally planned economies. *American Economic Review* **61** (2):422–29.

Portes, R., and Winter, D. 1977. The supply of consumption goods in centrally planned economies. *Journal of Comparative Economics* **1**:351–65.

1978. The demand for money and for consumption goods in centrally planned economies. *Review of Economics and Statistics* **60**(1):8–18.

1980. Disequilibrium estimates for consumption goods markets in centrally planned economies. *Review of Economic Studies* 47:137–59.

Quandt, R. E. 1978. Tests of equilibrium vs disequilibrium hypotheses. *International Economic Review*. **19**: 435–52.

1986. Unemployment, disequilibrium and the short run Phillips curve: an econometric approach. *Journal of Applied Econometrics* 1:235–53.

1988. *The Conflict between Equilibrium and Disequilibrium Theories: The Case of the U.S. Labor Market*. Kalamazoo, MI: W.E. Upjohn Institute for Employment Research.

1988. *The Econometrics of Disequilibrium*. Oxford: Basil Blackwell.

1992. Introduction. In *The Collected Essays of Richard E. Quandt*. Cheltenham: Edward Elgar, xiii-xxi.

Quandt, R. E., and Rosen, H. S. 1978. Estimation of a disequilibrium aggregate labor market. *Review of Economics and Statistics* **60** (3):371–79.

Reder, M. W. 1979. Review of Malinvaud 1977. *Journal of Political Economy* **87**(3):662–69.

Rizvi, S. A. T. 1994. The microfoundations project in general equilibrium theory. *Cambridge Journal of Economics* **18**: 357–77.

Robertson, D.H. 1922. *Money*. London: Nisbet.

1936. Some notes on Mr. Keynes' general theory of employment. *Quarterly Journal of Economics* **51** (1):68–91.

Robinson, J. 1937. *Essays in the Theory of Employment*. London: Macmillan.

1956. *The Accumulation of Capital*. London: Macmillan.

Rodgers, D. T. 2011. *Age of Fracture*. Cambridge, MA: Belknap Press of Harvard University Press.

Rose, H. 1973. Effective demand in the long run. In J. A. Mirrlees and N. H. Stern (eds.) *Models of Economic Growth*. London: Macmillan, 23–47.

Rotemberg, J. 1982. Monopolistic price adjustment and aggregate output. *Review of Economic Studies* **49**(4):517–31.

Rotemberg, J., and Woodford, M. 1992. Oligopolistic pricing and the effects of aggregate demand on economic activity. *Journal of Political Economy* **100**(6): 1153–1207.

1995. Dynamic general equilibrium models with imperfectly competitive product markets. In T. F. Cooley (ed.) *Frontiers of Business Cycle Research*. Princeton, NJ: Princeton University Press, chap. 9.

Rubin, G. 2002. From equilibrium to disequilibrium: the genesis of Don Patinkin's interpretation of Keynesian theory. *European Journal of the History of Economic Thought* **9** (2):205–25.

2007. Oskar Lange and the Origins of Walrasian Macroeconomics. Unpublished manuscript.

Samuelson, P. A. 1947. *Foundations of Economic Analysis*. Cambridge, MA: Harvard University Press.

1948. *Economics*. New York: McGraw-Hill.

1955. *Economics*. 3rd ed. New York: McGraw-Hill.

1958. An exact consumption-loan model of interest with or without the social contrivance of money. *Journal of Political Economy* **66**: 467–82.

1997. Credo of a lucky textbook author. *Journal of Economic Perspectives* **11**(2):153–60.

2003. Edmund Phelps: insider-economists' insider. In P. Aghion, R. Frydman, J. Stiglitz and M. Woodford (eds.) *Knowledge, Information, and Expectations in Modern Macroeconomics in Honor of Edmund S. Phelps*. Princeton, NJ: Princeton University Press, 1–2.

Samuelson, P. A., and Solow, R. M. 1960. Analytical aspects of anti-inflation policy. *American Economic Review* **50**(2, Papers and Proceedings):177–94.

Savage, L. J. 1954. *The Foundations of Statistics*. New York: Wiley.

Scarf, H. 1960. Some examples of global instability of the competitive equilibrium. *International Economic Review* **1**:157–72.

Schwödiauer, G. (ed.) 1978. *Equilibrium and Disequilibrium in Economic Theory*. Dordrecht: Reidel.

Sebastiani, M. (ed.) 1992. *The notion of equilibrium in Keynesian theory*. New York: St. Martin's Press.

Shackle, G. L. S. 1961. Recent theories concerning the nature and role of interest. *Economic Journal* **71**: 209–54.

1967. *The Years of High Theory*. Cambridge: Cambridge University Press.

Silvestre, J. 1992. Notes on the non-Walrasian approach to macroeconomics. In A. Vercelli and N. Dimitri (eds.) *Macroeconomics: A Survey of Research Strategies*. Oxford: Oxford University Press, 87–126.

Sims, C. 1980. Macroeconomics and reality. *Econometrica* **48**(1):1–48.

1996. Macroeconomics and methodology. *Journal of Economic Perspectives* **10**(1):105–20.

Snowdon, B. 2004. Outside the mainstream: Axel Leijonhufvud on twentieth century macroeconomics. *Macroeconomic Dynamics* **8**:117–45.

Snowdon, B., and Vane, H. R. 1998. Transforming macroeconomics: An interview with Robert E. Lucas Jr. *Journal of Economic Methodology* **5**:115–46.

1999. *Conversations with Leading Economists*. Cheltenham: Elgar.

2005. *Modern Macroeconomics: Its Origins, Development and Current State*. Cheltenham: Edward Elgar.

Snowdon, B., Vane, H. R., and Wynarczyk, P. 1994. *A Modern Guide to Macroeconomics*. Aldershot: Edward Elgar.

Solow, R. M. 1979. Alternative approaches to macroeconomics: A partial view. *Canadian Journal of Economics* **12**(3):339–54.

1980. What to do (macroeconomically) when OPEC comes. In S. Fischer (ed.) *Rational Expectations and Economic Policy*. Chicago: University of Chicago Press, 249–68.

1991. Cowles and the tradition of macroeconomics. In *Cowles Fiftieth Anniversary: Four Essays and an Index of Publications*, by Arrow, K. J., G. Debreu, E. Malinvaud, and R. Solow. New Haven, CT: Cowles Foundation for Research in Economics at Yale University, pp. 81–108. Online at http://cowles.econ.yale.edu/archive/reprints/50th-solow.htm.

1997. How did economics get that way and what way did it get? *Daedalus* **126**(1):39–58.

2000. Toward a macroeconomics of the medium run. *Journal of Economic Perspectives* **14**:151–58.

Solow, R. M., and Stiglitz, J. E. 1968. Output, employment and wages in the short run. *Quarterly Journal of Economics* **82**(4):537–60.

Sonnenschein, H. 1972. Market Excess Demand Functions. *Econometrica* **40**(3):549–63.

Sraffa, P. 1960. *Production of Commodites by Means of Commodities*. Cambridge: Cambridge University Press.

Stiglitz, J. E. 1972. On the optimality of the stock market allocation of investment. *Quarterly Journal of Economics* **86**(1):25–60.

1992. Methodological issues and the New Keynesian economics. In A. Vercelli and N. Dimitri (eds) *Macroeconomics: A Survey of Research Strategies*. Oxford: Oxford University Press, pp. 38–86.

1993. Reflections on economics and on being and becoming an economist. In A. Heertje (ed.) *The Makers of Modern Economics*, vol. 1. Brighton: Harverster Wheatsheaf, 140–83.

2001. Autobiography. Available from http://nobelprize.org/economics/laureates/2001/stiglitz-autobio.html.

2002. *Globalization and its Discontents*. London: Allen Lane.

Stoneman, P. 1979. A simple diagrammatic apparatus for the investigation of a macro-economic model of temporary equilibria. *Economica* **46**:61–66.

Svensson, L. E. O. 1986. Sticky goods prices, flexible asset prices, monopolistic competition and monetary policy. *Review of Economic Studies* **53**(3):385–405.

Tarshis, L. 1947. *The Elements of Economics: An Introduction to the Theory of Price and Employment.* Boston: Houghton Mifflin.

1980. Post-Keynesain economics: A promise that bounced? *American Economic Review* **70** (Papers and Proceedings):10–14.

Taylor, J. 1980. Aggregate dynamics and staggered contracts. *Journal of Political Economy* **88**:1–23.

Telser, L. G. 1972. *Competition, Collusion and Game Theory.* London: Macmillan.

Tobin, J. 1955. A dynamic aggregative model. *Journal of Political Economy* **63**(2):103–15.

1971. *Essays in Economics*, vol. 1 (Macroeconomics). Amsterdam: North Holland.

1980. Are new classical models plausible enough to guide policy? *Journal of Money, Credit and Banking* **12**(4):788–99.

Townshend, H. 1937. Liquidity-premium and the theory of value. *Economic Journal* **47**:157–69.

Van Ees, H., and Garretsen, H. 1990. The right answers to the wrong question? An assessment of the microfoundations debate. *De Economist* **138**(2):123–45.

Wald, A. 1933–34. Über die Produktionsgleichungen der ökonomischen Wertlehre. *Ergbnisse eines mathematischen Kolloquiums* **7**:1–6.

Walker, D. A., ed. 1984. *Money and Markets: Essays of Robert W. Clower.* Cambridge: Cambridge University Press.

Walras, L. 1874/1877. *Eléments d'économie politique pure ou Théorie de la richesse sociale.* Lausanne : Imprimerie L. Corbaz.

Warsh, D. 2006. *Knowledge and the Wealth of Nations: A Story of Economic Discovery.* New York: W. W. Norton.

Weintraub, E. R. 1969. *Stability of Stochastic General Equilibrium Systems.* Ph.D. diss., University of Pennsylvania, Philadelphia.

1970. Stochastic stability of a general equilibrium model. *American Economic Review* **60**(2):380–84.

1972. An Approach to General Equilibrium Dynamics. Unpublished typescript.

1974. *Conflict and Cooperation in Economics.* London: Macmillan.

1975. *General Equilibrium Theory.* London: Macmillan.

1977. The microfoundations of macroeconomics: A critical survey. *Journal of Economic Literature* **15**(1):1–23.

1979. *Microfoundations.* Cambridge: Cambridge University Press.

1985. *General Equilibrium Analysis: Studies in Appraisal.* Cambridge: Cambridge University Press.

1991. *Stabilizing Dynamics: Constructing Economic Knowledge.* Cambridge: Cambridge University Press.

2002. *How Economics Became a Mathematical Science.* Durham, NC: Duke University Press.

2008. Microfoundations. In W. Darity (ed.) *The International Encyclopedia of Social Sciences*, 2nd ed. New York: Macmillan.

2011. Lionel W. McKenzie and the proof of the existence of a competitive equilibrium. *Journal of Economic Perspectives* **25**(2):199–215.

Weintraub, E. R., and Gayer, T. 2001. Equilibrium proofmaking. *Journal of the History of Economic Thought* **23**(4):421–42.

Weintraub, S. 1956. A microeconomic approach to the theory of wages. *American Economic Review* **65**(5):835–56.

1957. The micro-foundations of aggregate demand and supply. *Economic Journal* **67**:455–70.

1958. *An Approach to the Theory of Income Distribution*. Philadelphia: Chilton.

Wicksell, K. 1898. *Interest and Prices*. Translated by R. F. Kahn, 1936. Reprinted 1965, New York: A.M. Kelley.

Woodford, M. 1994. Structural Slumps. *Journal of Economic Literature* **32**: 1784–1815.

1999. Revolution and Evolution in Twentieth-Century Macroeconomics. Available from http://www.columbia.edu/~mw2230/macro20C.pdf.

2003. *Interest and Prices: Foundations of a Theory of Monetary Policy*. Princeton, NJ: Princeton University Press.

2009. Convergence in macroeconomics: Elements of the new synthesis. *American Economic Journal: Macroeconomics* **1**(1):267–79.

2010. Financial intermediation and macroeconomic analysis. *Journal of Economic Perspectives* **24**(4):21–44.

Yellen, J. 1980. On Keynesian economics and the economics of the Post-Keynesians. *American Economic Review* **70** (Papers and Proceedings):15–19.

Younès, Y. 1972. Indices prospectifs quantitatifs et procedures decentralisees d'elaboration des plans. *Econometrica* **40**:137–46.

1975. On the role of money in the process of exchange and the existence of a non-Walrasian equilibrium. *Review of Economic Studies* **42**:489–501.

Young, W. 1987. *Interpreting Mr Keynes: The IS-LM Enigma*. Boulder, CO: Westview Press.

Index

Printed in the United States
By Bookmasters